VISUAL *difference*

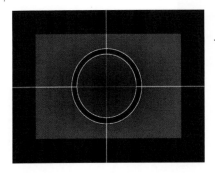

FRAMING FILM
The History & Art of Cinema

Frank Beaver, *General Editor*

Vol. 8

The Framing Film series is part of the Peter Lang
Media and Communication list.
Every volume is peer reviewed and meets
the highest quality standards for content and production.

PETER LANG
New York • Washington, D.C./Baltimore • Bern
Frankfurt • Berlin • Brussels • Vienna • Oxford

ELIZABETH HEFFELFINGER • LAURA WRIGHT

VISUAL *difference*

Postcolonial Studies and Intercultural Cinema

PETER LANG
New York • Washington, D.C./Baltimore • Bern
Frankfurt • Berlin • Brussels • Vienna • Oxford

Library of Congress Cataloging-in-Publication Data

Heffelfinger, Elizabeth.
Visual difference: postcolonial studies and intercultural cinema /
Elizabeth Heffelfinger, Laura Wright.
p. cm. — (Framing film; v. 8)
Includes bibliographical references and index.
1. Intercultural communication in motion pictures.
2. Multiculturalism in motion pictures. 3. Imperialism in motion pictures.
4. Culture in motion pictures. 5. Minorities in motion pictures.
6. Motion pictures—Developing countries. I. Wright, Laura. II. Title.
PN1995.9.I55H54   302.23'43—dc22   2010014245
ISBN 978-1-4331-0595-1
ISSN 1524-7821

Bibliographic information published by **Die Deutsche Nationalbibliothek.**
Die Deutsche Nationalbibliothek lists this publication in the "Deutsche
Nationalbibliografie"; detailed bibliographic data is available
on the Internet at http://dnb.d-nb.de/.

Cover: Still from *Heading South* (2005, France) a.k.a. *Vers le sud*
Directed by Laurent Cantet; Shown: Charlotte Rampling, Menothy Cesar
Credit: Shadow Distribution/Photofest © Shadow Distribution

The paper in this book meets the guidelines for permanence and durability
of the Committee on Production Guidelines for Book Longevity
of the Council of Library Resources.

© 2011 Peter Lang Publishing, Inc., New York
29 Broadway, 18th floor, New York, NY 10006
www.peterlang.com

Printed in the United States of America

Table of Contents
ೞಐೞ

Acknowledgments

***

We owe a debt of gratitude to the many friends and colleagues who provided us with financial, intellectual, and moral support over the years that this book was in production. We are grateful to our former department head Elizabeth Addison for encouraging us to team teach the special topics course, "Postcolonial Film," which inspired us to begin this book. We want to thank the students in that class, all of whom provided insights and interpretations that have found their way into this work. Many of them were teachers in North Carolina public schools who have since incorporated the literature and film from this course into their curriculum. We are humbled and grateful that our time together in the classroom had such real world applications. We want to particularly acknowledge three students, LeShay Maltry, Laurie Calvert, and Paul Denkenberger, who accompanied us to the British Commonwealth and Postcolonial Studies conference in 2008 to present work on the representations of Africa in the special *Vanity Fair* "Africa" issue. The audience for our roundtable discussion at the conference provided valuable feedback, as did the audience for our presentations at that conference in 2009 and 2010, where we presented excerpted work from several chapters.

Our colleagues at Western Carolina were unfailingly supportive and more than generous in sometimes shouldering additional burdens so that we could take on this work. Brian Gastle, our current department head, and Scott Higgins, Dean of the Graduate School, found funding for production costs including the purchase of the beautiful film stills. We would like to thank as well the staff at Hunter Library for their professional assistance and courtesy, specifically Dan Wendel in the media center for managing our consistent demands for film. We also want to thank Dr. Frank Beaver, editor of the Peter Lang series "Framing Film: The History and Art of Cinema," for choosing our manuscript for this collection, and for guiding it through the review process. For their support in the production of this manuscript, Caitlin Lavelle, our editor, and production head Sophie Appel, have been unfailingly professional and patient.

This project has been a wonderful and supportive collaboratiive experience in which we were able to combine out mutual love of film with rewarding experiences in the classroom. Nevertheless, we each wrote individual chapters for which we are responsible. Laura Wright wrote Chapter 2: Witness the Gangster in the Interregnum: Adapting Fugard's *Tsotsi*; Chapter 3: Reclaiming the Maoriland Romance: Inventing Tradition in *Once were Warriors* and *Whale Rider*, and Chapter 6: NRI: The Transnational Class and Transnational Class in the Films of Deepa Mehta. Elizabeth Heffelfinger wrote Chapter 1: "This is Africa," or How Leonardo Dicaprio Imagines Sierra Leone; Chapter 4: The New Voy(age)eur: White Women, Black Bodies, and the Spectacle of Sexual Abandon; and Chapter 5: NRI: The Transnational Class and Transnational Class in the Films of Mira Nair.

***

Elizabeth

The life of an academic spouse is not to be envied. Over the course of the three years in which I sequestered myself with this book, I have relied on the good humor and patience of my wonderful husband, Harry Alter. My parents have been especially generous. I thank my siblings, Tom and Katie, and my father-in-law, Paul Alter, for their steady encouragement.

***

Laura

I would, as always, like to thank Jason for his support and encouragement throughout the course of my work on this project. Thanks also to my parents and my sister, LeeAnn, and to Dorsey, for listening me talk about and theorize the ideas that have shaped my writing. Finally, thanks to Brent and Brian for sitting on either side of me during Avatar.

***

For permission to use the images included in the text, the authors would like to thank Shadow Distribution, Miramax Films, Fine Line Features, Newmarket Films, TriStar, Warner Bros. Pictures, Fox Searchlight, Focus Features, IFC Films, MGM, TNT, and New Line Cinema. We would like to thank Photofest for its assistance in securing these images.

Introduction
Situating Intercultural Film

***

In positing a postcolonial study of intercultural film, we feel that it is important, first and foremost, to define our terms and to situate our approach within (and outside of) the matrix of extant ways of seeing and discussing film about and from the so-called third world; in this sense, it is important to posit what this study is *not*. Our text seeks to utilize the influence and terminology of extant methodology—particularly the theoretical lenses of postcolonialism, as well as global, accented, and third cinema—but we are not dealing with films that fall neatly into these categories. Instead, we seek to differentiate our approach in terms of the scope of our exploration and the parameters that we consider herein. To begin to explore our particular subject position, it is necessary to state that there is considerable debate over the precise parameters of the scope and the definition of the term "postcolonial." In her 1999 study of intercultural cinema, *The Skin of the Film* (Duke UP), Laura U. Marks comments on the reasons for her resistance to the term "postcolonial" in her analysis of films produced by artists in the diaspora: "postcolonialism," she argues, has become a conceptually carnivorous term that swallows distinctions of nation, location, period, and agency," but she also notes that "an advantage of the term 'postcolonial' is that it emphasizes the history of power relations between the entities it designates" (8). Our text seeks to investigate the ways that films, produced in the West and in formerly colonized nations, generate, perpetuate, and subvert postcolonial readings, while simultaneously constructing images of specific postcolonies. In this introduction, we foreground the theoretical readings that follow by focusing on pedagogical strategies for teaching such films—in conjunction with various works of postcolonial and canonical literature and film, as well as with the aid of historical and theoretical grounding.

One of the reasons why we have chosen "intercultural" as our method-ology is because the chapters herein reveal the role of American film and culture in the films we analyze—Hollywood representations of the gangster, of blackness, of hip-hop and black music culture have been and continue to be an accessible toolbox, touchstone, paradigm, and reference point. Amy Kaplan ("Left Alone") locates American claims to hegemony within a discourse of imperialism that recognizes the international will to power as "inseparable from the social relations and cultural discourses of race, gender, ethnicity, and class at home" (16),[1] and Laura Marks notes in her rationale for choosing "intercultural" rather than the myriad other terms that might accomplish similar aims, including "multicultural" or "hybrid," that there is a theoretical bonus for reinvigorating a term rather than inventing a new concept, one that might prematurely foreclose the problems and possibilities signified by the previous one (6). We position our work as "intercultural" because it is a term that is easily parsed, and we focus predominantly on films that foreground personal, social, and political exchanges between cultures. These exchanges are never equivalent or equitable. Instead, relationships of power between dominant and minority cultures are often explicitly constructed by and through the histories, geographies, and experiences of imperialism, and these forces are embedded in many of the films we investigate. Our concern throughout the book is to articulate the multiple discourse communities in which these films circulate; the multiple and contentious communities that produce, publicize, review, and analyze these productions. We are particularly indebted, therefore, to Marks's explanation of the relationship between production and knowledge that "intercultural" makes manifest: "It accounts for the encounter between different cultural organizations of knowledge, which is one of the sources of intercultural cinema's synthesis of new forms of expression and new kinds of knowledge" (7).

Furthermore, we recognize that we do not engage with the experimental, noncommercial films made in the decade between 1985 and 1995 by filmmakers at the cultural, financial, and political margins that Marks identifies as an intercultural cinema *movement*. Rather, fifteen years later, we have intervened at a moment that she predicted in which "intercultural cinema" has become an increasingly popular genre of "theatrically released films that deal explicitly with the contemporary mixing of cultures in metropolitan centers, sometimes in formally experimental ways" (3). Hamid Naficy identifies an analogous trajectory in *An Accented Cinema*. In his consistent return throughout his text to Armenian-Canadian filmmaker Atom Egoyan, Naficy plots the trajectory that Egoyan has traveled as an independent filmmaker, one whose multicultural identity and sense of cultural difference informs his film production and style, but a filmmaker who has also garnered mainstream critical acclaim and success (36–37). We do not see this co-optation of independent voices, styles, or histories by a global audience as *necessarily* regressive; rather, we see this oscillation between the margins and the mainstream as a site to explore the tensions and contentions that characterize culture itself.

Our approach borrows from and respects various groupings—intercultural, global, third, and accented—while simultaneously seeking to make manifest an alternate space of signification; to date, no text exists that focuses exclusively on the concept of postcolonial film as a framework for identifying films produced within and outside of various formerly colonized nations, nor is there a scholarly text that addresses pedagogical issues about and frameworks for teaching such films. What feels like a mainstream approach is pedagogically necessary in terms of access, both financial and physical, to the films discussed herein, given that this text proposes models for teaching these works at the university and secondary levels. The focus of this work is therefore twofold: to provide the methodology to read and teach postcolonial film and to provide analyses in which we, as scholars and teachers, explore the ways that the films examined herein work to further and complicate our understanding of "postcolonial" as a fraught and evolving theoretical stance. The text contains a framework for theorizing both about film and about postcoloniality, as well as a rationale for why, particularly in the current historical moment, it is important to consider these two fields of study in conjunction with one another. In an increasingly global and visually oriented culture, film operates as a prime medium of historical and cultural exchange between nations.

***

We situate our study within the context of several recent texts that examine the works of specific filmmakers or works from specific locales from a postcolonial perspective. These include, for example, Reena Dube's 2005 work *The Chess Players and Postcolonial Film Theory* (Palgrave Macmillan), Roy Armes's *Postcolonial Images: Studies in North African Film* (Indiana UP 2005), and Jinga Desai's *Beyond Bollywood: The Cultural Politics of South Asian Film* (Routledge 2003). Other current studies such as Bishnupriya Ghosh and Brinda Bose's edited 1997 collection *Interventions: Feminist Dialogues on Third World Women's Literature and Film* (Garland) and Anthony Guneratne and Wimal Dissanayake's 2003 *Rethinking Third Cinema* (Routledge) theorize and re-examine the 1980's concept of Third-World (or just Third) Film as an area of scholarly exploration influenced by but distinct from Western cinema. The more broadly defined concept of World Cinema is examined and theorized in such current works as editor John Hill's *World Cinema:*

Critical Approaches (Oxford UP 2000), and Julie Codell's 2006 edited collection *Genre, Gender, Race and World Cinema* (Wiley-Blackwell). Similarly, the essays in *Transnational Cinema: The Film Reader*, edited by Elizabeth Ezra and Terry Rowden (Routledge 2006), examine world cinema within the context of globalization. Finally, Kate Gamm's recent *Teaching World Cinema* (British Film Institute 2008) explores the concepts of national and world cinemas and provides case studies of films from Hong Kong, Scandinavia, and France.

The theoretical lenses through which scholars historically have approached various categorizations of non-Western film fall into four main categories: global cinema, accented cinema, third cinema, and, most recently, intercultural cinema. We flesh out and define those analytical paradigms below. In terms of the role that the United States has played in the globalization of cinema, Mark Shiel notes that

> if cinema may be said to have been one of the first truly globalizing industries in terms of its organization, it may also be said to have long been at the cutting edge of globalization as a process of integration and homogenization. The hugely disproportionate dominance of the United States historically in many areas of culture, economics, and politics has rarely been more tangible and overt than in the dominance of Hollywood cinema, which has for decades now been widely recognized as a threat to discrete national and regional cultures. (10–11)

Furthermore, Hollywood as a conveyer of global culture has always been post-modern because of "its particular combination of both sign and image (culture) and manufactured goods (industry, technology, capital), it may also be recognized as central to, rather than merely reflecting, the process known as globalization" (11). In our analysis of *Blood Diamond*, we explore the role that Hollywood plays in the construction of various imagined postcolonial communities and the way that those images are disseminated across the globe, and we begin our study with an exploration of filmic representations of contemporary white, Western male interpretations of Africa as the "heart of darkness," in this film and in *The Last King of Scotland*. The influence of Hollywood is apparent in the films that we examine from non-Western cultures as well, from the tsotsi (gangster) culture that pervades Soweto in *Tsotsi* to the south-central Los Angeles inspired Aukland imagined and manifested in *Once Were Warriors*. Hollywood, as a cite of cultural dissemination is a prevalent, social, and commercial force in the shaping of many of the films that we examine in this text, and we feel that Hollywood's representations, of both postcolonial and marginalized U.S. populations, deserve careful scrutiny, particularly as Hollywood-generated minority U.S. representations influence and shape the way that various non-Western Others are rendered in intercultural film. The second framework, Accented Cinema, is the cinema of exile and the diaspora, created by filmmakers who have left their homelands to work in the West. Hamid Naficy states that

> accented filmmakers came to live and make films in the West in two general groupings. The first group was displaced or lured to the West from the late 1950s to the mid-1970s by Third World decolonization, wars of liberation, the Soviet Union's invasion of Poland and Czechoslovakia, Westernization, and a kind of 'internal decolonization' in the West itself, involving various civil rights, counterculture, and antiwar movements. (10)

He notes that the second wave of accented filmmakers

> emerged in the 1980s and 1990s as a result of the failure of nationalism, social-ism, and communism; the ruptures caused by the emergence of postindustrial global economies, the rise of militant forces of Islam, the return of religious and ethnic wars, and the fragmentation of nation-states; the changes in the European, Australian, and American immigration policies encouraging non-Western immigration; and the unprecedented technological developments and consolidation in computers and media. (10–11)

The non-resident Indian (NRI) filmmakers that we examine in chapter five, Mira Nair and Deepa Mehta, are most closely aligned with this category; both live in the West but often choose India as the locale and foci of their work, forever seeking to present an "authentic"—a highly contested term—Indian reality. The concern with authenticity arises from an anxiety of exile, and the filmmakers' status as similarly authentic is often challenged from within India.

While many of the films included in this study are postcolonial in the sense that they are by and about postcolonial peoples, none of them constitutes Third Cinema, the reactionary mode of filmmaking that emerged in Latin America in the 1960s and 1970s in direct response to capitalism, neocolonialism, and Hollywood. According to Anthony R. Guneratne, "Third-Cinema theory is the only major branch of film theory that did not originate within a specifically Euro-American context. No other theory of cinema is so imbued with historical specificities, none so specific in its ideological orientation, and yet none so universal in the throes of resisting Neocolonialism" (7). Robert Stam asserts that Third Cinema "offered a Fanon-inflected version of Brechtian aesthetics, along with a dash of 'national culture' and 'Third Cinema' represented a valid alternative to the dominant Hollywood model in an early period" (31). Our work, in that it examines films that are accessible to a broad (and often Western) audience and that are, in some cases, Western interpretations of postcolonial locations—like *Blood Diamond* and *The Last King of Scotland*, for example—is impossible to categorize in terms of this framework. Likewise, the works we examine that originate within postcolonial locations, like *Once Were Warriors, Tsotsi,* and *Whale Rider,* for example, are only marginally (if at all) interested in generating narratives of resistance to the auspices of colonization.

As mentioned above, films coming out of the West have historically operated as a kind of colonizing agent, that which not only manufactures Western ideas about postcolonial "Others" for Western consumption but is also initially replicated by colonial and postcolonial filmmakers. For example, in "Towards a Critical Theory of Third-World Films," Teshome H. Gabriel formulates a postcolonial film theory influenced by Frantz Fanon's work on decolonization and outlines three phases in postcolonial filmmaking. There is first a period of unqualified assimilation in which third-world filmmakers imitate Hollywood; second, a "remembrance" phase during which there is "indigenization of control of talents, production, exhibition and distribution" (342) and during which films very often feature the return of the exile; and third, the combative phase during which the struggle of third-world peoples is the predominant theme.

The primary section of our book takes this theoretical model as its starting place and then explores how international co-productions, new delivery systems, and other signs of films' global transformation have complicated many of the traditional frames of analysis, including "national" and "Third" cinemas. Arjun Appadurai's "Disjuncture and Difference in the Global Cultural Economy" suggests that the "complex transnational construction of imaginary landscapes" (327) requires analysis of multiple discourses; we offer a theoretically rich but accessible range of investigation in the case-study section of the text.

***

Several overarching themes and issues emerge with regard to the concept of postcolonial intercultural film. First, the influence of the Hollywood film industry is pervasive and responsible for Western interpretations of various non-Western locations while simultaneously shaping the cultures of those locations. We will discuss this idea further in subsequent chapters, particularly as Hollywood has shaped and dictated fashion, consumption, and identity politics in, for example, South Africa and New Zealand via its filmic representations of gangster culture.

Second, the anxiety of authenticity—of "real" representations by cultural insiders—plays a significant role in the discourse that surrounds and shapes our understandings of these works. In our special topics "Postcolonial Film" graduate seminar, a way to get students to begin thinking about the relationships between representation, discourse, power, and pedagogy was to give them a discourse deliberation assignment that called upon them to reflect on our in-class investigations of the ways that various formerly colonized locations are rendered through literature and film and, similarly, how such loci are "packaged" for U.S. consumption. We worked with a class in which many of the students are also secondary education teachers and who are interested in teaching contemporary, non-Western texts to their middle and high school students. As a class, we generated a discourse analysis that examined how our understanding of Africa is shaped by the popular media. For this assignment, our students examined the following texts: *Vanity Fair*'s July 2007 special issue on Africa; Joel Foreman and David R. Shumway's essay, "Cultural Studies: Reading Visual Texts;" *Blood Diamond;* and *The Last King of Scotland.*

We began with the *Vanity Fair* Africa issue as our object of study; we asked the question, "What understandings of Africa does this magazine encourage and deter, authorize and prevent?" What follows is a brief summary of our students' discoveries that demonstrates both a methodology and its results. A "media sensation," this issue was guest-edited by Bono, lead singer of the global rock b(r)and U2, and a human rights activist who (with Bobby Shriver) started "Project Red," a marketing campaign that encourages corporations to create "red" products, a percentage of the sales proceeds support the global AIDS fund. Our choice of *Vanity Fair* was dictated in part by the magazine's timely release, Project Red's familiarity to consumers (like our students), the wealth of visual information provided by the 20 different covers, all photographed by Annie Leibovitz, and the easy availability of the images online. Photographed against a deep red background (given the Project Red/Bono organization of the issue, the color "red" is over-determined as "about Africa"), Leibovitz's covers visually express the defining theme of the issue: "conversations about Africa." Her subjects include stars, celebrities and public figures who are easily recognizable (then-President George Bush, Don Cheadle, Muhammad Ali); or, recognized as social investors in Africa (Archbishop Desmond Tutu, Bill and Melinda Gates); or, both (Brad Pitt, Oprah Winfrey).

These photographs seem to say that the conversation that "we" are having—this can also be read as "the conversation that is being had" by a cultural elite—is both global (Queen Rania of Jordan) and local (George Clooney, Chris Rock).

Although it is difficult to distinguish the local from the global in the realm of American popular culture (Madonna and Brad Pitt live abroad and both are global stars), the issue is dominated by Americans (roughly three-quarters of the subjects are American); American political influence (George Bush, Barack Obama, Condoleezza Rice) and its celebrity philanthropists (Brad Pitt, Oprah Winfrey, Bill and Melinda Gates) are the key players in the photographic conversation. Only three of the subjects, Archbishop Tutu, the fashion model Iman, and the actor Djimon Hounsou are identifiable as "authentically" African. The cover's more-than-equal representation of African-Americans indicates that Africa can be best represented by black American celebrities, including Condoleezza Rice, Oprah Winfrey, and Muhammad Ali.

The metaphor at work in each individual photograph, and in the relation-ship between them (since they can be viewed sequentially, like a frieze), is that we can touch each other, talk to one another, cross the boundaries that divide us and start conversations in other political, social, and cultural arenas. This conversation is frequently not an easy one, as the photos suggest, and the news is sometimes disturbing, difficult to understand, or requires attentive and serious listening. Condoleezza Rice seems to impart information to George Bush who may not be listening; in the next photograph, Bush and Archbishop Desmond Tutu are posed in deep conversation, Tutu with his hands folded as if in prayer, contemplating his next words. The following photo creates a revealing juxtaposi-tion: a now-smiling Tutu casually clasps the shoulders of Brad Pitt, who sits, arms folded, in the center of the image, looking off-screen. The next photo is equally casual: Brad Pitt and Djimon Hounsou stand together in a medium shot, both facing the camera, Pitt's arm casually draped across Hounsou's shoulder.

These informal photos are in contrast to those more classically posed: Hounsou seems to lean in to the next photo to speak to Madonna who effects the pose of Rodin's "The Thinker," hand to forehead, gazing into space. Hounsou, an actor from Benin who was nominated for an Oscar for his supporting role as Solomon Vandy in *Blood Diamond* (2006), is not the star that Madonna is, and he approaches her carefully. Equally important to our analysis is the extra-textual information we bring to these photographs, information that can subvert their intended meaning: in 2005, in a widely publicized adoption, Angelina Jolie (Brad Pitt's partner) adopted Zahara, an Ethiopian orphan who is rumored to have a parent still living (Bevan). In 2009, Madonna's adoption of a second child required a court order to overturn Malawi residency laws. CNN reports that the child's alleged father opposes the adoption: "she [the child] is a Malawian," said James Kambewa, "so [I] need her to grow as a Malawian, as well with our culture"

("Madonna Wins"). The Malawi high court accepted Madonna's considerable charity work as proof enough of her commitment to the country: "in this global village a man can have more than one place at which he resides" ("Madonna Wins"). Celebrity commitment to Africa brings both necessary attention to human rights issues and a heightened circulation of those images—of war, genocide, disease, famine—that most define the continent and require intervention and, in the case of international adoption, removal.

The representatives from Africa included in *Vanity Fair* reveal there are multiple contradictions at play in the issue. Djimon Hounsou serves as a consultant for the issue's portfolio, "Spirit of Africa," which highlights the accomplishments of African leaders, teachers, economists, and artists, yet confines them to the ghetto of a separate section. As case studies of progress, this inclusion and separation draws attention to the central paradox that guides the discourse of the issue: attributing agency to Africans themselves in order to forestall a dynamic that gestures towards the constructs of colonial racism. Hounsou acknowledges the issue's tendency towards white paternalism: "The goal of the African people is to become self-sufficient, [otherwise]…it does feel like the white man's burden" (54). Hounsou makes clear that the relationship between Western philanthropy and African need should not be read as demeaningly charitable: "We are not looking for a handout" (54). Former fashion model Iman Abdulmajid, CEO of Iman cosmetics, a line of beauty products for women of color, and the global ambassador for Keep a Child Alive, a non-profit that provides lifesaving antiretroviral (ARV) drugs to children, points to the role of the media in fostering consistently negative perceptions of Africa: "I get insulted when I see only images of our dying, our wars, our AIDS victims…not our doctors, our nurses, our teachers"; in response, she proposes a feminist solution: "Africa must find its own saviors: the salvation of Africa is in the hands of African women" (56). Iman's reframing of the debate in terms of a separate African agenda is provocatively represented in her cover image: she wears a dress by American designer Donna Karan, yet its navel-grazing draped neckline, the turban she wears, her gaze and pose (56) evoke the iconic image of Darfur rebels, who appear later in the same issue (128)—a co-optation of the magazine's dominant discourse of Africa as a place of chaos. It is relevant to note here that the charity, Keep a Child Alive, is responsible for the "I am African" campaign to raise public awareness of AIDS in Africa; this campaign features celebrities like Richard Gere, Heidi Klum, Gwyneth Paltrow, and Seal, and Lenny Kravitz "tattooed" with colorful faux-tribal designs and ornamentation. The campaign, according to its website, makes a transnational connection based on biology: we can all trace our DNA to African ancestors, claims Iman, and thus are all part of the "human family" that now needs our help ("About I am African"). Robin Givhan writes that many bloggers, fashion followers, and media informers were skeptical of both (Product) Red and the "I am African" campaign, noting that Gwyneth Paltrow's "I am African" ad seemed to generate the most ire. A parody quickly appeared: titled "I am Gwyneth Paltrow" and featuring an African woman with two stripes of paint under her eye, the caption reads, in part, "Help us stop the shameless fame whores from using the suffering of those dying from AIDS in Africa to bolster their pathetic careers..." (Mohney).

We read the covers of *Vanity Fair* in the kind of detailed fashion that Foreman and Shumway encourage when they guide readers (and viewers) to note the formal elements of visual texts, such as "typography, corporate logos, icons, discrete images of people and other things...light, clothing, adornments, posture" that combine to give the coherent, unified image (whether advertisement, art, or film) its emotional and ideological authority (253). In Louis Althusser's terms, the image "hails" the viewer, makes the organization of the social relations in the image appear natural and "true," and situates the viewer in "a subject-position that represents the cultural and historical contingencies of the moment" (255).

As a way of foregrounding our examination of the way that culture is generated and commodified via film, we want to look briefly at the advertising in this issue of the magazine to expand this analysis into a critique of the values and beliefs that should govern our investment in Africa. Much of the advertising in this issue of *Vanity Fair* places an expectation on the consumer to practice philanthropic capitalism and to act as an agent of social change. (Product) Red is the dominant framework for advertising in the issue. Touted not as a charity but as a business model, (Product) Red encourages first-world consumers to buy the "red" version of manufacturers' products, easily identified by the (Red) logo; in turn, corporations such as the Gap and Nike contribute part of their profits to fight AIDS. According to "The (Red) Manifesto," which is reproduced in the center of the issue, this is a new relationship of consumer to capitalism. Much as it seeks to produce the frisson of "The Communist Manifesto," in its alignment of a radical proposition and Bolshevik "red," this re-working of the traditional relationship of consumer to producer allows corporate capitalism to practice social responsibility without undermining any social relationships or make any structural changes.

While companies "partner" with (Product) Red to offer consumers the choice of a Red product, our students were quick to note that this merchandise seems to cost more, indicating that these companies retain their profits by increasing the price of Red products. Motorola Motorazr, Emporio Armani, and Gap are (Product) Red advertisers in the issue; all promote the idea that the Red product, in the words of the Motorazr ad, is "designed to help eliminate AIDS in Africa" (37). The Gap (Product) Red ads are iconic, and the clothes, emblazoned with words that incorporate the movement's mission—Inspi(red), Discove(red)—easily identify the philanthropic consumer. In one Gap ad, Natalie Maines, the controversial Dixie Chicks singer who publicly denounced George Bush and set off a firestorm of publicity denouncing her patriotism, is wearing a Gap (Product) Red cashmere sweater. The facing page states, "Every generation has a voice." In another ad, child actress Abigail Breslin, wearing a Gap T-shirt with "Inspi(red)" across the front, holds her favorite stuffed animal, Curious George. George is wearing a matching Babygap (Product) Red T-shirt. The statement that accompanies this photograph is: "Inspire the next generation to change the world." Here we note that the close reading of the visual image reveals that the West's intention to help Africa is imbricated in a complex web of ambiguous meanings around this notion of Africa. Curious George has a long history in Africa: both the children's book and the 2006 animated feature film adaptation directed by Matthew O'Callaghan privilege an intervention-ist, exploitative relationship with Africa, as we detail more fully in the first case study.

The extended discourse analysis of *Blood Diamond* and *The Last King of Scotland* is the subject of our first case study—an example of the kind of criti-cal analysis generated by this methodology and that guides the remaining case studies. Foreman and Shumway's essay, "Cultural Studies: *Reading Visual Texts*," was developed for precisely the reason we deployed it in our classroom: as a primer for teachers that details both a theoretical paradigm that justifies the role of cultural studies in the classroom and as a methodology for the kind of textual analysis that we do throughout this book. Cultural studies recognizes that culture is a "site of struggle" (244). We are particularly concerned with visual texts that articulate the practices and habits, narratives and texts of everyday life that explicate the strategies and tensions of postcolonialism; as Foreman and Shumway note, it is important that students feel empowered to discuss images they choose, and we will detail the discoveries of our students in a moment. As they note as well, and as we observed in our classroom, students do not need a reminder that the social relations of race, gender, and class exist and that these discriminations mean that culture is a site of dissent (248). Rather, it is more important to discuss hierarchies of power, the relationships between dominant and subordinate groups, economies, and nations. In any analysis of cultural representations, an acknowledgment that relationships of power are both sustained by representations and interrogated by them, is perhaps the most challenging assumption of cultural studies.

We found it useful at this juncture to introduce the notion of discourse, as a way to recognize that representations operate in competition with one another, sometimes harmoniously, sometimes in stark opposition, that identity groups can share concerns while fashioning distinct spaces, and that representations seek to situate the reader and viewer as a subject. To quote Paul Bove in the chapter on "Discourse" in *Critical Terms for Literary Study*, discourses "produce knowledge about humans and their society," and an analysis of discourse aims to "describe the surface linkages between power, knowledge, institutions, intellectuals, the control of populations, and the modern state" as these intersect in systems of thought, and as represented in texts (55–56). We asked our students—and ourselves—to consider that we come to an understanding of Africa, for example, through visual texts such as *Vanity Fair*, *Blood Diamond*, and *The Last King of Scotland*, and that this understanding of Africa is constructed under specific conditions of production. We wanted our students to be able to discuss how these mass culture products *construct* the political, economic, and cultural conditions for the understanding of "Africa" at this particular moment.

This cultural studies approach proved most productive because it mobilized student participation and recognized progressive and regressive contradictions, tensions and advances. We asked that our students generate a discourse analysis that examines how their understanding of Africa—as a "real" and metaphorical entity—is shaped not only by the literature that we read in this class, but also by the contemporary popular media that they view outside of it, in the form of television, film, advertisements, and various other media. In order to do this, our students needed to find and analyze a magazine advertisement or story or scene from a film that depicts Africa and/or Africans. The idea was to generate an analysis in which our students examine the "image of Africa" that the text generates for a specific audience—exactly what Chinua Achebe does in his famous 1975 lecture "An Image of Africa." In this lecture, Achebe examines how Joseph Conrad's depiction of some homogenous concept of "Africa" in *Heart of Darkness* serves to silence various other—and perhaps more authentic—African realities. We have replicated this assignment, in various ways, in other course contexts: for example, both of us currently use an application on our electronic course interface that allows students to post popular media representations of the cultures that we study in class. Not only are the various manifestations of this project important because we hope to reach teachers and the next generations of students, but because (as we document more fully in the conclusion) these discourses, on Africa for example, continue to manifest themselves. By viewing such instances as contemporary representations of Obama as a monkey and the "next top model" employing blackface, we find these conjunctures important sites of analysis. The chapters that follow are examples and models of this analytical practice, focusing on race, gender, and class issues while recognizing how national cinemas and Hollywood productions collaborate with, compliment, and antagonize each other.

In the "Introduction" to their co-edited volume *Multiculturalism, Postcoloniality and Transnational Media*, Ella Shohat and Robert Stam encourage teachers to try "multiculturalizing and transnationalizing the media studies curriculum," as a critical step in curing students of their geographic and cultural provincialism, an ignorance fed in part by mainstream media (4–5). Although we did not want to retune "multiculturalism" as a keyword in this study, since it is a too-polarized word in education policy and administration, we did answer their call with the curriculum that formed the foundation of this book. One of our central conceits was the pairing of canonical texts with revisionist works: *Jane Eyre* with *Wide Sargasso Sea*, for example, or the pairing of exploitative representations of Haiti in Wes Craven's film *The Serpent and the Rainbow* (1988)—based on Wade Davis's 1985 book of the same name—with the investigation of social relations in Laurent Cantet's *Heading South*. We wanted to introduce students to a wide range of styles and questions, including: how did the experience of colonization affect those who were colonized while also influencing the colonizers? What were the forms of resistance against colonial control? How did colonial education and language influence the culture and identity of the colonized? How did Western science, technology, and medicine change existing knowledge systems? What are the emergent forms of postcolonial identity after the departure of the colonizers? How has film—both independent and Hollywood productions, fiction and non-fiction forms—perpetuated colonial control, or allowed filmmakers to create postcolonial identities? To what extent has decolonization (a reconstruction free from colonial influence) been possible? How do gender, race, and class function in colonial and postcolonial discourse? How are issues of gender, race, and class visually constructed?

Several of the students who were in our course participated in the annual Commonwealth and Postcolonial Studies Conference sponsored by Georgia Southern University and were able to present their work to their academic peers—fellow graduate students and faculty—but also to formalize the ways that they incorporated the discourse analysis into their own teaching. One student states:

> Of course, your course completely changed the way I teach English II. I bring
> in so many works from other cultures, and I spend a great deal of time on
> the concept of postcolonial writing. The first year, I taught the Africa works
> in "chronological order," *Heart of Darkness, Things Fall Apart,* and then *Tsotsi.*
> However, students advised me in a survey at the end of the course that *Tsotsi*
> was one of their favorite books, so I moved it up in the year. I think I wrote
> to you that I've had trouble with *Heart of Darkness,* so now we read only parts
> of it and the Achebe criticism ["An Image of Africa'], and we watch *Rabbit
> Proof Fence* as a way to explore binaries and the effects of colonialism.I got
> *Tsotsi* approved for the county and teach it to all of the 10th grade courses.
> We look at the first part of the film to get a sense of the environment and
> the characters. Last year, by the end of the semester, students had become
> concerned about world poverty, so we set a goal of raising $250 to send animals
> to other countries via Heifer International. When we exceeded our goals and
> were able to send a goat, a sheep, a flock of chicks, and two hives of bees, I let
> them have a pizza party and watch the whole movie—including the alternate
> endings. I put *Once Were Warriors* on a book club list along with literature from
> other cultures, and it was popular with many (but not all) students. I also got
> [Alexander McCall Smith's] *Ladies' No. 1 Detective Agency* approved for the whole
> class, and the standard class said it was their favorite book.

Another student notes that "many of the books I help purchase through
Title I funds [for my students] include nonfiction selections with post-colonial
terms. For instance, I worked with a group of fourth graders with a text about
the history of China, which included information about Western influence and
colonization. In a similar situation, but in a separate classroom (the books ordered
are shared school-wide depending on student reading levels) I overheard a Title
I assistant working with another small group discussing the term apartheid."

***

Our study provides an expanded demonstration of our discourse-based methodology. The first chapter, "'This is Africa,' or How Leonardo DiCaprio Imagines
Sierra Leone," examines contemporary filmic narratives of the "white man in
Africa" story. This chapter is the result of the discourse project highlighted
above that explores the circulation of images and films that represent Africa
to largely American, Western audiences in order to understand the emotional
transformation of white men. In our first case study, we examine the inven-

tion of Africa in two 2006 films that focus on historical events in two African countries, Edward Zwick's *Blood Diamond*, about the mining of so-called "blood diamonds" in Sierra Leone in the 1990s, and Kevin Macdonald's *The Last King of Scotland*, about Idi Amin's rule in Uganda in the 1970s. Both films were produced in the West, and we read them through the lens of Chinua Achebe's aforementioned famous 1975 lecture at the University of Massachusetts, "An Image of Africa," in which Achebe accuses Joseph Conrad of creating a racist depiction of a generalization known as "Africa" in *Heart of Darkness*. Similarly, while these films are about two specific African countries, the protagonists in these films (played by American actors Leonardo DiCaprio and Scottish actor James McAvoy) both claim, at various points in the narrative, that "this is Africa," and both perpetuate Conrad's project in *Heart of Darkness* in that they depict "Africa" as a generalization, a dark mirror for the Western conscience, and a backdrop for the emotionally transformative journey of white men. These films were released at a significant conjuncture: the emergence of what has been called the "celebrity-philanthropy complex," with celebrities assuming international diplomatic roles and endorsing campaigns, such as One with its "Project Red" and Red Manifesto, begun by Bono, that transcend traditional rubrics of diplomacy and turn consumers towards philanthropy in their critique of capitalism. The first chapter is related to the second in that both show two different narrative strategies for representing Africa and African political and social subjects—in the first, representations emanate from outside of Africa and in the second, representations emanate from within. In the Hollywood films discussed in the first chapter, there seems a real emphasis on the happy ending, on the recovery of the individual self, while in *Tsotsi*, the South African film discussed in the next chapter, some ambiguity remains, indicating that, perhaps, South Africans are not trying to elide their social or political history.

The second chapter, "Witness the Gangster in the Interregnum: Adapting Fugard's *Tsotsi*," provides a kind of counterpoint to its predecessor in that it examines a work written, produced, and acted by South Africans, Gavin Hood's 2005 film adaptation of playwright Athol Fugard's only novel to date, *Tsotsi*, which was written in 1960 and published 20 years later. The novel tells the story of an unnamed "tsotsi" (gangster) living in the black township of Sophiatown in the 1950s and follows Tsotsi's spiritual progression from an unfeeling murderer to an empathetic being capable of identification with other victims. Fugard's notes on the novel indicate a sense of uncertainty about how to end the story: "In the end, rushing to save the child as the bulldozer moves in. The wall collapses on both. Or alive?" (230). The ambiguity inherent in the novel's ending reflects a state of South African consciousness that Nadine Gordimer describes in her 1982 essay "Living in the Interregnum," in which she applies Antonio Gramsci's theoretical interregnum—the political space during which an old order is dying but a new order cannot as yet be born—to apartheid-era South Africa in the 1970s and 1980s. Gordimer claims that the interregnum is "not only between two social orders but also between two identities, one known and discarded, the other unknown and undetermined" (269–70). Furthermore, after apartheid ended in 1994, the "new" South Africa has in many ways found itself in a "second interregnum" (Ohlson and Stedman 2). The psychology of this second interregnum is apparent in Gavin Hood's award winning film adaptation of *Tsotsi*. The film, set in the post-apartheid township of Soweto, changes several key elements of Fugard's novel: for example, the film depicts a black African middle-class that would not have existed in the 1950s world of Fugard's text. Like Fugard, Hood had difficulty concluding the film. Hood shot three different endings, each revealing contrasting social and ideological consequences; however, the film, unlike the novel, also took into account other factors when constructing the ending, including the responses of test screening audiences. Both film and novel point to the difficulty, during and after apartheid, of imagining a positive future for black township South Africans. Furthermore, both works point to the difficulty—perhaps impossibility—that white writers and filmmakers such as Fugard, Hood, and Gordimer face in depicting South Africa in its various interregnum moments.

The third chapter, "Reclaiming the Maoriland Romance: Inventing Tradition in *Once Were Warriors* and *Whale Rider*," examines the retelling and reinvention of the Maoriland romance genre, prevalent in the literature and film of New Zealand in the early to mid-twentieth century. Even before the signing of the much contested Treaty of Waitangi in 1840, the indigenous Maori population of New Zealand had been decimated by intertribal warfare and the introduction of unfamiliar diseases, particularly influenza, brought by European settlers who had been exploring and settling the area since the mid-seventeenth century, and by the beginning of the twentieth century, the Maori had lost the majority of their land. The oral culture of the Maori, as well as Maori myths and traditions, have, therefore, been subsumed by colonial interference and influence, and the Maoriland romance genre—generated by white authors and filmmakers—functioned to mythologize the Maori in terms of the European imagination. By the 1980s and 1990s, however, a distinct body of New Zealand literature—including Keri Hulme's 1984 novel *the bone people*, Witi Ihimaera's 1987 novel *Whale Rider*, and Alan Duff's 1990 novel *Once Were Warriors*, for example—imagined, for both

Maori and white or Pakeha populations, new cultural narratives in the production of a contemporary Maori mythology that were dependent upon the reclamation and adaptation of traditional Maori institutions. Lee Tamahori's 1994 film adaptation of Duff's novel depicts protagonist Beth Heke's struggle to save herself and her children from marginalization and the abuse of her husband Jake, and Niki Caro's 2002 adaptation of Ihimaera's narrative depicts the ascendance of Paikea Apirana, a girl who, according to tradition, cannot claim status as chief. Both films (and novels) place the responsibility for Maori cultural persistence squarely on the shoulders of the Maori—particularly Maori women; in these depictions, white colonial intrusion is marginalized. This chapter positions these two films as works that speak back to and reclaim the Maoriland romance fiction genre of the late nineteenth and early twentieth centuries, in which Pakeha authors and filmmakers imagined and depicted the Maori as heroic warriors and seductive maidens.

The three films in the case study that constitutes the fourth chapter, "The New Voy(age)eur: White Women, Black Bodies, and the Spectacle of Sexual Abandon"—*I Walked with a Zombie, Wide Sargasso Sea* and *Heading South*—share an exotic locale: Caribbean nations exploited by colonial rule. In these narratives, the "exotic" is over-determined: "San Sebastian," Jamaica, and Haiti represent liminal[2] spaces in which narratives of sexual pleasure are complicated by the politics of colonial exploitation. Jacques Tourneur's 1943 horror film, *I Walked with a Zombie* and John Duigan's 1993 screen adaptation of Jean Rhys's *Wide Sargasso Sea* are significant texts in postcolonial analysis because they revise Charlotte Brontë's *Jane Eyre*, the quintessential novel of female independence acted out against the normative demands of British colonialism, by restoring the character of Rochester's wife or by visually invoking the exotic mise-en-scène of the Caribbean that *Jane Eyre* only obliquely imagines. By invoking "voodoo" at key moments in the text, the directors negotiate female sexual freedom or abandon in interesting ways.

Heading South, Laurent Cantet's 2005 film in which women "of a certain age" pay young black Caribbean men for sex and companionship, inverts a trope familiar in *Jane Eyre* and its adaptations. In *Heading South,* three North American women arrive at a resort in Haiti in the late 1970s; sexual tourists, they take young local men as lovers for the summer, while remaining mostly oblivious to the political and social conditions of their everyday lives amidst the poverty and violence unleashed by the regime of Baby Doc Duvalier and his security force, the vicious Tonton Macoute. While Cantet focuses mainly on the personal lives of the women and the problematic exchange system they have entered into, he frequently leaves them behind to follow Legba, the most sought-after gigolo, in his daily life. Cantet's style is interrogatory: all of the main characters except Legba address the camera in a self-revealing monologue and, rightly, many critics have addressed the politics of excluding Legba from this engagement with the viewer. Legba assumes another role: in Haitian Voodoo, Legba is an emissary between the living and the spirit world; indeed, in the narrative of the film, Legba's murder is the crisis that renegotiates the terms of Western sexual abandon and economic exploitation.

In the fifth and sixth chapters, "NRI: The Transnational Class and Transnational Class in Films from the Indian Diaspora," we examine the ways that the supposed authenticity of female Indian filmmakers—Mira Nair in chapter five and Deepa Mehta in chapter six—is complicated by their status as non-resident Indians. *Bollywood* and *Hollywood* continue to resonate as monolithic filmmaking centers that produce fairly generic products for global audiences through standardized modes of production. Lately, the two giants have seemingly entered into a fruitful relationship with films such as Gurinder Chadha's *Bride and Prejudice* (tagline: "Bollywood meets Hollywood...And it's a perfect match") melding a Bollywood aesthetic to traditional Western texts, employing bankable stars, and benefitting from Hollywood's marketing and distribution hegemony. This chapter focuses on the problematic conjunctures that have surfaced from collaborations between Bollywood, Hollywood, and the global filmmaking community by focusing specifically on films made by non-resident Indian (NRI) directors.

Films made by non-resident Indian directors reveal a range of cultural anxieties and ideological angst that not only interrogates Indian nationality and culture but also re-invigorates questions about class, sexual and gender identities, and nationality for diaspora and Western audiences. For example, social tensions in India have flared when films by non-resident Indians introduced the stories of previously marginalized subjects into the visual space of India, as Deepa Mehta did in her trilogy: *Fire, Earth* and *Water*. Similarly, a clash of values complicated a typical celebrity charity endorsement when Hollywood superstar Richard Gere spontaneously kissed Bollywood superstar Shilpa Shetty, resulting in an obscenity lawsuit in India against Gere.

In Mira Nair's *Monsoon Wedding*, the traditional arranged marriage finds its liberal expression when true love is privileged and a class-appropriate marriage is made; while issues of caste are largely absent (or ignored) in American films, they are reintroduced here. Non-resident Indian directors, this chapter argues, are participating in more than just a transnational industry; they are participating in multiple cinematic and public discourses that seek to organize global and national political and social spaces.

We conclude our study with an examination of three films, Steve Jacobs's *Disgrace*, Neill Blomkamp's *District 9*, and Clint Eastwood's *Invictus*, all of which reached North American screens in 2009 and all of which depict South Africa in various post-apartheid moments. A brief analysis of this trinity of narratives allows us to map, in the current moment, a theory of the intercultural as a space both transnational and specific, delineated by a concern with the interstitial, and perhaps preoccupied with the concept of truth. All three films are, to varying degrees, political, but each deals with South African politics in vastly different ways, *District 9* through allegory, *Disgrace* through the personal, and *Invictus* through sentimentalism. Finally, we read James Cameron's *Avatar*, the highest grossing film in history, as a failed intercultural narrative: in creating a completely fictional culture and landscape to colonize, Cameron is still utilizing familiar and highly essentializing notions of real peoples and cultures in order to generate a composite Other.

Notes

1. According to Bhabha, the "Nation itself, alienated from its eternal self-generation, becomes a liminal form of social representation a space that is internally marked by cultural difference and the heterogeneous histories of contending peoples, antagonistic authorities, and tense cultural locations" (299); "it is from the liminal movement of the culture of the nation—at once opened up and held together—that minority discourse emerges" (305).

One

"This is Africa," or How Leonardo DiCaprio Imagines Sierra Leone

***

Edward Zwick's *Blood Diamond* (2006), about the mining of conflict diamonds in Sierra Leone in the late 1990s, and Kevin Macdonald's *The Last King of Scotland* (2006), about Idi Amin's rule in Uganda in the 1970s, are two recent and popular films that seem to offer at least a superficial critique of the history of colonial intervention in Africa. *The Last King of Scotland* suggests that colonial rule not only eradicated African societies, but ill-prepared new nations for independence. In one scene, Idi Amin reminds an assembly of British and Ugandan officials that Africa, *black* Africa, before colonialism destroyed its unique cultures, was once a center of arts and learning. *Blood Diamond* suggests that the West's indiscriminate love of "bling" has brought untold destruction to the people, especially the children, of Sierra Leone. Released during a period of the West's intense scrutiny of African famine, genocide, civil war, and political disruptions, both films affirm through archival footage and documentary-style cinematography that Africa is in crisis. Not surprisingly, both films feature American and British actors in lead roles as white characters that articulate the collapse of Africa after colonialism. *Blood Diamond* stars Leonardo DiCaprio as Danny Archer, a Zimbabwean mercenary eager to get his hands on an enormous pink diamond, while *The Last King of Scotland* stars James McAvoy as Idi Amin's Scottish physician and confidant. *Blood Diamond* and *The Last King of Scotland* are prescriptive; both films provide "First World" audiences with an explanation of the continent's state of disorder and a rationale for Western intervention.

In explaining the way Africa "works" to Westerners who want less corruption, less bloodshed, and less chaos—an Africa that "makes sense" to them—both protagonists dismiss these desires by deploying the acronym T.I.A.: "This is Africa," at significant moments in the narrative. Both films are mired in what Hannah Longreen calls the "development gaze," a "way of seeing" that privileges European intervention in the lives of the African Other (230).

Barbara Heron, in *Desire for Development*, suggests that the acronym "T.I.A.: This is Africa" indicates the ideological contradictions provoked by this gaze: it is a response deployed by the development community to negotiate the feeling of "resignation" when aid workers are faced with what appear to be intransigent African conditions, marked by violence, corruption, and confusion. Its mobilization as an explanation of the "state of things" draws distinctions between superior Northern bourgeois "knowledges and practices" and Southern inferior African lives (Heron 82–83). In these films, Hollywood's fantasy Africa provides an ideologically evocative mise-en-scène, a backdrop for the emotionally transformative journey of white men who enunciate the state of things on the "dark continent."

Read through the lens of Chinua Achebe's famous 1975 lecture, "An Image of Africa," it is evident that both films offer viewers invented, imaginary Africas. Achebe strives to dislodge Conrad's classic novella of British colonial exploration from the canon because the novel "projects" an image of Africa rooted in racism; it perpetuates stereotypes of the continent as "the antithesis of Europe and therefore of civilization, a place where man's vaunted intelligence and refinement are finally mocked by triumphant bestiality" (3). Achebe argues that Conrad's novel, at the level of style and story, reaffirms Europe's superiority, despite the assertions of critics who suggest the novel is not complicit with the project of colonialism because of Conrad's authorial remove from the action (10).

On the contrary, argues Achebe, Conrad gives no language to the Other, and no alternative ethics or epistemologies are offered (11). Instead, Conrad's exploration of the deteriorating mind of the European, warped by fraternization with his inferiors, reveals the psychic consequences of colonialism, and it is precisely the use of Africa as "setting and backdrop," and the diminishment of Africans to subhuman, that proves the racism of the novel (12). The novel permits Europeans to imagine their superiority by projecting inferiority. Achebe notes that *Heart of Darkness* is only one book among many that fulfills the Western desire to represent Africa as a "place of negations at once remote and vaguely familiar, in comparison with which Europe's own state of spiritual grace will be manifest" (3). In Conrad's novel, as in *Blood Diamond* and *Last King of Scotland*, "Africa" functions as a palimpsest for the writing and rewriting of Western stories.

Kenneth Cameron, in *Africa on Film*, provides an encyclopedic summary of the more than 400 American and British films that comprise a genre of films in which *Blood Diamond* and *The Last King of Scotland* are exemplars. According to Cameron, the continent is represented mainly in terms of white exploration and exploitation, without much differentiation between Africa's many cultures, traditions, landscapes, or languages (Cameron 12). Ruth Mayer, in *Artificial Africas*, confirms that the West's production of an imaginary Africa effaces African cultures, identities, and geographies and replaces or reinscribes it with stories about the West. She asserts: "Africa is an artificial entity, invented and conceived by colonialism" (1). Her notion of *"Africanity*…the artificial concoctions of Africa" produced by the Western world, explains that the "speculations, projections, fantasies, and fears" that accompany images of Africa reinvigorate colonial histories and imperial fantasies (1).

Achebe's project to dislodge *Heart of Darkness* from the canon is not merely rhetorical; it yields a heuristic approach for the reading performed here of *Blood Diamond* and *The Last King of Scotland*. I want to suggest that *Heart of Darkness* might likewise provide a method of identifying and investigating the discourses that surround the films' release, particularly *Blood Diamond*'s examination of the politics of penetration: a justification of the West's access to African resources, and a wrestling with its attendant guilt and rationalizations. In Conrad's novel, Marlow travels deep into the Congo to recover Kurtz, the Company's man, who is rumored to have descended into barbarism and to have relinquished his hold on civilization. At Kurtz's camp, Marlow discovers ivory, "heaps of it, stacks of it….You would think there was not a single tusk left either above or below the ground in the whole country," and Marlow loads this bounty into the steamboat (64). In addition, he discovers Kurtz's research: the "International Society for the Suppression of Savage Customs, had entrusted him with the making of its report, for its future guidance" (65). At the end of the novella, Marlow, recovering from a near-fatal illness, returns to Europe with Kurtz's pamphlet with its ominous postscript, "Exterminate all the brutes"; a selection of personal letters; and a portrait. Marlow will not relinquish any documents to a Company official, despite his threats of legal action or his assertion that the report contributes to scientific inquiry. To a journalist, however, Marlow does turn over the report. Conrad reminds us that competing claims to knowledge about "savage custom" circulate as commerce, as science, and through the media. I make this long segue through *Heart of Darkness* because the two films discussed here make central to their narratives the dissemination of information—from the right source, into the right hands—about this place called "Africa." Thus, *Blood Diamond* and its challenge to conflict diamond mining, and the competing claims, complaints, and revelations that seek to explain the exploitation of "Africa," exceed the confines of the film itself.

I end this chapter with a brief survey of two other films about Africa released in 2006: *The Librarian: Return to King Solomon's Mines* (Frakes) and *Curious George* (O'Callaghan). Unlike *Blood Diamond*, a loose adaptation of H. Rider Haggard's 1885 novel, *King Solomon's Mines, The Librarian: Return to King Solomon's Mines* does not mediate the politics of its source but resuscitates the validity of the colonial-era fable in which lost treasure is discovered by European explorers with the help of a noble African companion. *The Librarian: Return to King Solomon's Mines* and *Curious George* are both film adaptations of literature with long histories of representing Africa as a locus of Western penetration and interrogation.

The "imaginary Africa" represented in the claim, "This is Africa," and the emergent, repressed, and disavowed discourses in contemporary mass culture that also state "This is Africa" in a much different register are the objects of this extended analysis.

The Last King of Scotland

The Last King of Scotland, adapted from the 1998 novel by British writer Giles Foden, is Scottish director Kevin Macdonald's first feature film. The film stars Forest Whitaker as the historical Idi Amin, Uganda's charismatic and deadly dictator. Scottish actor James McAvoy portrays the completely fictional Nicholas Garrigan, a young doctor who becomes Amin's personal physician and confidant; Simon McBurney, the well-respected British character actor, is Stone, the British envoy; and Kerry Washington, an American actress, is Amin's third wife, Kay. Although Whitaker is American, he has often been mistaken for a British citizen following his convincing performance in *The Crying Game* (Collier 150). Whitaker's uncanny resemblance to Amin, and MacDonald's clever use of archival footage of the Ugandan president that substantiates the similarities between them, adds to the confusion over Whitaker's nationality. The film was produced with British and Scottish funds and released through Fox Searchlight, an American studio; it was filmed on location in Uganda and features Ugandan actors and music. I draw attention to this triangle of casting, production, and geography because the relationships between English, Scottish, and Ugandan characters, and their respective national affiliations, figure prominently in *The Last King of Scotland's* construction of postcolonial "Africa." The film negotiates and renegotiates the tripartite relationship between England, Uganda, and Scotland, as represented by the characters of Stone, Amin, and Garrigan, respectively. By emphasizing the bond between the two men who reject England's will to empire—Garrigan, a Scotsmen, and Amin, a pretender to the Scottish throne—the film critiques England's consistent interference in Ugandan nation-building and provides a sustained exploration of the politics of transition between the colonial and postcolonial eras. Yet in its representation of the civil unrest, corruption, and violence that attended the end of colonial rule, the film undermines its critique of the ideology of imperialism in a number of ways that draw attention to the discomfort the West might feel in explorations of the postcolonial condition. Ultimately, *The Last King of Scotland* concludes that Africa is not a place for white Europeans by indulging nostalgia for the "civilizing" influences of the West, thus reinforcing a notion that Africa is a place of *real* and monstrous horror.

Much of the film's excellent reputation hinges on Whitaker's Oscar-winning performance, and his prominence in the marketing of the film might lead one to conclude that *Last King of Scotland* is an Idi Amin biopic. However, the film is explicitly a "white-man-in-Africa" coming-of-age story. Garrigan, a fictional character acting against the backdrop of Amin's reign, is introduced before the title credits. A newly minted doctor, his future seems determined: he will join in family practice with his well-meaning but arrogant father who congratulates his son by noting that Garrigan's degree is not as good as his own, while measuring out a wee drop of sherry in celebration. Alone in his room, Garrigan smokes a forbidden cigarette, drinks from a bottle of whiskey, and contemplates the bland and boring future laid out before him. His discontented howl is immediately met with an inquiry from his repressive parents; his confinement in his parent's stultifying middle-class home is absolute. In rebellion, Garrigan grabs a globe and tells himself that he will go wherever in the world his finger lands: his finger lands on Canada. Canada, like Scotland, is too closely associated with the British empire and not the radically different geography required for such a break with tradition. The second spin of the globe yields Uganda, a nation granted independence from Great Britain in 1962.

In contrast to gray, dull, and provincial Scotland, Uganda is sunny, vibrant, and exotic. On a crowded bus, we reconnect with Garrigan as the opening credits roll. A friendly and engaging explorer, Garrigan talks to an old woman and crowds to the windows of the bus with the other passengers to catch a glimpse of Amin, stopped with his entourage by the side of the road. Garrigan learns that there has been a coup and that Amin's triumph is a day of celebration. Garrigan is fascinated by the differences between Scotland and Uganda, and he can maintain pride in his heritage yet laugh at its idiosyncrasies. On seeing monkeys, a fellow passenger on the bus asks Garrigan if there are monkeys in Scotland. Garrigan replies, "No," but if there were, he jokes, the Scots would deep fry them. As he travels deeper into the heart of Uganda, Garrigan enthusiastically embraces the nation and its people. He begins his seduction of a young woman on the bus by bragging: "I'm a licensed physician." At her stop, they consummate their flirtation. His yell while pinned beneath her, "I am a medical officer overseas," reveals his belief that certain privileges and benefits accrue to his position. As Nigel Penn notes in his analysis of the African pastoral (in *Out of Africa* and other films set in Kenya), Africa serves as a natural paradise in which Europeans act out sexual relationships free from the strictures of the metropole (169). Indeed, shortly after Garrigan arrives at the health clinic in the countryside where he is to practice, he attempts to seduce the doctor's bored wife (Gillian Anderson), who ultimately chooses their good works over a dalliance with such a charming cad. Garrigan's youthful promiscuity meshes well with the film's historical moment: miniskirts, bell bottoms, and an appropriate soundtrack, including Ugandan singer Angela Kalule covering Kris Kristofferson's "Me and Bobby Magee" at a Holiday Inn bar, evoke the counter-culture aesthetic of the 1970s. The West's penetration, both literal and figurative, of the newly postcolonial African nation and its consequences are explored through the unlikely friendship that develops between Idi Amin and Garrigan.

Garrigan's compassionate care of the general's paranoid hypochondria endears him to Amin, who finds the young physician's naïve bluntness and his willingness to speak "truth to power" refreshing. Amin's delight in immoderation—of body, of speech, and of rule—manifests in the pomp and circumstance of official spectacle, liberal speeches of black power, and a lavish lifestyle, all equally delightful to Garrigan, who quickly becomes enamored of the perks of his job: a lovely convertible Mercedes-Benz, a flirtation with Kay, and the power attendant on access to the throne. Amin's promise to include Garrigan in creating a progressive health care system provides Garrigan with the moral stature of a missionary participating in the development process, visually enforced by images emblematic of modernity, including the bustling capital city of Kampala, the grand Presidential palace, the clean hospital, and other examples of modern architecture.[1] Most important, Garrigan and Amin share a love of all things Scottish, which binds them in a common disdain for the British who worked behind the scenes to place Amin in power. Prior to Ugandan independence, Amin was a member of the King's African Rifles (Britain's colonial African regiment) and served under Scottish officers, who he remembers fondly. In honor of his Scottish "heritage," Amin named two of his children who figure prominently in the film "Mackenzie" and "Campbell," and incorporated some of the trappings of Scottish ceremony including bagpipe players and kilted soldiers into Ugandan national spectacles. In one scene in the film, Amin, wearing a kilt, entertains Garrigan and his court with Scottish songs.

Amin's adaptation of Scotland's national dress and song appear as a politically astute appropriation of a recognizably Western culture with, ironically, anti-colonial dreams of its own. As Homi Bhabha notes in his analysis of "mimicry," an imitative discursive formation is the means by which the West hopes to reproduce colonized subjects whose adoption of their norms, values, and beliefs appears to secure colonial authority. What results, however, is a destabilizing occupation in which the oppressive politics of "almost the same, but not quite" become transparent and the hybrid colonized subject lives a double existence, both accommodating and menacing (Bhabha 86).

Amin's threat to British power is in his identification of Uganda with Scotland as a place "almost the same, but not quite" like its English neighbor; his offer to free Scotland from English control when he becomes the "last king of Scotland" critiques Britain's imperial mission. "Scotland" thus becomes a liminal site, an unstable signifier suggestive of Amin and Garrigan's ambiguous relationship with England. "England" is negated and negotiated at the first meeting between Amin and Garrigan. Garrigan attends Amin when the general is injured in a car accident just outside the village where Garrigan practices. At this, their first meeting, Garrigan grabs the general's gun and kills the cow, writhing in pain on the road, that has caused the accident. This assumption of the general's authority results in a tense standoff between Amin's heavily armed soldiers, Garrigan (suddenly aware of his brashness), and Amin—who confronts Garrigan and assumes that he is British. When Garrigan clarifies that he is Scottish, Amin immediately defuses the situation. Amin, enamored of Scotland, asks for Garrigan's Scottish soccer jersey as a present for his son; in exchange, Garrigan dons the voluminous shirt of the general's uniform, complete with its medals.

After their initial encounter, Garrigan and Amin part, yet Amin, impressed by Garrigan's abilities, wants Garrigan as his personal physician and sends a car for him. Garrigan, enjoying the luxury of the President's limousine, pretends to be Amin, waving to Ugandans who mistake Garrigan for the President. Garrigan also mimics the "royal wave" and thus masquerades as both a European monarch and the "last king of Scotland." The film consistently discriminates between England and Scotland, a distinction central to the formation of the friendship between Garrigan and Amin, but one that is complex and frequently ambiguous, complicated as it is by the film's simultaneous negotiation of Garrigan in another register: Western and white.

Garrigan easily assumes the role of Amin's trusted advisor. As he gets closer to Amin, he earns more power and usurps more of its perquisites: Garrigan takes Amin's place at a meeting; he replaces him in Kay's affections; he mistakenly informs on Amin's other "most trusted" advisor, Jonah Wasswa (Stephen Rwangyezi), the Minister of Health, resulting in his disappearance; and he acts as "official spokesperson" in rationalizing Wasswa's disappearance to a *London Times* reporter. Garrigan is especially contemptuous of Nigel Stone, the British diplomatic envoy who reveals that Wasswa is missing and implies that the increasing violence of Amin's regime signals political repression. Unaware of, or unable to recognize the extent of Amin's murderous regime, Garrigan explains to Stone that "This is Africa": violence must be met with violence to create a nation independent of the British. Garrigan is uncompromisingly naïve in believing that he is in some significant way different from the attachés of the British government because he condemns Stone's constant request for "clarifications," information about Amin that might assist the British as they monitor Amin's government. While Stone's stooped shoulders, ferret-like demeanor and obtuse diplomatic rhetoric perfectly embody the sneaky machinations of Uganda's former overlord, the film does not wholly repudiate the Crown's supervision or the necessity of Western surveillance. Stone's concern for the health minister stems from their mutual and productive working relationship and a humanitarian desire to deliver penicillin to Ugandans, and it is Stone's monitoring of human rights abuses that provides the documentation of Amin's murderous excesses.

In creating such a distinction between England and Scotland, the film explores the competing histories of Britain's "four nations" and the nationalist rebellions of Ireland, Scotland, and Wales against the more dominant English military and culture. Linda Colley, in "Britishness and Otherness: An Argument," acknowledges that attention to individual nation building is important, but warns that ethnic affiliations waned when "Otherness" threatened greater Britain. Beginning in the 1700s, these disparate groups united consistently against the threat of Catholicism; similarly, they united again once Britain's empire moved East: "Whatever their own individual ethnic background, Britons could join together vis-à-vis the empire and act out the flattering parts of heroic conqueror, humane judge, and civilizing agent" (324–325). Scots were not exempt from the nation's will to empire, joining with Scots-Irish and Anglo-Irish in the exploration and administration of the empire "quite disproportionate to their total numbers back home" (324). For Garrigan, "Africa" is a place where he can assert a politically and personally liberal ethnic identity (that is not empowering at home) within the reassuring parameters of postcolonial expectations for African behavior—until Amin becomes less the rational, Western-leaning leader and more the stereotypically savage African despot. The film then reestablishes the West and "home" as normative.

When it becomes evident that Garrigan must leave the country, he discovers that his room has been ransacked, and in straightening it up he lingers over an old photograph of him with his father—he also discovers that a Ugandan passport has replaced his own. Desperate for British protection, Garrigan goes to Stone to restore his national identity. Stone's terms are severe: in order to return to his own father, Garrigan must kill Amin, the father of Uganda, and restore this postcolonial African nation to Western norms of ethical and political rule.

Amin exploits, as well, the personal-as-political disjuncture between Scotland and England. When Garrigan, sensing the end of his tenure as Amin's trusted advisor, wants to return to Scotland, Amin says: "Are you like all the other British, here to fuck and take away?" Since Garrigan has recently consummated his flirtation with Amin's third wife, Kay, his inability to provide a ready answer to the literal question creates additional suspense and serves to confirm not only Garrigan's guilt but also his very tenuous position. Amin provides Garrigan with the answer to the political question: "No." Amin insists that Garrigan remain in Uganda because he has become like a son to the dictator. Although Garrigan reaffirms that he is Scottish and must return home, Amin insists that he stay: "You have stepped deep into the heart of my country, Uganda embraces you." As he is swallowed by Amin's bulk, the camera focuses on Garrigan's reluctant return of Amin's embrace. In the director's commentary, Kevin Macdonald notes that this scene represents Garrigan's ultimate subjection. Yet the oblique reference to Conrad's *Heart of Darkness* and what it entails is telling, for in the film's resolution of their friendship we can see in Garrigan's dilemma what Gyan Prakash noted as a psychic split in the Western experience of colonialism: intellectuals like Joseph Conrad and George Orwell hated the tyranny of empire and the "space of its enunciation" (193). The film dissolves the difference between England and Scotland, the foundation of its critique of imperialism, in favor of a shared *Western* horror of African excess. The film documents not the kind of political violence that Garrigan imagines is necessary for African independence, but a constructed cinematic horror that invokes clichés of Africa: a visual representation of tribal or traditional African practices that are horrific, and a depiction of black African women as overtly sexual and pornographic.

The film consistently reaffirms the relevance of simple binaries: civilization, modernity, and the West on the one hand and barbarism, tribalism, and Africa on the other. Throughout the film, Amin performs and privileges non-Western customs and beliefs. Following the coup, Amin reassures his followers that he is a humble man and joins the villagers in a traditional dance. He believes that he has seen his death in a dream, and despite his modern hospital and health care system, Amin thinks that his epileptic son should be isolated. Perhaps the most shocking and catalytic scenes in the film occur when Amin extracts what the film represents as traditional forms of revenge: Amin punishes Kay and Garrigan for their affair and punishes Garrigan for attempting to assassinate him.

It is unclear when Amin begins to suspect the relationship between his friend and Kay, but there is a clear indication of its evolution when, in a rare shot from Amin's point of view, we intrude on a moment of significant eye contact between Kay and Garrigan. Garrigan and Kay meet again at a party in which half-clothed women dance before a fire; Amin, dressed like an American cowboy, rides a white horse and ropes a guest, and, according to the director's commentary, an epic poet from northern Uganda plays the part of a naked reveler.[2] This pastiche of disparate yet resonate signs—the abandon of black women dancing to African drums; the recognizable Western iconography, emblematic of imperial ambition; and the privileging of the carnivalesque over the Homeric, indicate Garrigan's increasingly intoxicated condition, in which his life in Africa has ceased to make coherent sense. Garrigan and Kay escape this chaos to make love, and the camera lingers on Kerry Washington's bottom. On the commentary track, Macdonald lingers on this shot as well, noting that Washington has a particularly fine bottom and that at the film's preview male moviegoers were also quick to praise her derrière. I mention the director's indulgent gaze because it evokes Europe's fascination with Saartjie Baartman, a Khoikhoi with a steatopygous rump, displayed in the early 1800s throughout Britain and Europe as the "Hottentot Venus" (Lindfors 56). According to the mythmakers of the time, Baartman's larger posterior and the real and imagined differences in Khoikhoi female genitalia (and other differences of physiognomy) were an indication of black African racial inferiority (57). I note this history because the camera directs our gaze to Washington's posterior and reduces her to a body part (a cliché of Western filmmaking). More significantly, the film finds in the mutilated female body of Kay one of its most graphic representation of an Africa that is profoundly uncivilized and barbaric.

Kay discovers she is pregnant with Garrigan's child and becomes hysterical: she must risk discovery by Amin or go to a village and have an abortion. By the time Garrigan tracks Kay down, she has been murdered, her body dismembered, and then sutured together with arms and legs transposed. In the "making of" documentary, *Capturing Idi Amin*, Macdonald recognizes the liberties he has taken with representing Amin's third wife as a prosthetic grotesque. Kay Amin did have an affair and she was brutally murdered, although her murderer was never identified and her body was not mutilated. The reconstituted Kay, sewn together like Frankenstein's monster, serves as a metaphor for the dictator's psychic collapse and allows the film to return to the repressed colonial imagination in which the tribal and the village—the place of the "back room" abortion that Kay fears—are legitimately sites of uncivilized horror.

After witnessing Kay's mutilated body, Garrigan is forced to confront Amin's true nature and he is now willing to assassinate him. As he races to the Presidential palace, the film utilizes a surrealist montage to represent Garrigan and Amin's mental deterioration. Both feel the betrayal of their friendship; both realize that anarchy is at hand. The shots include, significantly, scenes from early in the film in which Garrigan surreptitiously watched a witchdoctor try to cure one of his patients at the clinic; shots of Amin and his men watching *Deep Throat* (Damiano 1972) and shots from *Deep Throat* and a shot of Kay, dead in the hospital. With this collection of images, the film establishes an imaginative and regressive history of a nation in its early postcolonial period with scenes that trace a de-evolution from superstition into the excesses of pornography. When Garrigan arrives in Amin's room, Amin asks if it is true that Linda Lovelace has a clitoris in her throat. Garrigan responds, purposefully, that all aberrations of nature are possible.

In the conclusion of the film, Garrigan has failed at his mission to murder Amin and is caught and beaten by Amin's men. Amin, aware of Garrigan's many betrayals, details Garrigan's psychology: Garrigan thought, wrongly, says Amin, that he would come to Africa and play the white man among the natives. Amin, holding Garrigan's head between his hands like a lover, a repeated gesture throughout the film that demonstrates Amin's Oedipal dominance over Garrigan, tells him: "I am the father of this nation, Nicholas, and you have most grossly offended your father." For this offense, Garrigan will suffer a distinctly Ugandan torture: to be hauled up by hooks piercing his skin and left to hang until dead. In the final cathartic moments of the film, in a conclusion that marks his ascent to adult masculine subject, Garrigan switches the terms of the father/son paradigm. Grabbing Amin by his uniform and pulling him closer, Garrigan tells him, "You're a child, and that is what makes you so fucking scary."

Jan Nederveen Pieterse, in *White on Black: Images of Africa and Blacks in Western Popular Culture*, his exhaustive catalogue of the visual construction of Africa and Africans across a number of texts, identifies the dialectic encoded here: colonial paternalism in the late nineteenth century established (during a period of relative stability) a "new mythology" accompanied by a shift in visual imagery that replaced the "savage" with a more malleable political subject: the child (88). Like the Western texts that constructed the story of African political promise and failure in the age of Conrad, *The Last King of Scotland* tells us that the "child and savage" cannot be separated, thus this early attempt at Ugandan political independence has failed. At the conclusion of the film, Dr. Junju (David Oyelowo), a physician who has always been skeptical of Garrigan's motives, rescues Garrigan and gets him on a plane back to Europe. This act of pity is necessary, Dr. Junju tells Garrigan, because Garrigan is white and it is his report about Uganda that people will believe. Both *The Last King of Scotland* and *Blood Diamond* dramatize this moment that transfers authority to the white characters to tell stories *about* Africa *to* the West. *Blood Diamond*, as I will demonstrate, engenders a wide-ranging critical discussion of a range of issues central to Africa, including diamond mining and consumer responsibility, child labor, resource exploitation, and the legacy of colonialism; however, the parameters of these discourses are negotiated and defined by the West.

Blood Diamond

Blood Diamond, released in December 2006, was not an unqualified hit despite its big-budget production values, exotic location shooting, well-reviewed performances by an A-list cast including Academy Award winner Jennifer Connelly, Academy Award nominees Leonardo DiCaprio and Djimon Hounsou, and director Edward Zwick's previous success with *The Last Samurai*, a film that reimagined the colonial presence in Japan from the point of view of Tom Cruise. In *Blood Diamond*, Danny Archer (DiCaprio) and Solomon Vandy (Hounsou) find themselves aligned across a complicated racial divide as each seeks an enormous pink diamond that will deliver them both from the violence and poverty of Sierra Leone. The film opens as Revolutionary United Front (RUF) soldiers raid Vandy's village, kidnap his son to serve as a child soldier, and force Vandy to work in an RUF diamond field that provides the diamonds the rebels exchange for weapons. When Vandy comes across the fabulous uncut gem, he hides it moments before government forces raid the mine. Imprisoned, Vandy crosses paths with Archer, who is serving time for smuggling diamonds across the Sierra Leone border into Liberia on behalf of Colonel Coetzee, Archer's former commander in the South African Border War and now an employee of Van De Kaap diamond company. Archer and Vandy come to an arrangement: Vandy will give Archer the pink diamond in exchange for locating his family. In exchange for the news story of conflict diamonds, Maddy Bowen (Jennifer

Connelly), an American journalist who develops a romantic attachment to Archer, uses her press credentials to guide them through the war-torn area.

The attraction between Maddy and Archer is established quite early in the film. They meet at a bar, and their repartee reveals the sexy magnetism of opposing worldviews: Maddy is smart, steely, and optimistic, while Archer is world-weary and cynical. While Maddy believes that her work can inspire the West to stop its material exploitation of the continent, Archer responds: "T.I.A."—his is an Africa that cannot be helped. The coming together of Maddy and Archer might be fruitfully understood as representing a juncture that marks the transition from colonialism to postcolonialism and hinges on white subjectivity as it defines and identifies diachronic visions of the "real" Africa. Danny Archer's peregrinations across Africa indicate the way that European influence has been able to persist on the continent, if only as nostalgia for a pre-Independence colonial era. Born in Rhodesia (Archer refuses to call the nation "Zimbabwe"), his parents were killed by African national groups in the rebellion against the former British colonizers who opposed black majority rule. Ironically, Archer served in South Africa with the South African Defense Force that helped in the liberation of Angola while crushing majority rule in South Africa. As a mercenary, he now works in the interest of a renegade ex-military force determined to rob the continent of more of its resources. The mercenary is a stock character of African adventure films. Kenneth Cameron describes him as the "soldier-emeritus of one of the great European armies…. He will necessarily be cynical, proficient, sentimental (about children, whores, and comrades), and masculine" (146). He is profoundly racist: freed from the politics of national affiliation and loyalties, he represents the last ditch efforts of whites to exert their hegemony in the face of black independence movements on the continent. Not surprisingly, Cameron is able to date the emergence of this archetype to the 1960s, the eve of independence, and to *Dark of the Sun* (Cardiff 1968), a tale of mercenaries in the Congo whose mission is to extract diamonds for Belgian officials (146). Archer's sentimental memories of the loss of his family and his home, a history of colonial transition, which he reveals to Maddy, is an emotionally compelling moment in the film that gives us access to what "This is Africa" means for him. Without his land (Rhodesia), and without his family, he feels no investment in the future of the continent or its people. Through his relationship with Maddy, a representative of the textual enunciation of Africa's ills through her reporting and of the missionary ideals that she brings to bear, we witness a transformation from the West's exploitative present to its humanitarian future.

Figure 1. Danny Archer (Leonardo DiCaprio) appears to single-handedly rescue Vandy's son, Dia (Kagiso Kuypers) from the RUF. (Warner Bros/Photofest)

While Vandy and Archer set off on foot to find the diamond, journeying across a predictable African landscpe of lush jungles and snow-capped mountains, the film works through the racism that subtends the colonial and postcolonial histories of these two men, within the norms of the action-adventure genre. Gina Marchetti argues that the genre frequently narrates the story of a white hero, "a mercenary, a treasure-hunter" (188) who navigates exotic locations in search of a local exploitable treasure with the help of a non-white "buddy" (195). The genre's principal themes, including the "rights of possession and property; the definition of the national, ethnic, racial self as opposed to 'other'; the propriety of intervening in other nations' or other cultures' affairs; the moral consequences of violence; and the meaning of masculinity and male prerogatives" (188) adequately summarize the trajectory of *Blood Diamond* and the ideological valences of the film. Archer consistently treats Vandy with contempt. In one scene, he calls Vandy a "kafir"; he bullies him with a gun; and in the most explicitly racist scene (because it evokes the evolutionary racism dating to the height of the colonial era), Archer skins a small primate and equates this animal with Vandy. Archer's success over the RUF, in which he single-handedly appears to eradicate a much larger and more threatening force of black Africans, is a Hollywood cliché.

One is inclined to agree with Marchetti when she suggests that this type of narrative affirms Western superiority: "…Since action-adventure tales generally involve a white American [or Western] hero going to battle with non-white foreign villains, the fact that the hero's buddy may be part of that alien culture assures the viewer of the moral right of the hero to combat the alien nation violently" (195). Del Hornbuckle, in a review of the film on the *Pambazuka News* website, a site targeted to a pan-African community, articulates a similar pattern in Zwick's film, which grants much of the narrative to Archer, a white African with a commitment to the colonial past of his parents and a man who upholds the mercenary stereotype in his quest for diamonds: "Thus unfolds the classic Africa saga—an almost unimaginable story of courage and horror becomes a lush, breathtaking African backdrop of white redemption, black, power-hungry, violent, psychopathic rebels, and the good-as-gold, innocent African caught up in the madness." Monohla Dargis, in a *New York Times* review, notes that *Blood Diamond*, like *The Constant Gardener* (and one might add, *The Last King of Scotland*), consistently projects "an almost quasi-touristic fascination with images of black Africans, who function principally as colorful scenery or, as in the gruesome scenes inside rebel training camps, manifestations of pure evil." Nathan Lee in the *Village Voice* offers a scathing critique of this representation of black Africa's perennial descent into chaos, proposing another acronym in place of Archer's resigned "T.I.A.": "T.I.A.P.U.O.M.A.A.C.Y.W.B.T. T.S.S.O.B. W.P.W.S. H.A.T.I.G.R.B.S. T.W.N.A./O.V.A: This Is Africa Propped Up Once More As A Colorful Yet Wrenching Backdrop To The Stupid Story Of Boring White People Whose Sham Heroics Are Thrown Into Greater Relief By Surrounding Them With Noble And/Or Vicious Africans."[3]

Djimon Hounsou, a native of Benin, was much praised for his acting, yet like so many black characters before him, Solomon ("the wise") embodies the moral compass of the film; he leads the white man across Africa and teaches him the meaning of humanity, family, and justice. Stephanie Zacharek, in a review in *Salon*, calls Hounsou the "soul of the picture." As Paul Arendt complains, "While Leo and Jennifer have good crunchy characters to play with, the always brilliant Hounsou is stuck with an underwritten, saintly tribesman type." Hounsou, as Zwick notes in the commentary, plays Vandy as basically humble and passive, a victim of circumstance, and one who does not give rise to anger against this racial treatment. In fact, Vandy, perhaps learning his own lessons from Archer, wonders if Africa was not better off under colonial rule.

The film rewards Vandy's complacency by reuniting him with his family while denying his relationship with his country or with his nation's economic resources.

Once Archer and Vandy find the diamond and rescue Vandy's child, Archer has a change of heart: he now recognizes the "just use" of the diamond. With his own blood mixing with the red African soil, Archer dies reconnected to his heritage and to the land, defending Vandy and his son from his mercenary comrades. Vandy's fate is somewhat different. At the film's conclusion, Vandy does not look at the diamond that he passes over to the Van De Kaap representative because the exchange of this precious stone for his family is an equitable one. However, there is no homeland represented in the film other than the one Archer had with his family in Rhodesia—for Vandy, there is family (now refugees) but no land. In the last scene of the film, Vandy attends a conference on the Kimberly process, the agreement that will regulate the exportation of conflict diamonds to Western consumers. Maddy's investigation has resulted in an article that reveals the complicity of the West in the violence that surrounds diamond production, a synechdochal gesture towards the larger public and political investigation of this industry. As Vandy waits to be admitted to the conference, he reads the article, and his gaze falls on a photograph of Archer, reminding us of the role he has played in rectifying the abuses of the industry. Yet when Vandy is introduced as the "voice of Africa" by the conference's white, male delegate and called to the podium as a representative of the people whose lives have been most traumatically disrupted by exploitation, his voice is silenced. Although the word "voice" is invoked at least three times to describe Vandy's authority to "speak for" the material conditions of the continent, he does not actually talk in this final scene.

Blood Diamond had a profound effect on public perception of the acceptable relationship between the West and resource extraction in Africa. The film ignited a firestorm of publicity for its explicit message to consumers that they have a role to play in ending the mining of conflict diamonds in Africa. In response, and even before the film was released, the diamond industry moved to contain public opinion, hired a crisis manager to deal with consumer fallout and mounted a diamond-industry-wide media campaign in response to the perceived threat of the film (Snead). I want to conclude this chapter by detailing the convergence of multiple media forces and outlets around the problem of resource exploitation in Africa.

According to reporter Elizabeth Snead, Amnesty International's celebrity outreach program sought to capitalize on the publicity attendant on the film by reaching out to other celebrities who might be willing to focus attention on human rights abuses. Because he works with De Beers on a line of jewelry, hip-hop artist and jewelry entrepreneur Russell Simmons was one celebrity and businessman that Amnesty International wanted to reach with a special screening of the film (Snead). Simmons, co-founder of the influential hip-hop label Def Jam, is also

(TNT/Photofest)

(MGM/Photofest)

Figure 2. White Western men remain in the foreground of the frame, a composition both visual and ideological that remains relatively stable. On top, Noah Wylie in *The Librarian: Return to King Solomon's Mines* (2006) and on the bottom, a still from *Mogambo* (Ford 1953), with Ava Gardner, Grace Kelly, and Clark Gable. Nostaliga for an era when African adventure stories might be screened without repercussions ripples through some mainstream reviews. In his review of *Blood Diamond*, *Los Angeles Times* film critic Kenneth Turan wished that DiCaprio's performance evidenced the compelling masculinity of "white hunter" Clark Gable.

the founder (with his ex-wife Kimora Lee Simmons) of the Simmons Jewelry Co. In addition, he is the Advisory Board Chairman of the Diamond Empowerment Fund (DEF), a non-profit organization sponsored by Simmons Jewelry. According to the organization's mission statement, it was "[E]stablished by individuals and businesses in the diamond and jewelry industries and others who are committed to the empowerment of Africa" ("Mission and Vision Statement"). DEF encourages the industry to contribute to education projects in Africa and urges consumers to buy products that support the foundation. This mediated position that returns profits to the country in the form of charity appears to be only marginally success-ful. Kim Kardashian appeared on David Letterman in October 2009 to promote the Fund's work in Botswana with the message that profits from the diamond industry support "pretty much the entire country." The audience responded with general laughter, and David Letterman wondered if there might be another side to the story, namely that local people are exploited. Kanye West takes a slightly different position. In one variation of his video, "Diamonds Are Forever," West juxtaposes the old money of Prague with images of children mining diamonds in Sierra Leone to point to the consequences of the demand for diamonds. The video ends with a message to consumers to buy conflict-free diamonds.[4]

Two films that appeared in 2006, *The Librarian: Return to King Solomon's Mines* and *Curious George,* challenge progressive deliberations on extractive practices in Africa. The popular TNT cable television program, *The Librarian: Return to King Solomon's Mines* (2006), starring Noah Wylie, is only the most recent adaptation of Haggard's late-nineteenth-century novel, *King Solomon's Mines.* In the novel, British adventurer Alan Quatermain is hired by a young woman to find her father, who disappears while seeking the fabled Biblical lost treasure with the help of Umbopa, an African king in disguise. First adapted in 1918, its versions include a 1950 MGM Technicolor extravaganza starring Deborah Kerr and Stewart Granger; a 1985 action/comedy hybrid modeled on Indiana Jones films; and a 2004 television version starring Patrick Swayze. In *The Librarian* series, of which *Return to King Solomon's Mines* is one iteration, Flynn Carsen travels to all corners of the globe in search of lost treasures, acting out adventures against a backdrop of exotic locations peopled with saintly, incompetent, or terrifying inhabitants. Whatever artifact the Librarian discovers or recovers on his adventures—the Spear of Destiny, the Judas Chalis—is returned to the safety of the Metropoli-tan Library, an institution that houses the world's most important and sacred texts and objects, and collects knowledge about the Other for the benefit of the West. *King Solomon's Mines*—its 1885 original and 2006 reincarnation—is, as Cameron notes, a "myth of empire, the wealth of Africa proposed as the goal of the white hero's quest" and one made all the more immediate to Haggard's generation by the discovery of the Kimberley diamonds and the Rand gold deposits (24). Alessandra Stanley, writing for the *New York Times*, surmises that contemporary viewers are indulging this myth, "because it promised the simplicity and cozy exoticism of an old Saturday-afternoon movie or a Tintin comic."

Curious George, another film that imagined Africa, was also released in 2006. In this animated adaptation, the "Man in the Yellow Hat" is named Ted (voice by Will Ferrell). Although he may have been a poacher in the very popular 1941 children's book, in the film he is the curator of a museum that has fallen on hard times. Ted is a bit timid, but, in desperation, he becomes an explorer and adventurer who travels to Africa to steal a priceless idol to save the museum. George is a precocious monkey who follows him back to New York. Over the course of their relationship, George teaches Ted to be more outgoing, to explore and to play and, eventually, to romance Maggie (Drew Barrymore), a teacher. George, ever curious, is taught to behave, to become the good child, or subject, of white culture. In the film, George's penchant for mischief is a source of humor, and closely monitored; in the PBS children's television series that followed quickly on the heels of the film, the behavioral lessons so prominent in the book are reinforced. June Cummins, in her analysis of the children's book series, argues that the books are a parable of colonial-era slavery: captured by the white man, the African subject, represented as a childish little monkey, learns proper behavior from the appropriate authority figure (69–70). George is not the only "object" removed from Africa, the priceless idol that Ted pilfers is a resource whose value to Africa is ignored by the filmmakers. The filmmakers did debate whether stealing cultural artifacts is ethical, but decided that any explanation of this kind of resource grabbing was much too advanced for the animated films' audience: "We just felt it was the wrong audience to explain it to," says director Matthew O'Callaghan. "I understand the criticism, I really do. But we couldn't come up with a solution. There wasn't an entertaining way to deal with it" (qtd. in "Insider"). The film, like the book, is recognizably pedagogical, and the director's explanation of the conditions under which the West acquires Africa's resources is disturbingly flippant. The image of Africa that functions as a narrative device in *Curious George* circulates in products geared for children. In *Buy, Buy Baby*, Susan Gregory Thomas warns that all areas of children's lives, from school time to naptime to mealtime, are infiltrated by products emblazoned with the licensed image of George, including books, plush toys, sheets, cookie jars, and salt and pepper shakers (168). Cummins asks us to consider the pedagogical upshot of this popular series that has forty titles and twenty million copies in print: "By portraying and excusing imperialism, the books coerce children into accepting their own and each others' colonization" (70).

Curious George and *The Librarian* are two films in which colonial histories, and imperial discourses and forms, are once again recuperated to serve as a dark mirror for the conscience of even the youngest Western viewer. It seems appropriate, therefore, to return to Achebe's condemnation of *Heart of Darkness* and his resistance to its inclusion in the canon (in what amounts to an institutional endorsement of colonial memory). At the end of *Blood Diamond*, Maddy publishes her story about conflict diamonds in a magazine (much like *Vanity Fair*). Like the reports, portrait, and papers that Marlow brings back to Europe to document Africa, Maddy's story is just one compilation of worn-out images of "Africa" that we have watched her take throughout the film. At the conclusion of *Things Fall Apart*, Achebe critiques the premise that white people have the authority to speak about these cultures by mocking *Heart of Darkness* and the West's production of knowledge about Africa:

> The Commissioner went away, taking three or four of the soldiers with him.... As he walked back to the court he thought about that book. Every day brought him some new material. The story of this man who had killed a messenger and hanged himself would make interesting reading. One could almost write a whole chapter on him. Perhaps not a whole chapter but a reasonable paragraph at any rate. There was so much else to include, and one must be firm in cutting out details. He had already chosen the title of the book, after much thought: *The Pacification of the Primitive Tribes of the Lower Niger*. (171)

In the following chapter, we examine a very different vision of Africa: Gavin Hood's 2005 film adaptation of Athol Fugard's novel, *Tsotsi*. Made by South Africans in South Africa, *Tsotsi* works through the nation's history of economic and racial discrimination. The film retains Fugard's ambiguous ending, an indication that the narrative is still coming to grips with the nation's difficult past.

Notes

1. In Foden's novel, Garrigan is the son of a Scottish Presbyterian minister. Ironically, according to an interview with Sally Vincent, James McAvoy also wanted to be a missionary until personal qualms about the Catholic Church's mission in Africa dissuaded him.

2. Macdonald's DVD commentary consistently draws attention to his inability to accommodate in the film Uganda's unique culture or the accomplishments of individual Ugandans. For example, the epic poet from northern Uganda for whom no other role could be found agreed to full frontal nudity, although, as Macdonald claims, the Ugandans are a particularly modest people.

3. Lee also notes that Connelly is "so ready" for her "'I am African' poster." As we note in the Introduction, the "I am African" campaign generated a similar debate around issues of "authentic" or appropriate representations of Africa and Africans.

4. American music culture, particularly rap and hip-hop, is enormously influential in Africa. See our analysis of its influence on the film *Tsotsi* in chapter two.

Two

Witness the Gangster in the Interregnum: Adapting Fugard's *Tsotsi*

***

"God Bless Africa."

Gavin Hood, from his 2006 Oscar acceptance speech

South African playwright Athol Fugard's only novel to date, *Tsotsi*, written in 1960 but unpublished until 1980, is the story of an unnamed "tsotsi" (gangster) living in the black township of Sophiatown in the 1950s. The novel follows Tsotsi's spiritual progression via the recovery of repressed memory from an unfeeling murderer to an empathetic being capable of identification with other victims of South Africa's apartheid era government—an abused dog, an abandoned baby, and an elderly man crippled in a mining accident. Fugard's notes on the novel, self-published in his *Notebooks: 1960-1977*, indicate a sense of uncertainty about how to end the story in terms of whether to allow his title character to live or die: "the end—a life saved. (A useless life saved? Old man?) Hold and refusing to let go. Carried, cherished—dying with it? Love" (11). Of Tsotsi's fate, he writes "in the end, rushing to save the child as the bulldozer moves in. The wall collapses on both. Or alive?" (12–13). The ending he chose forecloses his ambiguity: while trying to rescue the abandoned baby, Tsotsi dies as Sophiatown, once the site of a South African multi-racial renaissance, is razed to make way for a white settlement. Such narrative finality characterizes a period situated at the height of the apartheid era just prior to the emerging state of South African consciousness that Nadine Gordimer describes in her 1982 essay "Living in the Interregnum," in which she applies Antonio Gramsci's theoretical interregnum—the political space during which an old order is dying but a new order cannot as yet be born—to apartheid era South Africa in the 1970s. In this now famous and oft referenced work, Gordimer claims that the interregnum is "not only between two social orders but also between two identities, one known and discarded, the other unknown and undetermined" (269–70); the "known" identity of which

Gordimer speaks is apartheid, still very much in place and manifest in Fugard's novel in Tsotsi's fate at the end of the narrative. The future into which he could emerge after resurrecting repressed memories of his traumatic past is marked by the complete destruction of Sophiatown. Tsotsi's continued persistence at this point in history—late 1950's South Africa, a moment just prior to the Sharpeville massacre of 1960, which followed Fugard's completion of the novel in 1960—is a bleak prospect, and Fugard's tragic ending is testament to that reality.

After apartheid ended in 1994, the so-called "new" South Africa has in many ways found itself, as various critics have claimed, in a "second interregnum." According to Thomas Ohlson and Stephen John Stedman, this uncertain period "differs from that of the 1980s in two important respects. People's expectations about and demands for change have grown, and profound uncertainty about what form that change would take has raised the political stakes for all concerned" (2). It is in the unknown space of this second interregnum that South African director Gavin Hood has situated his 2005 film adaptation of *Tsotsi*, the second most internationally successful South African film to date.[1] The psychology of this second interregnum and the political and social concerns that mark it are apparent in the film, which stars Presley Chweneyagae in the title role, particularly in terms of the film's alteration of several key components of the narrative. These include a focus on black male power struggles as opposed to Fugard's novel's tacit attention to the demise of black women, both as mothers and as victims of sexual violence perpetrated by black men; a shift in the treatment of Tsotsi's repressed memory of the violent death of his childhood dog at the hands of his father; and the creation of an ambiguous ending of the narrative illustrative of the unknown and undetermined nature of the new South Africa. In the film, the baby is safely returned to his parents, but the fate of Tsotsi is unclear, and Hood shot three endings, all of which are included on the DVD. In many ways, the film substantially softens the violence inherent in the original text; in fact, Lindiwe Dovey points out that Hood was quite angry when real tsotsis criticized Chweneyagae's performance as "too soft" to be believable (152–3).

As an artist whose work deals explicitly with the black experience of apartheid, Fugard, like fellow white writers Alan Paton and Nadine Gordimer, has been criticized for sentimentalizing and patronizing the experiences of black South Africans, experiences from which his privileged position has protected and insulated him. Of this white authored "literature of sympathy," Derek Cohen claims that "white art which is concerned with black life often tends to distill the vast ocean of black life into a single drop of pain and suffering, seeming unable or unwilling to acknowledge the wholeness and completeness of life" (373).

Cohen goes further in his criticism of *Tsotsi*: "for all its excellences and inherent impetuses, *Tsotsi* is, by obtrusive design, a novel of sympathy and Christian redemption which sets out to celebrate the virtues of pain and suffering and the salvation that follows from the experiences these provide" (374). Similarly, Hood has had to defend his position to critics who suggest that black township life lies outside the scope of his experience and that he speaks for a position beyond his realm of comprehension: "first of all, this happens to be my pigmentation, but I've spent more time in the shanty towns than some of my actors. I hate to be boxed in because of my heritage" (qtd. in Archibald 46). My main concern in this chapter is to examine how Hood's visual adaptation translates Fugard's text to generate a dialogic narrative of witness that resists an overarching and singular reading of Tsotsi's—or any South African's—"truth" and points instead to the need for open discussion of the connection between and progression from two historical South African moments: one that marked the apartheid-era end of Sophiatown's thriving multi-racial culture and one that marks the current moment of post-apartheid uncertainty, characterized by a multi-racial democracy on the one hand and violence and HIV/AIDS on the other.

The concept of witnessing is of particular importance in terms of a discussion of Fugard's novel and Hood's adaptation of that novel, especially given the controversial role that witnessing has played in what Archbishop Desmond Tutu refers to as the "restorative justice" sought by South Africa's post-apartheid Truth and Reconciliation Commission (TRC). In his introduction to Jillian Edelstein's photographic account *Truth and Lies: Stories from the Truth and Reconciliation Commission in South Africa*, Michael Ignatieff describes the nature of the testimony that took place when the commission met from 1995 to 2001, during which time perpetrators could appeal for amnesty for crimes committed during apartheid, if they could prove that those crimes were politically motivated. Ignatieff asserts that in terms of the commission, "it was always a question of just how much anyone could stand: the witnesses, the victims, the watching audience. No one who was there was sure that such a bitter catharsis was always a good thing for the country or the individuals to go through," and he states, "there is an African proverb: Truth is good, but not all truth is good to say" (16). In the context of the TRC—or of the reiteration or confession of any traumatic event—the personal and the political may be, it seems, too closely elided for so much "truth" to be healthy, and, furthermore, whatever is confessed may never prove to be *enough* truth for the victim.[2]

American poet Carolyn Forché has argued for the need for a third place of signification that is neither the personal nor the political; she calls this space "the social," and she argues that poetry situated in this space

> cannot be judged by simplistic notions of "accuracy" or "truth to life." It
> will have to be judged, as Ludwig Wittgenstein said of confession, by its
> consequences, not by our ability to verify its truth. In fact, the poem might be
> our only evidence that an event has occurred: it exists for us as the sole trace
> of an occurrence. As such, there is nothing for us to base the poem on, no
> independent account that will tell us whether or not we can see a given text as
> being "objectively" true. Poem as trace, poem as evidence. (16)

In terms of Fugard's project in *Tsotsi* and Hood's modernization of that work,
this discussion of the social as conceived of by Forché is particularly relevant. In
many ways, Fugard's novel exists as trace evidence to the once thriving culture of
Sophiatown, and the work positions Tsotsi as witness to the destruction of that
culture—and the individuals who inhabit it—at the hands of state. Through this
narrative strategy, rather than attempt to provide an authentic—or true—voice of
Tsotsi's experience, the third-person narration eschews any attempt to represent
some objective truth, to establish any sense of verisimilitude. Conversely, film,
as a visual medium, is uniquely situated to position the audience as witness, and
Hood's adaptation of Fugard's novel capitalizes on this reality. Not only does the
film lack the narrative perspective of the novel, which highlights Tsotsi's inner
turmoil, but Tsotsi seldom speaks throughout the film; in fact, during the film's
lengthy final scene, he remains entirely mute. Therefore, the viewer inhabits the
social space identified by Forché, realizing that, except for a roll of the dice—the
image that opens Hood's film—as Hood suggests, Tsotsi's reality "could have
been your destiny" ("The Making of"). The viewer must bear witness to and
engage in dialogue with the truths revealed in the film,[3] most significantly, the
struggle to define the role of black men within contemporary post-apartheid
South Africa.

***

Athol Fugard is one of South Africa's most prominent white playwrights, an
Afrikaner who writes in English, and whose literary career spans from 1958,
with the performance of *No-Good Friday* at the Bantu Men's Social Center in
Johannesburg (Wertheim vii) to the present. Fugard's fame is international in
scope; as Albert Wertheim claims,

> if one were to list the six or seven most significant English-language playwrights
> alive during the last decade of the twentieth century, that list would undoubtedly
> include the names of Arthur Miller, Tom Stoppard, Harold Pinter, Edward

Albee, and perhaps August Wilson and David Hare. It would also surely include
South African playwright, director, and actor Athol Fugard. (vii)

According to Francis Donahue, Fugard's plays "stand as judgmental *witnesses* to
the true nature of the South African experience as lived by the immense majority of the country's non-white population in the second half of the twentieth
century" (323, my emphasis). Indeed, since *No-Good Friday*'s performance a
decade after the National Party's implementation of apartheid, Fugard's entire
body of work has been a testament to the devastation engendered by such a
system and to the subsequent struggles South Africans have had to face in the
wake of apartheid's demise in 1994. The story of *Tsotsi*'s genesis in 1960, disappearance for two decades, and eventual resurrection and publication in 1980,
are events that are chronicled by David Hogg, the first scholar to write about
the novel, Stephen Gray, who edited Fugard's manuscript for publication, and
Barrie Hough, Gray's student. Hogg's 1978 essay, "Unpublished Fugard Novel,"
provides an extensive summary of the work, which, at the time of Hogg's writing,
was "housed in the Pringle Collection at Rhodes University" and had "no title,
though Fugard proposed to call it *Tsotsi*, after its main character" (60). Gray
discusses early critical consensus of the work, which "appeared for a while to be
much the same as Fugard's own" (57) as expressed in his *Notebooks*: "read what
I had written to Sheila. Her silence—my own feelings as I progressed from one
muddled paragraph to another, were enough. I tore it up" (51).

Despite Fugard's insistence after foregoing the manuscript that "I am a
playwright" (*Notebooks* 51), he later agreed to let Stephen Gray edit and eventually publish the work, with a caveat that a note be included to indicate that the
novel was not a new text. Of the work's foundational status, Rita Barnard claims
that *Tsotsi* "is the ur-text for Fugard's literary investigations of the relationship
between person and place. Though it languished for years in manuscript at the
National English Literary Museum, it is a work that Fugard was to mine, however
unconsciously, for motifs and dramatic ideas he would explore in his plays"
(103). Initially, Gray claims that Fugard did not even remember having written
the novel, so Gray had to piece together the time frame for its writing, and Gray
disagrees with Hogg's assertion that the work was written between 1952 and
1954, claiming instead that the work would have to have been written after 1958
when Fugard moved to Johannesburg. It would have been during this time that
Fugard would have come to know Sophiatown, the "'freehold' township where
blacks had historically been allowed to own title to their properties" (Kaplan xiii).

According to Jonathan Kaplan, in his 2006 introduction to the Grove Press edition of the novel, Sophiatown's "lively jazz and shebeen culture, where black and white could drink and dance together, formed the febrile center of urban African renaissance and theater" (xiii), and David Goodhew, in his study *Respectability and Resistance: A History of Sophiatown*, states that the Western Areas of Johannesburg (Newclare, Sophiatown, and Western Native Township) "formed the most significant black center of population…in South Africa in the 1940s and 1950s. The district was a seedbed of political activism by the ANC and the Communist Party as well as a fertile environment for black culture" (xv). In the late 1950s, black writers such as Bloke Modisane, Can Themba, and Lewis Nkosi were thriving in Sophiatown, writing for *Drum* magazine. The 1955 Western Areas Removal Act, however, implemented the clearance of Sophiatown; the process was complete by 1963 when the area was rebuilt as a white settlement and renamed Triompf, Afrikaans for "triumph." The clearance process is described early in the novel:

> The slum clearance men had been at work in that area and a few more roofs were down and the walls, without doors and windows, gaped like skulls in the fading light and you could still see the dust settling inside while you remembered the disbelief, the angry impotence, the confusion of faces that had followed the cart loaded high with sticks of furniture. (6)

Because Fugard discarded the novel after writing it, its description of life in Sophiatown in the period just prior to its compete clearance and prior to the Sharpeville Massacre of 1960—the event that brought Fugard back to South Africa from London where he had been in search of theatrical experience—was not banned, as were the majority of works that explored or arose from the Sophiatown renaissance. As Stephen Gray claims, "for a South African reader in the 1980s, Tsotsi is almost the only reminder available that such a complex and richly rewarding, and disturbing, past in the arts not only could have existed, but actually did exist" (61). In Forché's sense, novel as trace, novel as evidence—and the above passage's use of "you" positions the reader as witness to a South African cultural movement that was all but destroyed.[3] *Tsotsi* is, according to Barrie Hough, "about the metaphysical journey of a man in search of his soul" (74), a man suffering from "ontological insecurity" who "has no sense of himself as a being in space or time" (75). In it, Fugard explores one facet of the "lost generation" (Glaser 1) of South Africa, the male specific, violent, anti-establishment, and completely disenfranchised tsotsi subculture that thrived in and around Johannesburg during the late 1950s. The titular character is the leader of a gang made up of himself, Butcher, Die Aap, and Boston, and the four prowl the streets, killing indiscriminately. According to Clive Glaser in his study *Bo-Tsotsi: The Youth Gangs of Soweto, 1930-1976*, the tsotsi phenomenon was not specific to this particular urban area, but "it represents the biggest concentration of urban Africans in South Africa and…[Soweto] was the cauldron of the 1976 uprising" (2). Tsotsidom arose, at least in part, out of the failure of the Bantu education system:

> There is significant evidence to suggest that the better-educated young men were as, or even more, likely to be unemployed than those without much education. Rather than offering a ladder of opportunity that parents hoped for, education was encouraging hopes that the system tended to frustrate. By contrast, tsotsidom offered glamour and a sense of importance. (Goodhew 98)

Significantly, much of the style sensibility of the tsotsis was based on American culture, particularly American film: "the most important source of American fashion was, of course, Hollywood. Tsotsis were heavily influenced by cowboy, gangster, and black American jazz movies" (Glaser 69). In fact, according to Jonathan Kaplan, "the word tsotsi may have been derived from an Africanisation of 'zoot-suit'" (Fugard, *Tsotsi* ix),[4] and such a reality speaks to the influence of the Hollywood film industry—particularly the imagined gangster identity depicted in film during the 1930s and 1940s—on the lives of urban, black South African males. The language spoken by tsotsis is called tsotsitaal, a creole that varied from township to township, made up of English, Afrikaans, and indigenous African languages like Xhosa and Zulu.

Despite these historically verifiable specificities of language and dress, as I stated earlier, Fugard's novel is entirely unconcerned with verisimilitude and with generating an "accurate" external picture of the tsotsis; the novel contains almost no physical description of any of the characters, nor is there much dialogue. The narrator often comments on the fact that the characters are speaking, but the focus is on the act of speaking, not on what is being said:

> Tsotsi told them what they would be doing that night. He told it slowly, taking his time, the words coming in an easy rhythm between the swallows of beer… and other interruptions like leaving the room for the backyard where *you* rested against the hot corrugated iron fence with an outstretched arm…. When he got back he would ask, where was I, and sometimes someone remembered and most times no one cared because it wasn't important. All that mattered was that his voiced filled that last reluctant hour of an afternoon that was heavy with the weight of idle hands. (2, my emphasis)

The narrative's insistence, in this instance as elsewhere, that what Tsotsi says "wasn't important" is, in my reading, not a negation or silencing of black South Africans but rather underscores a major strength of the work: the specifics surrounding Tsotsi's speech are unimportant as compared with the inarticulate experiences of trauma, repressed memory, and violence of apartheid that have an impact on not only Tsotsi but are written on the bodies and inscribed within the psyches of all South Africans. Furthermore, the shift in the passage above from the pronoun "he" to "you" and back to "he" indicts the reader for her or his collusion with apartheid even as it posits that "he"—Tsotsi—could be "you" the (ostensibly) white reader. What dialogue there is, is spoken in English, although Fugard will occasionally include a non-English word and then translate it for his audience: Butcher "turned to Tsotsi and smiled and said, 'Nyama,' which means meat" (66). The predominant "voice" in the novel, then, is that of the third-person narrator who, at various points, occupies space inside the consciousnesses of Tsotsi, Boston, Gumboot, Miriam, and Morris in order to weave their distinct stories together in such a way that there emerges one overarching theme of a man who, according to Hough, "leaves his pregnant wife at home while he goes to find work; he does not return, and the baby has to grow up fatherless" (77). And this lack of physical description of either characters or their surroundings, while it highlights the space of the social, also has much to do with Fugard's status as a playwright, an artist interested in creating frameworks to be inhabited by actors who would shape and fully realize the roles.

Fugard's novel is about Tsotsi's carefully guarded silence and his aversion to words, to memory, to questions, and to dreams, as he seeks to exist in the here and now; in this context, silence is significant, as it is both what Tsotsi seeks as well as that which exists in place of Tsotsi's self-defining narrative. Of the four gangsters, Boston is the only one with an education, and he alone feels remorse for their crimes, which cause him to become physically ill. It is his attempt to make Tsotsi aware of the concept of "decency" that causes Tsotsi to lash out and beat Boston nearly to death: "Maybe you had a woman. Ja, that's right. And when she let you down, or she left you, it hurt inside. Hey?…Not one?…Your folks, Tsotsi. Your mother…or father. Sister? Jesus! What about a dog?" (26). Tsotsi does not remember his past and does not recall his name. The narrator claims

> Tsotsi hated the questions for a profound but simple reason. He did not know the answers…. He allowed himself no thought of himself, he remembered no yesterdays, and tomorrow existed only when it was the present, living moment. He was as old as that moment, and his name was the name, in a way, of all men. (20–21)

This sense that the unnamed tsotsi is representative of "all men" again underscores the narrative's focus on the audience's ability to identify with Tsotsi and to see his plight as part of a larger framework, apartheid, that affected all men (and all women) in South Africa. His repressed memories surface after he begins to care for a baby that is handed to him by a terrified woman he plans to rape. While the baby triggers Tsotsi's memory of his mother's arrest and the events that transpire thereafter, it is Boston's mention of the dog that sets Tsotsi's journey in motion. Dogs, literal and figurative, appear throughout the text, from an initial description of the street as "sharp with stones, and eyes, and dog's teeth" (5), to Butcher's claim that Boston is sick "like a dog" (13) after the four murder Gumboot Dhlamini. The references to dogs appear more frequently—as if to force their way into the consciousness of the novel's protagonist—on the pages between Tsotsi's beating of Boston for asking about "a dog" and his encounter with the baby. For example, as he walks away from the shebeen after beating Boston, Tsotsi ignores "the curses that snapped at his heels like small dogs" (30), and he attempts to shut out all sound, "dog barking, dog whining, the thin notes of a penny whistle…, a baby born" (30). The first memory that breaks through Tsotsi's consciousness is initiated by Boston's questions and is of "a dog, a yellow bitch…in great pain" (57); he realizes that "the two were tied up together, somehow, the baby and the dog" (58). Finally, it is the crippled Morris Tshabalala's cry, "whelp of a yellow bitch!" (98) when Tsotsi steps on his hand that causes Tsotsi to follow but not kill Morris; it is this man who "looked like a dog who had been pulled up short by a savage jerk of its leash" (100) that causes Tsotsi to realize that "he has an alternative" (Post 418) to killing.

I have written extensively elsewhere about the role of dogs in South African history and literature, particularly in terms of the work of another white South African author, J. M. Coetzee.[5] I do not intend to replicate that research here, except to state that in my reading, dogs, both literal (appearing as embodied beings in the work) and figurative (as in to start over "like a dog"[6]), function in particular ways in South African literature, especially in literature written by white authors up to the end of apartheid, from Olive Schreiner's 1883 novel *Story of an African Farm* to Marlene van Niekerk's 1994 novel *Triomf*, to, of course, almost everything written by Coetzee up until 1999. The use of the animal as metaphor for subjected groups of individuals is a common way of Othering various humans, and as such, the animal body becomes the locus of oppositional thinking, the foundational example of all subsequent forms of human Othering (it is easier, therefore, for whites to subjugate black South Africans if they are rhetorically constructed as animals). But dogs are a particular kind of animal, creatures that negotiate the space between animal and human; they are boundary keepers, and they are our companions. Donna Haraway, in her *Companion Species Manifesto*, asserts that dogs have been our "partners in the crime of human evolution, they are in the garden from the get-go, wily as Coyote" (5), and Carolyn Parkhurst claims, "the conclusion I have reached is that, above all, dogs are witnesses. They are allowed access to our most private moments. They are there when we think we are alone…. If they could tell us everything they have seen, all the gaps of our lives would stitch themselves together" (14).

In his 1963 autobiography *Blame Me on History*, Bloke Modisane's memoir of life in Sophiatown, Modisane writes of a girlfriend who worked in a white household and gave Modisane the meat prepared for the dogs "which were fed more nutritiously than the children of the locations" (56). After SPCA members see township dogs eat from latrines, the SPCA reacts by lobbying to restrict African pet ownership. In response, Modisane says, "it was easy for them to be publicly appalled, they did not have to live with it, they did not, as did the Africans, have to hate themselves for being unable to feed both the children and their dogs" (179). The dog as pet is positioned in a place of privilege within white South African households, usurping the position of nameless black South Africans who suffer *like dogs*, but what Modisane's assertion that Africans have to hate themselves for not being able to feed their "children and their dogs" makes clear is the focus of the white South African SPCA on the plight of the animals and not the plight of the children and their parents. In this reading, black South Africans occupy a space within white South African consciousness that is *beneath* the dog, and in Fugard's novel, Tsotsi and his companions prowl the streets of Sophiatown, like "mad dogs" who "bite their own people" (Fugard, *Tsotsi* 94).

The dog as metaphor appears throughout *Tsotsi*, first to draw attention to the way that life under apartheid rhetorically constructs black South Africans as dogs; for example, after Morris Tshabalala is crippled while working in a gold mine, he questions why he continues to live, claiming "I am not better than a dog" (79) who crawls "with his tail between his legs" (87). The metaphor also connects Tsotsi to his literal childhood dog, the yellow "bitch" crippled and killed by his father in a fit of desperate anger after he returns home to find that his wife has been arrested. Tsotsi remembers the yellow dog only after he begins to care for the baby: soon after Miriam says of the baby Tsotsi brings her to feed, "a bitch in the backyard would look after its puppies better" (139), Tsotsi remembers how his injured dog "gave birth to the stillborn litter, and then died beside them" (161). This memory evokes, for both the reader and for Tsotsi—although he never articulates it—the ways that the experiences of all the characters in Fugard's novel are linked by a common set of apartheid-specific circumstances to which the yellow dog is both primary witness and primary victim: the fragmentation the black family and the subsequent atrophying of potential and hope for the children. This scenario arises from a confluence of the alienation of men who, during apartheid, worked far from their families (in the mines or in the cities), the victimization of women and the necessity that women raise children without the presence of the children's father, the resultant disenfranchisement of black South Africans, particularly male youth, and that contingent's perpetuation of murder and rape, actions that serve as outlets for displaced rage at the apartheid machine. In Fugard's novel, the initial object of this displacement is a mother, Tsotsi's childhood dog.

This scenario of absent fathers and subsequent abandonment and victimization of women and children is first demonstrated in Fugard's novel when Tsotsi's gang murders Gumboot Dhlamini, a man who has left his pregnant wife "a thousand miles away" (8) so that he can work in Johannesburg, the "Golden City in a purple distance" (9). Tsotsi decides to murder Gumboot on a train, after he sees his victim smile, and his smile, "white as light" (10), makes him stand out in the long line of men waiting at the entrance of the station. This scenario is repeated in the character of Miriam Ngidi (who Tsotsi forces to breastfeed the baby), whose husband leaves to go to work and never returns. We never find out what happened to her husband, only that he worked six miles from home during "the time of the bus boycott and all the people were walking and Simon was that sort of man that when the people walked, he walked…. No sign of him, no word, no memory" (132). She is eight months pregnant when he disappears, and her baby, also named Simon, is six months old when Tsotsi forces her to breastfeed "his" baby.

Initially, Miriam believes that Tsotsi plans to rape her, and rape plays a significant role in the confluence of these events; after murdering Gumboot, Butcher and Die Aap rape a woman named Rosie, to whom Boston refers to as "that poor bitch" (24). Tsotsi runs after beating Boston, and, when he encounters a woman, he plans to rape her: "he caught her by one arm and swung her into the darkness…. A second move forced her against a tree and there, with…a knee already between her legs…, he looked into her eyes" (40–41). A noise emanating from a shoebox she is carrying causes him to stop, and when he releases her, she forces the shoebox into his hands and runs away, sobbing. When Tsotsi looks into the box, he sees "a face that was small and black and older than anything he had ever seen in his life. …The sound that had stopped him, and saved the woman, was the cry of a baby" (41). All of these interwoven narratives—of fractured families and male brutality, particularly against women—trigger Tsotsi's memory of the abduction of his mother by white police forces who break into their house and drag her from her bed after asking for the pass that they do not give her time to produce. According to Derek Cohen, in this scene,

> The novel springs into hellish life—activity and loud voices, blows and shouts engulf the little boy's consciousness that Tstotsi has recaptured. The reader is suddenly thrust into a nightmarish world where the senses of time and place are distorted by the hideous shock of the child. The still night bursting into frenetic wakefulness as the full meaning of a malevolent white domination is brought home. (282)

This intrusion amounts to more than a figurative rape of Tsotsi's mother; it is the physical violation of the woman's space and her rights, as the white policemen "put their boots down on her protests, and even her plea for a dress" (151) and drag her into the waiting van. The events that precede this attack mirror the experiences of Gumboot and Miriam: Tsotsi, who, at this point in the narrative recalls that his name is David, is raised by his mother, who tells him that his father, "a big man, a gentle man, a laughing man" would return "one day" (148), and that day coincides with the day after David's mother's abduction. The father has been absent so long that David has no memory of him, and when the man returns home to find David's mother gone, he, in a moment of displaced anger, kicks and mortally wounds the dog when she growls at him:

> He had kicked her and she was walking around in circles, biting at her own back legs and rolling over and over in the sand.... On she came, until a foot or so away [from David] the chain stopped her, and although she pulled at this with her teeth until her breathing was tense and rattled she could go no further, so she lay down there...and...she gave birth to the stillborn litter, and then died beside them. (161)

The traumatized David flees to join "a ragged pack of mongrel beings" (161), a group of parentless children. While black women are consistently the victims of violent assault in Fugard's novel, black men, particularly black fathers, are disfigured by the apartheid system. David is unable to see the loving father his mother describes because, at the moment of his father's return, he is transformed into a violent man whose literal aggression against the dog is later mirrored in Tsotsi's beating of Boston—which, in turn, is provoked by Boston's question about a dog; after regaining his memory, Tsotsi goes to speak to Boston and is told by Marty, "you worked him like he is.... I wouldn't do that to a dog" (186).

But Tsotsi's recovered memory of his father's violence against the dog also allows Tsotsi to symbolically redress those wrongs he and the dog suffer under apartheid. If by beating him Tsotsi has treated Boston as his father treated the dog, then he not only also works to redeem both actions but to enact the role of his, the baby's, and Boston's absent mothers when he carries the unconscious Boston, who has "messed in his trousers" (187)—like the abandoned baby—back to Tsotsi's home where he cares for him. Furthermore, Tsotsi declares that things are "finished" (174) between him and Die Aap, the man who, Tsotsi thinks "stayed and followed me like a dog follows a man" (173). They are finished, he thinks, because of "my mother.... My father. The bitch. The river. A spider spinning a web—but most of all my mother" (172)

At the moment that Tsotsi declares his allegiances to his gang "finished," he fully inhabits the present instance as a space shaped by a past he has only now begun to access via the recovery of the repressed memories that is instigated by Boston's question about the dog. The baby "had become the repository of Tsotsi's past. The baby and David, himself that is, at first confused, had now merged into one and the same person," and, for the first time, David can imagine a "future awaiting the baby" (175), albeit a bleak one: "He could sympathize with it in its defenselessness against the terrible events awaiting it" (175). It is, of course, for his former child self that he feels sympathy as well, as he finds himself situated, at the end of the novel, finally in a position to "to remember" (225), to bear witness to his own experiences and to tell his own narrative. The novel ends with explicit reference to the destruction of this past as Tsotsi, who has recently remembered that his name is David Madondo, attempts to save the baby from the ruins of a building. The narrator states, "the slum clearance had entered a second and decisive phase. The white township had grown impatient" (225). David reaches the building just as the bulldozer plows into the wall: "then it was too late for anything; and the wall came down on top of him, flattening him into the dust" (225). When he is unearthed moments later, he is smiling. The crowd "agreed that it was hard to believe what the back of his head looked like when you saw the smile" (226).

***

The narrative finality of Fugard's novel is not characteristic of his plays. Francis Donahue points out, to most of his nine anti-apartheid plays, Fugard

> gives an open ending, by which he seems to say "what happens after this is up to you, the public." For South Africa's nonwhites, this represents a call for

continued resistance, for its white playgoers, a grave rebuke, and for audiences outside the country, an appeal for solidarity and political pressure to be brought to bear on the Pretoria government. (324)

This lack of resolution is indicative both of the dialogism inherent in theater and of the African oral form of the dilemma tale, "prose narratives that leave the listeners with a choice among alternatives…. The choices are difficult ones and usually involve discrimination on ethical, moral, or legal grounds" (Bascom 1). The dilemma is phrased as a question and invites discussion and debate. Similarly, according to Lindiwe Dovey, "what tends to distinguish African films in general is not necessarily their realism, but rather the dialogic manner in which they attempt to engage realities, and [Gavin Hood's] *Tsotsi* is no exception to this rule" (152); as Hood has claimed, he leaves his ending open so that the audience will be forced to answer the question, "would you forgive?" ("The Making of"). Rod Hay claims that the success of Hood's film adaptation of Fugard's novel—which won South Africa its first Oscar (Maingard 511)—"is a prime example of the new democratic South Africa embracing a subject and character that would have been completely out of bounds 15 years ago" (72), and, indeed, a brief overview of South African film history illustrates the truth of this assertion.

Jacqueline Maingard notes that "the history of South African cinema is intertwined with the appropriation, negation and dissemination of the nation in South Africa" (*South African National* 2), and Robert Cancel chronicles cinematic representations of apartheid during three eras of South African history, beginning after the codification of apartheid in 1948 when "for nearly 30 years, the South African Information Service kept American schools and even public movie theaters supplied with films about South Africa. These were offered at low or no cost, had high production values, and invariably sought to explain South Africa's apartheid system in positive terms" (15). After the Sharpeville massacre in 1960, international audiences began to see more documentaries, many of which were filmed illegally, that chronicled the other side of apartheid. Of particular note is Nana Mahomo's 1974 documentary *Last Grave in Dimbaza*. More such documentaries followed the Soweto uprising in 1976, and the Information Service reacted, releasing counter-documentaries such as *To Act a Lie* in 1980 (Cancel 20).

More anti-apartheid films, many adapted from novels and short stories, were made in the 1980s, including six films adapted from Nadine Gordimer's short stories, including "Six Feet of the Country" and "A Chip of Glass Ruby," that were made for international television release in 1982–3 (Cancel 23). According to Josef Gugler, "it took the major Western studios until the mid-1980s to address the anti-apartheid struggle," and he cites as examples such films as Richard Attenborough's *Cry Freedom* (1987) and Euzhan Palcy's *A Dry White Season* (1989), adapted from Andre Brink's novel of the same name. Rod Hay examines several landmark South African films made by white filmmakers, including Zoltan Korda's 1951 adaptation of Alan Paton's 1948 novel *Cry the Beloved Country*, and Jamie Uys's 1974 *Animals are Beautiful People* and 1980 *The Gods Must Be Crazy*, and he notes that during the apartheid era, "apartheid laws forced characters to speak in one official language" (73), Afrikaans.[7] Furthermore, not only was there negligible funding for black films, but what films were made would have had no chance of being seen by a white audience; in fact, under the National Film Subsidy, "films made for black audiences had to have at least 75 percent of the dialogue in a 'recognized South African Bantu language' in order to qualify for the subsidy" (Maingard, *South African National* 127). By 1988, the year that Keyan Tomaselli's *The Cinema of Apartheid* was published, only one critical film, Gibson Kente's *How Long* (1976) had been made and financed by a black South African (Tomaselli 23).[8] The commercial international success of Uys's *The Gods Must Be Crazy* sparked debates about South African cinema from outside of that country, and there was international condemnation of the film and a call to boycott it based on its problematic racial politics (Tomaselli 10).

Conversely, British filmmaker Richard Attenborough's 1987 *Cry Freedom* was banned in South Africa because of its treatment of the life and death of Black Conscious Movement leader Steve Biko, and under apartheid, censorship was part of a film industry that aimed to present apartheid as normal (Tomaselli 11). Certain films were only screened for white audiences, and the 1963 Publications and Entertainments Act increased censorship of internally produced films and "a differentiated censorship based on race became commonplace and appeals had to be made directly to the Minister of the Interior" (Tomaselli 16).[9] Under this act, about one in every three films approved for whites was banned for black audiences, "the most ridiculous example being the ban on Zulu viewers seeing the [1966] film *Zulu*" (Tomaselli 21). Within South Africa, cinema has historically been used to display and maintain the superiority of the colonial infrastructure and has, in many ways, looked to emulate models established by Hollywood, a circumstance vastly different from filmmakers elsewhere in Africa who have "largely sought emancipation from the Hollywood-derived cultural dependency" (Tomaselli 53). Dovey discusses South African cinema's relationship to Hollywood at the turn of the twentieth century: "South Africa's strong trade relations with the United States and the fact that English was a *lingua franca* provided fertile ground for Hollywood to appropriate South Africa's nascent film industry" (144). She reads Hollywood, an industry that produced Attenborough's *Cry Freedom*, Chris Menges's *A World Apart* (1988), and Palcy's *A Dry White Season*—all three of which are based on novels by white South African men—as a "colonizer" of South African stories on the one hand, and the machine that produced propaganda films for the National Party in 1948 on the other.

Maingard notes "the historic moment [that] marks South Africa's full entry into the frame of African cinema post-apartheid" as the 2005 nomination of the South African films *Drum* and *Zulu Love Letter* (both 2004) for the Golden Stallion of Yennenga Award given by the Panafrican Film and Television Festive of Ouagadougou (*South African National* 1), for which *Drum* won the award. Dovey provides an overview of post-apartheid cinema in South Africa, noting that there are many films that "mark a flourishing film industry since the end of apartheid in 1994, if we define 'flourishing' as the winning of international film awards" (144). She mentions, among others, Dimpho Di Kopane's films *U-Carmen eKhayelitsha* (2005) and *Son of Man* (2006), Darrell James Roodt's *Yesterday* (2004), the aforementioned Zola Maseko's *Drum* (2004), and Ian Gabriel's *Forgiveness* (2004). Dovey concurs with Tomaselli's assessment of South African cinema's dependence on Hollywood, noting that "a 'First Cinema' mode of production has become institutionalized in South Africa, characterized by high production values and an emphasis on the commercial rather than artistic value of the film" (145). Hood's *Tsotsi* is no exception to this rule, she contends, and she notes that *Tsotsi*, which was viewed by both black and white audiences in South Africa, outperformed Hollywood blockbusters. In terms of Hood's adaptation, Dovey notes that it, like black filmmaker Ramadan Suleman's 1997 adaptation of black writer Njabulo Ndebele's 1983 *Fools*, and colored director Mickey Madoda Dube's film adaptation *'Nagstappie* (1998) of colored author Alex LaGuma's *A Walk in the Night* (1962), follows a particular trend with regard to film adaptations, that "white filmmakers have tended to draw on texts written by white authors, black filmmakers on those by black writers, and colored filmmakers on those of colored writers" (146). In fact, the only cross-racial adaptation to date is Zola Maseko's *A Drink in the Passage* (2002), which is an adaptation of Alan Paton's 1963 short story of the same name (146).

Jacqueline Maingard has examined the history of the gangster film in South Africa, noting that "township and street gangsterism and violence will predict-ably continue to form a strong strand of representations of black identities" ("South African Cinema" 515). Joseph Gugler identifies the gangster film in South Africa as beginning with Oliver Schmitz and Thomas Mogotlane's 1988 film *Mapantsula*, "the first militant anti-apartheid film to be produced in South Africa. It was filmed in its entirety in Soweto and Johannesburg at the height of government repression under the third state of emergency" (91). The film is about a pantsula, the Zulu word for "gangster" or "hustler,"[10] named Panic who lives an amoral life of crime and whose victims, unlike Tsotsi's, are white. Panic becomes a police informer after he is arrested, but he undergoes an awakening of consciousness and refuses to inform on anti-government activists, "at the cost of his own freedom and well-being" (Cancel 28). Robert Cancel claims that

> Panic's power as a criminal is in part explained as the reaction to the impotence he has felt working menial jobs for racist white bosses. His posturing and violent assertion of territorial claims over criminal and sexual turf also depict a kind of power that is ambiguous in its elevation of a black man's agency while suggesting its regressive basis in selfishness and counterrevolutionary indifference. (28)

Despite the obvious influence of *Mapantsula* on *Tsotsi*, there are differences between the two films, many of which are the result of the apartheid and post-apartheid contexts in which the films were produced; Panic's rage is clearly directed at the white supremacist brutality of apartheid, and his behavior, which is initially indifferent to the swell of black activism taking place around him, is situated in a time of "growing violent protest and brutal government reaction" (28)—and in many ways, such is the case with Fugard's character as well. In Hood's adaptation, however, Tsotsi's violence and initial amorality exist in the void left by the fall of apartheid, the undefined space within which ostensible white domination is no longer a *visible* presence. In fact, the only white character in Hood's narrative is Police Captain Smit, played by Ian Roberts, and with perhaps two notable exceptions,[11] all of the power struggles within the film take place between black men. Despite these differences, both films leave the ending ambiguous; the audience does not learn what happens to Panic, whose fate is characterized by the first interregnum of which Gordimer speaks, after he refuses to inform, and Tsotsi is held at gunpoint by the white Captain Smits and two other officers, the black Zuma (Percy Matsemela) and a third, racially ambiguous and unnamed officer, played by Craig Palm.[12]

In Hood's adaptation, according to Dovey, "the problem surrounding Tsotsi's unlikely 'articulation' of his story [in Fugard's novel] is dropped and, in this sense, the film's depersonalized third person perspective offers a much more realistic representation of Tsotsi" (152), and Hood claims that he has used "images and interactions" to accomplish "what Fugard does so well" with language ("The

Making of"). Indeed, the interior narrative that is so present in the novel and that encourages the audience's identification with Tsotsi is entirely absent in the film. Presley Chweneyagae's performance is marked by silence, by the actor's ability to display upon his face and through his body his turmoil. Mood is set not through the third-person narrative voice as it is focalized through Tsotsi in Fugard's novel, but rather through the soundtrack, particularly the Johannesburg specific kwaito music of Zola, which underscores the violent, male-centric aspects of the film, and the more searching melodies of Mark Kilian and Paul Hepker, which indicate moments of Tsotsi's self-reflection and/or his attempts to connect with other characters—particularly the baby and Miriam (Terry Pheto).

As I mentioned earlier, Hood's adaptation changes various aspects of Fugard's novel, including its omission of what Dovey refers to as the novel's "redemptive Christian 'solution'...that...construes a silence around the particular foundation of Tsotsi's violent criminality" (150). The language in the film is not restricted to English as is Fugard's novel; in fact, Hood allowed the actors to translate their lines into tsotsi-taal in a move that contributes to the cacophonous nature of South African oral reality. Instead of retelling the narrative of the absent father and the displaced violence that such absence engenders, in a flashback, the film presents Tsotsi's father as present, a man who misunderstands the nature of AIDS from which his wife suffers, and who forbids his son from going near her lest he become sick as well. The film also creates a secondary story around the wealthy black family whose life is made chaotic after Tsotsi carjacks and shoots the mother, inadvertently abducting her child in the process. Finally, the Tsotsi of Hood's imagination is less violent (even though he does shoot the mother of the baby he mistakenly abducts) and softer than Fugard's thug.

The aforementioned criticism—by real tsotsis—of the film's inability to represent reality in terms of tsotsidom is significant in terms of the Forché's aforementioned social space of signification, which seeks to illuminate the trace as opposed to some monolithic truth. But such an assertion also reflects the kind of criticism voiced by Jordache Abner Ellapen who examines the fetishization of "township space" in South African cinema. According to Ellapen, "in South African cinema the 'township space' has been employed as a central location to represent black identity and culture" (113–114), and she notes the township's contemporary status as a hybrid space, existing at the intersection between the rural and the urban. Historically, even though the creation of townships is a modern phenomenon, life in the townships has been constructed as pre-modern, and since the end of apartheid, Ellapen claims that there has been "a sanitization and 'sanctification' of the township space" (121) that, in terms of cinema, functions as an "ideologically loaded representation that [has] resulted in the re-inscription of "Otherness' onto black identity and culture" (133).

Rita Barnard also comments on the depiction of township space in South African art as an immediately identifiable trope: "by the mid-1980s, the image of matchbox houses in serried ranks had become an all-too-familiar and ready-made trope. It had, of course, a certain kind of usefulness in the repertoire of writer and filmmaker alike, as an instant icon of apartheid's stark injustices." She goes on to critique the use of this trope, however, noting that "its Orwellian grimness may have exaggerated the extent of state control over the lives of urban residents. Is so doing, the recreation of 'ghetto atmosphere' may have unintentionally discouraged resistance instead of fostering it" (148). In Hood's film, the audience's engagement with township spaces is particularly intimate, with the township writ large as a familiar backdrop appearing infrequently during the film; more often, scenes take place inside of various residences, Tsotsi's, Miriam's, and the home of the baby's parents, whose affluent suburban house, enclosed behind a locked gate, alarmed by ADT security, feels more claustrophobic and cluttered than Tsotsi's hovel or Miriam's light and softly lit dwelling.[13] The implication in Hood's utilization of interior spaces, it seems, has little to do with the township as symbol for black African Otherness and more to say about the sense that personal space, at least for black South Africans, is a fraught and potentially non-existent concept, even a decade and a half after the fall of apartheid.

In terms of *Tsotsi*, Ellapen notes that the township is always shot from above or from the main street but hardly ever from Tsotsi's point of view (133), and this question of point of view is particularly important in terms of an analysis of how an audience might witness Hood's post-apartheid narrative of violence, HIV/AIDS, and redemption in terms of its verisimilitude with the "real" new South Africa. Unlike Dovey who reads this incarnation of Tsotsi as more realistic than Fugard's, I read Hood's narrative—as I read Fugard's—not in terms of its realism, which I find incredibly suspect and problematic, but instead in terms of those things about South Africa that this narrative, as a film that seeks to present a redemptive vision of post-apartheid democracy and a narrative that updates Fugard's novel, puts forth, particularly in terms of how black South African men fit into the various spaces depicted in the film. As Eleanor Ringel Gillespie asserts in her review of the film, Tsotsi "doesn't intend to be a realistic look at the hard-luck-life in Soweto any more than *Three Men and a Cradle* was meant to be a hard-eyed look at parenting. Rather, it's more like a compelling coming-of-age fable with a bittersweet ending," and film critic Liz Beardsworth calls the work "an inverse fairy tale." What is witnessed, then, at least in terms of the cinematic version of this narrative, is the nature of the aforementioned second interregnum rendered as a series of questions about black South African masculinity, and the film opens a space in which to discuss possible answers.

***

Critic Daniel Eagan claims that Hood's film "reduces moral issues to point-lessly simplistic levels. Using a baby to redeem a criminal is neither realistic nor honest, especially as it's enacted here" by Chweneyagae, who has "too pleasant a demeanor to project the menace his part requires.... As the widow who helps humanize him, Terry Pheto is improbably kind and beautiful" (Review), and other critics have noted the highly sentimentalized nature of the film as well. Hood responds to such claims and to claims that he softened, simplified, and depoliticized Fugard's apartheid-era story: "we've repoliticized the original" (Archibald 46) in that the film situates AIDS as the "elephant in the room" (45) in contrast with Fugard's representation of "the political reality of apartheid" (45) as the unstated antagonist. At three minutes into the film, as Tsotsi and his gang stalk a victim in a train station, the camera pulls back and up so that the banner hanging above them, which reads "we are all affected by HIV and AIDS," becomes the center of the visual frame. The banner appears again later in the film, as does a billboard containing the same text, situated on the left side of the frame while Boston (played by Mothusi Magano) vomits from a staircase beside it. In these scenes, the audience witnesses the specter of AIDS that looms large and pervasive in South African culture.

The film, set in the contemporary post-apartheid township of Soweto, the township to which many displaced Sophiatown residents moved in the late 1950s and 1960s, updates the narrative by positioning HIV/AIDS as the unspoken cause of Tsotsi's alienation from his family; in a flashback, we see his mother dying of AIDS and his father forbidding the boy from touching her. Even though the disease is never named, the camera's attention to the banner and billboard early in the film resonates in this later scene. In a recent *New York Times Magazine* article, Tina Rosenberg writes about the dangers that black South African women face not only with regard to AIDS, but of the dangers inherent in admitting to one's male partner that one has tested positive for HIV. According to Rosenberg, women fail to be tested or refuse to admit to a positive test out of fear that their partners might inflict physical harm upon them ("When a Pill"). This visual metaphor of the banner allows the audience to witness one major aspect of contemporary South Africa about which there is extensive silence and lack of black male accountability despite its being responsible, in large part, for a life expectancy rate of 53 years of age (Outwater et al. 135). South Africa is home to approximately ten percent of the entire world population of HIV/AIDS infected people, and, as of 2005, the estimated number of children orphaned because of the disease was 420,000 (Outwater et al. 137). Hood uses the visual and not the verbal to highlight the silence, shame, and misunderstanding that still surround the disease, and, in terms of these visual cues, the young, black South African men of Tsotsi's gang are implicated as potential perpetrators of the often unspoken AIDS epidemic.

Figure 3: Terry Pheto as Miriam and Presley Chweneyagae as Tsotsi. (Miramax Films/Photofest)

As I noted earlier, in terms of *Tsotsi*, Fugard situates the most profound physical suffering that takes place in the narrative on the body of a dog, a creature whose voiceless pain is caused by the displaced aggression that results from apartheid. In so doing, Fugard mediates his role as white authorial voice, opting instead for the ambiguity and silence that, via his repressed memory of the suffering of the dog, also shapes Fugard's protagonist's consciousness. The novel's opening line asserts such a reading: "there had been a silence" in which all four main characters "were suddenly without any more words" (2). Similarly, Hood states that in the film, "Tsotsi doesn't say very much so you have to focus on what he does" (Archibald 45), but in Hood's adaptation, the audience and not the dog or Tsotsi functions as literal witness to Tsotsi's transformation; whereas in Fugard's novel, the body of the suffering dog functions as (silent) text, in Hood's film, Tsotsi's body—through his stony and subsequently anguished facial expressions, his trembling hands late in the film when he visits Miriam, his violent shivering as he stands in the rain—is inscribed with a narrative of mute suffering, readable by the film's international audience. As Hood states:

> The challenge in this film was to draw the audience into the world of a very marginal, anti-social character and have them empathize with him.... So we shot most close-ups with eye-lines very tight to camera. I wanted to create a real sense of intimacy between audience and actor; to allow the audience to look almost directly into the actor's eyes. ("Making Tsotsi")

This strategy of filming in a way that requires the audience's eye contact with Tsotsi creates a sense of visual intimacy and a sense that the viewer exists in a space outside of Tsotsi's reality, a space for witnessing Tsotsi's nearly mute narrative of spiritual transformation as it is written on his body.[14] In fact, it is nearly eight minutes into the film before we hear Tsotsi utter his first words, which are spoken to Boston as he breaks down at the memory of the murder the four have recently committed: "What? Sick again?" The third-person narrative perspective of Fugard's novel is non-existent in Hood's film, and the gaze—both of the audience and of the character—is highly significant in terms of Hood's depiction of Tsotsi's evolution: early in the film, Tsotsi "stares down" Boston prior to beating him, but he looks away, uncertain where to cast his gaze, when Miriam breastfeeds the baby. And in the film's final scene during which Tsotsi does not utter a single word, he pleads visually, maintaining eye contact with the baby's parents—particularly the child's father—that is only broken when the police order him to surrender the baby. Similarly, Fugard's novel pays particular attention to Tsotsi's gaze as he witnesses the suffering of the dog, noting that "he had to open his eyes, and when he did he wished that he hadn't, because for all his tears and prayers he could not close them again until it was over" (160), but Hood's film allows the audience to gaze back.

Rhetorical dogs are less central to Hood's film, but the scene in which Tsotsi's father wounds[15] his son's dog is highly significant in terms of the changes that Hood makes to the narrative—as well as what those changes indicate about the nature of the second interregnum—in the ways the narrative links Tsotsi, his dying mother, the dying animal, and his violent father. In fact, the very dog has changed breed and possibly sex in the film: in Fugard's novel, Tsotsi's childhood dog is female and pregnant, the "yellow bitch" chained in the yard. The dog's sex and the fact that she is chained are both significant features in terms of what she represents, the maternal trapped within the confines of a system that alienates her from her offspring and often inscribes her as a victim of male violence.

Figure 4: A close-up of Presley Chweneyagae as Tsotsi. (Miramax Films/Photofest)

In Hood's adaptation, however, the dog is a Rottweiler that stands beside the young Tsotsi as his mother, dying from AIDS, beckons him to her bedside. After Tsotsi's father, in a drunken rage, kicks the dog, he tells his son to "leave *it*," and the use of the gender-neutral pronoun reduces the dog to a thing, an "it" to be destroyed and discarded by a character with whom it is nearly impossible to identify. Significantly, the use of the gender-neutral pronoun is repeated later in the film in reference to a male; when Tsotsi returns the baby to John and Pumla; he says, "I'll leave it here. . . . Your baby—I'll leave it here." In Fugard's novel, despite his violence against the dog, Tsotsi's father is a character with whom the reader can sympathize: he has returned from years away from his family only to discover that his wife has been abducted by the police. His anguish is apparent in his repeated utterance of his wife's name, "Tondi," which becomes "a cry . . . cried with a terrible sound" (160). The delivery of the dog's stillborn litter and her immediate death thereafter resonates in terms of the first interregnum, the space in which the old is dying but the new cannot *yet* be born, and through this symbol, the novel provides a harsh indictment of the role of apartheid in the destruction of the familial relationship—particularly the perversion of the role of the township mother.

Conversely, Hood's film alters this key symbol, replacing the female dog with a Rottweiler, a bully breed that often functions as a hyper-masculine attribute of gangster culture. This alteration of the dog clearly demonstrates the film's focus on the role of black South African men and minimizes the role of South African women, particularly the black South African mother. While the novel is primarily concerned with Tsotsi's integration of his memories of loss of two mothers, his own and the dog, the scene in which Tsotsi remembers his father's abuse of the Rottweiler in Hood's adaptation establishes one of the four black South African fathers depicted in the film: the ignorant and abusive drunk depicted as Tsotsi's father; the successful gangster Fela (played by Zola, the musician whose work comprises the majority of the film's score) who acts as a surrogate father figure and entices the young tsotsis to work for him; John Dube (Rapulana Seiphemo), the upper-class father who, within the context of the film, garners the most respect and has the most power—even going so far as to yell at the white police captain, demanding that he, first, find the missing child and, later, put away his weapon—and Tsotsi, who, for six days, serves as the "father" of the kidnapped baby. The focus on the paternal is evidenced early in the film when Boston questions Tsotsi. Instead of focusing on Tsotsi's sense of decency as it pertains to his feelings for his mother, as is the case in Fugard's novel when Boston says to Tsotsi "your folks, Tsotsi. Your mother... or father. Sister? Jesus! What about a dog?" (26), in the film, Boston says "your father—your father, Tsotsi. Your father, where is he? Your father and mother. Where are they? Jesus, Tsotsi! A dog? What about a dog?" The repetition of the word "father" four times foreshadows the four ways of being a father that the film both presents and critiques.

The focus on the role of various fathers undermines the role of women in the narrative, particularly in terms of their positions as mothers. Such a scenario is apparent when Tsotsi goes to Soekie's (Thembi Nyandemi) shebeen to claim Boston. Despite the fact that Soekie tries to get Boston to go back to school, offers him a job, and tells Aap (Kenneth Nkosi) to "leave him alone,"[16] as she cares for her wounds, Boston says to her, "you never had a child, did you?" When Tsotsi says that Boston can stay with him, Soekie protests. Tsotsi replies, "I remember when he first came here.... You gave him as much beer as he wanted.... And when he fell down in the street, sick from the beer you sold him, I found him, not you. Brother, who took care of you when you were lying in the street? Me or her?" The challenge that takes place in this scene is at once an affront to Soekie's inability to mother, inherent in Boston's assertion that she never had children (and is, therefore, bad at caring for him) and her entrepreneurial greed (she only cares about making money, not about Boston's well being). The implication is that, despite the fact that he is the cause of Boston's injuries, Tsotsi is his "brother," the familial member who must care for Boston in the face of an absent father and the ineffectual "mother" figure, Soekie.

In John and Pumla Dube (played by Nambitha Mpumlawana), Hood creates an upper-class black family that does not appear in Fugard's narrative, and Tsotsi inadvertently abducts the baby from this family after he shoots Pumla while stealing her car. But when the film focuses on this family's loss, the narrative is focalized through John, as he negotiates with police and later with Tsotsi. Pumla is paralyzed from the waist down as a result of the shooting, but the audience is never allowed access to her experience of either trauma or loss; what is witnessed, particularly when Tsotsi, Aap, and Butcher break into John and Pumla's house, is John's ability to negotiate the potentially dangerous encounter, and Tostsi and John's interaction thereafter. When John activates his home security system, via a control on his keychain, Butcher attacks but is killed by Tsotsi before he can hurt John. In what follows, there are no words, only the persistently blaring alarm as Tsotsi, hand shaking, slowly brings his gun down to John's temple, where he pauses, before lowering the gun and taking the control out of John's hand and deactivating the alarm. In the silence that follows, the two stare at each other, John with a look of disgust and defiance, Tsotsi on the verge of tears. The scene cuts between Tsotsi and John six times; the last shot of Tsotsi is from below, as he looks down at John from the balcony. John looks back up, and the camera remains on him after Tsotsi has left. This focus provides a glimpse into John's interiority as he sighs, looks down, and begins to cry; at no point in the film does the audience ever get a similar perspective with regard to Pumla. At the end of the film, it is John who takes the baby from Tsotsi, despite Pumla's command, "Boy, give me my son." John says to Tsotsi, in a moment that harkens back to Tsotsi's earlier statement of entreaty to Boston, "Brother, we don't want anyone to get hurt." John comes forward and takes the baby from Tsotsi, while Pumla sits behind the security gate and watches from her wheelchair. The mother in Hood's film, like the "yellow bitch" in Fugard's novel, while not dead, is paralyzed and effectively removed from the narrative.

As was the case with Fugard before him, "the ending seems to have been something of an enigma even to the filmmaker with Hood deciding to shoot three separate versions" (Hay 75), and Hood's ambiguous ending to the story is characteristic of the dialogic nature of African narrative, which invites the audience to participate in the construction of the character's fate. In an interview with Rebecca Murray, Hood has said that the film's ending "leaves it open where you go, 'Well, what is going to happen to him?' Then the natural question is, 'Well, what do you think should happen?' And that question kept people talking for far longer after screenings than either of the other endings." In one of the film's alternate endings, Tsotsi is shot by the police, in another he runs from them, and in the ending that Hood finally chose for the film, Tsotsi surrenders. The final scene of the film, punctuated by Mark Kilian and Paul Hepker's wailing refrain as it is sung by protest singer and poet Vusi Mahlasela, closes with a fadeout of Tsotsi, hands raised above his head. Both Tsotsi and the baby are alive at the end of Hood's retelling, but Tsotsi's fate remains uncertain. The ending that Hood had originally written for the film was the ending in which Tsotsi dies, but on a bonus film "The Making of *Tsotsi*" that is included on the DVD, he states that after he spoke with Athol Fugard about that decision, he realized that the novel depicts a very different time, "as apartheid was becoming more and more repressive."[17]

Hood claims that killing Tsotsi in the film just seemed wrong to him, "too sentimental," and evidence that "no matter what you do, you're screwed" ("The Making"). Of the ending he chose for the film, Hood has said that he did not kill Tsotsi because "there is far greater cause for hope today than there was during the sixties under apartheid" (Hood, "A Note"), but despite Hood's potentially more optimistic ending, both the novel and film point to the difficulty, during and after apartheid, of imagining a positive future for black township South Africans, and both works illustrate the politically fraught task that white writers and filmmakers like Fugard and Hood face in depicting black South Africa in its various, pre-and post-apartheid, interregnum moments. Furthermore, despite Hood's claim that his ending is "less tragic, more open-ended and even slightly more hopeful" (Rotten Tomatoes), a crucial aspect of Fugard's narrative is silenced: in his attempt to create a more positive ending, Hood's film clearly illustrates that, while there may be hope for the Tsotsi(s) of his imagination, the plight of black South African women is less hopeful and becomes, during the second interregnum, that which is unknowable and, in Hood's work, unspeakable. Dovey makes this case in her astute argument that the film's depicts "certain forms of contemporary violence at the expense of another, very pressing kind of violence in South Africa: violence against women and children" (151).

Nadine Gordimer takes the epigraph for her 1982 novel *July's People* from Antonio Gramsci's *Prison Notebooks*: "the old is dying and the new cannot be born; in this interregnum there arises a great diversity of morbid symptoms." Her protagonist Maureen Smales flees her white suburban life to follow her black servant July to his village during a fictional South African civil war. At the end of the novel, she hears a helicopter and runs toward it, through the river "like some member of a baptismal sect" not knowing whether the aircraft holds "saviors or murderers" (158). Stephen Clingman writes that Maureen "is running from old structures and relationships…but she is also running towards her revolutionary destiny. She does not know what that destiny may be…. All she knows is that it is the only authentic future awaiting her" (203). Similarly, Hood's film fades to black as Tsotsi raises his hands above his head in a gesture of surrender, according to Hood, "to whatever is going to happen next," particularly in terms of the way that the legal system and John and Pumla Dube will deal with Tsotsi ("The Making of"). South Africa has no death penalty, but it is possible that Tsotsi could go to prison for life for his crime. The audience, as primary witness to the truth of this narrative, must ask, should he? Should the Dubes plead for leniency, given his free admission of guilt and his attempt to make reparations? And what does this secular confession indicate within a culture only recently through its Truth and Reconciliation Commission? But there are other questions the film raises as well, particularly in terms of what roles are available to the tsotsis of South Africa's post-apartheid townships. How, we are left to wonder, does someone like Tsotsi become someone like John? During the second interregnum, a decade and a half after the fall of apartheid, Hood's film indicates that the answer to that question remains unknown and unforeseeable.

Notes

1. According to the "Official *Tsotsi* Film Site," the film took awards at international film festivals in Edinburgh, Toronto, Los Angeles, St. Louis, Cape Town, Denver, Thessaloniki, and Santa Barbara. It won the Jury Prize for best feature at the 2006 Pan African Film and Arts Festival and received two nominations at BAFTA. In addition, *Tsotsi* won South Africa its first Academy Award for Best Foreign Language Film of 2005. In 2009, *District 9* topped *Tsotsi*'s record.

2. According to J. M. Coetzee, confession always raises "problems regarding truthfulness, problems whose common factor seems to be a regression to infinity of self-awareness and self-doubt" ("Confession" 274).

3. Forché employs the same strategy in her poems; for example, the first line in her most anthologized poem "The Colonel" states that "what you have heard is true."

4. Louis Moluma, in *Tsotsi-taal: A Dictionary of the Language of Sophiatown*, offers another etymology for the word "tsotsi": "an alternative explanation of the roots of the words lie in the ethnic term Tutsi. It has been argued that the term gained currency in the early 1940s in the wake of the brutal ethnic conflicts experienced in central Africa in the 1930s and 1940s" (108).

5. See Wright, Laura *Writing "Out of All the Camps": J. M. Coetzee's Narratives of Displacement*, New York: Routledge, 2006, particularly chapter two, "Coetzee's Dogs from Simile to Signified: South African History, Environment, and Literature."

6. At the end of Coetzee's *Disgrace* (1999), Lucy Lurie, a white woman who has been raped by three black men who have also shot the dogs she kennels, agrees to marry her black overseer Petrus and give him her land in return for his protection. Lucy's father David is appalled at Lucy's decision to place herself in a position he views as humiliating, as a person forced to live "like a dog" (205). But for Lucy, this is a place of beginning, a place to "start from again" (205). By leveling the post-apartheid playing field and placing everyone in the position of the dog, Coetzee rewrites Franz Kafka's existential ending in *The Trial* when Joseph K proclaims his fate to be "like a dog" (231) and renders literal the condition of both humans and animals in the new South Africa: for change to

occur, it would seem, everyone must begin again from the same place, with the liberation of the land from its contested historical status. To begin "like a dog" is simply to start over, and the literary and historically negative connotation of this famous and persistent simile is itself essentially negated.

7. In *South African National Cinema*, Jacqueline Maingard discusses the National Film Subsidy scheme established by the government in 1956 that "created a strong division between films for black audiences, differentiated by language and ethnicity, and films for white audiences, differentiated by language" (125). The subsidy bolstered Afrikaans language films by promoting the genre of border war films (125).

8. During the filming of *How Long*, Kente was arrested in the Eastern Cape because "the production period had coincided with the nationwide unrest of that year [1976], which had made police extra-cautious with regard to scenes critical of the police" (Tomaselli 19).

9. A 1974 amendment to the act "cancelled the racial bias of censorship but retained the right to restrict films 'to persons in a specific category…or at a specific place'" (Tomaselli 16).

10. "Mapantsula" is the plural of "pantsula." The word "pantsula" is synonymous with "tsotsi" and, according to Gugler, "refers to an exaggerated way of talking, dressing, and swaggering originally derived from Hollywood gangster movies of the 1940s" (91).

11. I am thinking specifically about Tsotsi's shooting of the baby's mother Pumla and his demand that Miriam breastfeed the baby.

12. It seems significant that in the alternate ending in which Tsotsi is shot, it is this officer, not Smit or Zuma, who shoots him.

13. Hood notes that it was actually more difficult to film in the suburbs, as the space was more restrictive in terms of his ability to set up and maneuver his equipment ("The Making of").

14. After Tsotsi beats Boston early in the film, he starts to run from the bar but pauses and turns to look at the other bar patrons. The camera focuses only on

Tsotsi; the effect is that he seems to be looking—with a mixture of fear, anger, and sadness—directly at the viewer.

15. It is worth noting that the dog does not die in the film but appears to be paralyzed.

16. In Fugard's novel, Boston leaves school because "he was expelled for trying to rape a fellow student" (190). Boston explains that "I didn't do it. …Not the way they thought I did" (191), and the narrator asks, after Boston's explanation, "can you honestly say that he was to blame? Or the girl for that matter?" (192). In the film, the reason that Boston gives for not going to school is that he failed an exam; the rape narrative is omitted.

17. It is this ending, however, that made it onto a pirated copy of the DVD that sold for a fraction of the cost of a commercial DVD. Of the pirated copy, Hood has said, "When you buy a ticket and when you buy a genuine DVD, you are an investor in South African film as your money is going back to people who invest in local films…. But when you buy a DVD you are giving your money to criminals who are in the business of investing in nothing but their greedy souls" ("SA Pirates").

Three

Reclaiming the Maoriland Romance: Inventing Tradition in *Once Were Warriors* and *Whale Rider*

***

Even before the signing of the still-controversial Treaty of Waitangi in 1840, the indigenous Maori population of New Zealand had been decimated by intertribal warfare and the introduction of unfamiliar diseases, particularly influenza, brought by European settlers who had been exploring and settling the area since the mid-seventeenth century. By the beginning of the twentieth century, the Maori had lost the majority of their land. The discovery of another imperial commodity, gold, on the South Island of New Zealand in 1861 and that island's subsequently bolstered economy further divided the white settler population from the indigenous Maori, particularly since the majority of white settlers—who outnumbered the Maori by 1850—inhabited the South Island. The oral culture of the Maori, as well as Maori myths and traditions, has, therefore, been subsumed by colonial interference and influence.

In the 1980s and 1990s, a distinct body of New Zealand literature—including Keri Hulme's 1984 novel *the bone people*, Witi Ihimaera's 1987 novel *Whale Rider*, and Alan Duff's 1990 novel *Once Were Warriors*, for example—imagined, for both Maori and white or Pakeha populations, new cultural narratives in the production of a contemporary Maori mythology that were dependent upon the adaptation of traditional Maori institutions. Lee Tamahori's 1994 film adaptation of Duff's novel depicts protagonist Beth Heke's struggle to save herself and her children from marginalization and the abuse of her husband Jake, and Niki Caro's 2002 adaptation of Ihimaera's narrative depicts the ascendance of Paikea Apirana, a girl who, according to tradition, cannot claim status as chief. Both films (and novels) place the responsibility for Maori cultural persistence squarely on the shoulders of the Maori—particularly Maori women (as has been addressed by critics such as Pascale De Souza, Mary M. Wiles, and Maureen

Molloy); in these depictions, white colonial intrusion is marginalized. This chapter positions these two films as works that speak back to and reclaim the Maoriland romance fiction genre of the late nineteenth and early twentieth centuries, in which Pakeha authors and filmmakers imagined and depicted the Maori as heroic warriors and seductive maidens.

According to Jane Stafford and Mark Williams in *Maoriland: New Zealand Literature, 1872-1914:*

> Maoriland...is an archaic word with colonial associations, politically suspect in a postcolonial age. "Maoriland" suggests the smug paternalism of a period now regarded with embarrassment, a world in which Maori warriors in heroic attitudes and Maori maidens in seductive ones adorned romantic portraits and tourist postcards.... But for at least four decades of its short history, from the early 1880s to the late 1910s, once the first generation of Pakeha settlers had been replaced by a more modern, urban and self-inventing society, Maoriland was a literary synonym for New Zealand. (10)

Stafford and Williams's book examines literature written by white settlers during the late colonial period, "which came to register the first literary evidence of a national consciousness" (11) and notes the contradictory meaning of "Maori-land" as a term "that denies what it seems to state: that New Zealand is a land properly belonging to Maori. Maoriland is a land of settlers who, having claimed for themselves the designation 'New Zealanders' once reserved for Maori, now feel comfortable enough about their identity and security to borrow the name of those they have supplanted" (12).

Early New Zealand film, like its literature, was characterized by settler presentations of a romanticized Maori culture, and films like Georges Méliès's 1913 *Loved by a Maori Chieftess, Hinemoa,* and *How Chief Te Ponga Won His Bride* as well as George Tarr's 1914 *Hinemoa*[1] utilized Maori mythology and Maori cast members to depict the Maori culture as timeless, existing outside of history, and somehow uninvolved with the white culture that had, at that point, displaced it. Furthermore, such films portray Maori men as heroic warriors and eroticize Maori women. Both *Once Were Warriors* and *Whale Rider,* like traditional Maoriland romances, depict Maori experience as cut off from Pakeha culture, but the absence of white characters in both films serves to underscore the marginalization of the Maori as a result of colonial domination. And while both films, like their predecessors, are shaped by Maori legend, both rewrite traditional mythology in a way that, instead of sexualizing Maori women, positions them as saviors who will be responsible for the invention of contemporary Maori culture.

***

There have been several significant texts that chart the somewhat short and, until recently, sparse history of filmmaking in New Zealand, a country with a population of four million that did not have access to television until 1960 (Babington 1). Helen Martin and Sam Edwards's *New Zealand Film History* chronicles the history of New Zealand film from 1912 to 1996, and Bruce Babington's *A History of the New Zealand Fiction Feature Film* situates fictional filmic representations of New Zealand within various historical moments in that culture's past and present, extending the list of films covered by Martin and Edwards to include films made in the twenty-first century. Babington notes that "New Zealand ranks among the smallest [cinemas], sustained by a population of only four million, producing on average about five films a year, increasing with the advent of cheap digital production from seven in 2002 to an unprecedented sixteen in 2003" (7–8). Two other important studies, Martin Blythe's *Naming the Other* and Sacha Clelland-Stokes *Representing Aboriginality* examine specifically the way that New Zealand's indigenous population, the Maori, have been depicted—by Maori and Pakeha filmmakers alike—in New Zealand's cinema from its earliest incarnations in the early 1900s to the present. Clelland-Stokes asserts that

> The filmic representations of any group of people in a society become an important issue of control over the nature and value of that group of people's identity. For this reason, the representations of aboriginal peoples within a post-colonial society, and control of media forums within that society, is as important to aboriginal peoples themselves in their struggles against oppressive ruling hegemonies as it is to colonial and neo-colonial media-makers. (4)

What becomes apparent from studying texts like those mentioned above is the way that filmic representations of New Zealand and its people(s) were largely concerned, at least initially, with constructing narratives that romanticized the creation of New Zealand as a peaceful settler colonial nation and sought to cast "Maoriland" as a kind of prelapsarian—yet still extant—realm of native innocence and environmental beauty. As control of the visual frame has begun to shift from Pakeha male filmmakers to Maori and Pakeha women and Maori men, the national visual narrative has shifted as well, to call into question New Zealand's former image of itself as a peacefully colonized culture.

The primary reason for a belief in an amicably colonized New Zealand is the signing of the aforementioned Treaty of Waitangi that took place between

Governor William Hobson and approximately 500 Maori chiefs in 1840. The treaty, written in English and translated into Maori, was interpreted differently by both groups, and, as a result, "the legitimacy of this treaty has...been largely contested and discredited by revisionist historians over the past couple of decades" (Clelland-Stokes 149). The predominant Maori understanding of the treaty was that British sovereignty would extend only to British subjects, thereby allowing for the existence of two distinct realms, one Maori and one Pakeha. However, according to Clelland-Stokes, "the treaty was used as proof of an agreement between Maori and Pakeha to the sovereignty of Britain over Aotearoa/New Zealand and all of its inhabitants, despite the verbal explanations of the treaty to the contrary" (150). The 1980s were marked by explicit Maori activist challenges to the Treaty, and Donna Awatere's 1984 publication *Maori Sovereignty* gave voice to a desire for biculturalism in that it issued a call for Maori representation in Aotearoa, the Maori name for New Zealand. According to Martin Blythe, during the 1980s,

> There were endless public debates which turned on whether the Treaty now symbolized the Original Sin of imperial annexation, or the later desire for national integration, or the more recent desire for biculturalism, or the potential for Maori separatism. Obviously, it can represent any and all of these, but the recent opinion has been toward the segregation option...and whether this is unfortunate or not, the main casualty has been the mythology of New Zealand. (6)

According to Philippa Mein Smith in her *Concise History of New Zealand*, New Zealand took until the 1990s to consider itself a "multicultural" nation: "the country first had to grow more diverse before acknowledging cultural difference.... The multicultural idea transferred belatedly, from the 1980s in law and policy, and effectively from the 1990s" (242). The laws and policies of which Smith speaks include the Waitangi Tribunal, which formed in 1975, and the 1985 Treaty of Waitangi Amendment Act, which allowed the Tribunal to investigate land claims dating from 1840, when the Treaty of Waitangi was signed (Howard 199). With the explosion of the New Zealand mythology of a peacefully colonized—or annexed—"Maoriland," there also emerged a Maori cultural identification dependent upon perceived difference from the Pakeha.[2] As Clelland-Stokes asserts, such identification is imaginary and contradictory, focused on the one hand on a universalizing identity of "Maoriness" and on the other on the diversity of various *iwi*, or tribal affiliations that predate colonial intrusion. She says,

With the construction of an identity difference between Maori and Pakeha since the 1980s, *iwi* affiliation has simultaneously been collapsed and reasserted. A "Maori" Self has been imagined as an identity category against a Pakeha Other, and simultaneously, in the building of the Maori Self, increased emphasis has been placed on the Maoritanga (the Maori way of doing things), which inevitably recognizes the diversity of *iwi*. (148)

In terms of the imagined entities of both a unified New Zealand and, later, a unified Maori culture, film has played a significant role, particularly in terms of the vision of history and tradition that the nation has told to itself and to the rest of the world as well as in terms of the narrative of relationships—amicable, romantic, or hostile—between the Maori and Pakeha in New Zealand. Significantly, New Zealanders have had a contentious relationship with Hollywood, an industry that has acted as both influence and cultural colonizer, in terms of control of this mythology. From 1926 onwards, according to Blythe, when movie theaters opened across New Zealand, Hollywood studios block-booked them and supplied a steady flow of films. This action "resulted in an acrimonious debate within New Zealand's official culture, prompted partly by the British themselves, as to the dangerous affects of American films on the Dominion's British way of life" (10). This debate highlights a three-way collision between British, Maori, and American culture, characterized by Maori identification with American film stars[3] and characters as the Maori dressed like cowboys in the 1920s and 1930s and, in the 1980s, rastas, break dancers, and exotic primitives (Blythe 19).

In terms of the creation of a national mythology, Harrington Reynolds's 1922 film *The Birth of New Zealand*—obviously influenced by D. W. Griffith's successful 1915 film *Birth of a Nation*—"was widely praised for its educational value and morally uplifting qualities" (Martin and Edwards 29), and the New Zealand Government Publicity Office's 1925 *Glorious New Zealand* "confirms the myths of empty landscapes ripe for the plough which were perpetuated in the nineteenth century by companies attracting settlers to New Zealand from Europe" (36). Martin and Edwards's study begins with French filmmaker Gaston Méliès 1913 film *Loved by a Maori Chieftess*,[4] a film that examines the romance between a Maori woman and a Pakeha man, and Blythe notes that "easily the most popular story in New Zealand films and novels, even into the Eighties, features romantic liaisons between Maori and Pakeha" (34). Blythe characterizes filmic representations of the Maori during imperialism as being based on the idea of the native as either noble savage, ignoble savage, romantic savage, comic savage, or dying savage (24). Clelland-Stokes likewise characterizes various periods of New Zealand film history and examines the ways that the Maori are represented in each. She characterizes these periods as the timeless Maoriland romance period of 1910 through the 1930s during which the Maori are depicted as unaffected by history; the historical/interracial romance genre; the social problem documentaries of the 1950s, which were aimed at the Maori in order to expose them to the supposed benefits of Westernization; and the "Kiwi" national identity films of the 1960s. She notes that in all of these periods, up through the 1980s, "although Maori have been disproportionately visible in Aotearoa/New Zealand feature films, their roles within these films have been primarily as actors playing out Pakeha generated narratives of Maori Otherness" (167).

Blythe supports this assertion, noting that the Maori and Maori identity have always been a part of New Zealand's film history, "from scenarios and locales, to costume and extras, to the 'raw material' for fantasies of the erotic/exotic" (260). Blythe's study differs from Clelland-Stokes's in that Blythe chronicles New Zealand film through its filmmakers, from Rudall Hayward, "widely recognized as New Zealand's greatest pioneering filmmaker" (35) who worked in film from the 1920s until the 1970s, through Barry Barclay's 1987 film *Ngati*, which is regarded as the first Maori film (272). Alongside fictional feature films existed films made for the New Zealand Tourist Department during the 1920s and 30s, the newsreel propaganda of the 1940s, the social problem documentaries of the 1950s, and the arts and culture documentaries of the 1970s, which showcased a Maori revival and renaissance (Blythe 107). Along with films that highlighted Maori spirituality, the 1970s and 1980s also saw the birth of the Pakeha pilgrimage genre, which, according to Blythe, "became a final refuge for a Pakeha liberal humanism which, driven by a guilt complex derived from history, desires to renounce its authority and cede it to the Maori" (130).

If, according to Babington, the period in New Zealand film history from 1975–1985 is characterized by male-centered cinema and by the re-identification of New Zealand with its various landscapes (18), then by 1985, "the beginnings of a perceptible feminization of New Zealand films [is] observable, not only in subject matter and emphases, but in directing personnel" (113). The period in New Zealand film history between 1986 and 2005, Babington asserts, is characterized by the dominant status of many female New Zealand filmmakers—including Jane Campion, who, along with Vincent Ward and Peter Jackson, is among New Zealand's most internationally recognized filmmakers—changes in relationships between Maori and Pakeha, changes from the New Right, and the predominance of multiculturalism (179). This period saw a reinterpretation and reinvention of the "'Maoriland' romance, in which all but segregated Maori worlds are produced, but in contemporary settings...in which the European world is, if not entirely expelled, then extremely peripheral" (Babington 226). It is during this period, of course, that New Zealand's two top-grossing films, *Once Were Warriors* and *Whale Rider*, emerge to present first a dystopic and then utopian view of the mythical conception of "Maoriland," one shaped by female power and dependent upon the invention of new traditions in order to define Maori identity.

Historian Eric Hobsbawm has argued in *The Invention of Tradition* that "'traditions' which appear or claim to be old are often quite recent in origin and sometimes invented" (1). He continues:

> "Invented tradition" is taken to mean a set of practices, normally governed by overtly or tacitly accepted rules and of a ritual or symbolic nature, which seek to inculcate certain values and norms of behavior by repetition, which automatically implies continuity with the past. (1)

Through repetition and lack of variation, Hobsbawm asserts, ritual becomes codified as tradition in that it ultimately becomes linked with past action, even if only because the action is repeatedly performed over a short period of time. Given that a traditional—read "precolonial"—Maori culture is at once inaccessible and also a fiction (in that precolonially there was no conception of "Maoriness"), in the imaginative representations of Maori identity discussed throughout this chapter, what is considered "traditionally" Maori is necessarily an invention generated within the context of national narrative. What makes *Once Were Warriors* and *Whale Rider* unique within this framework is that both narratives are intensely conscious of the ways that Maori identity is largely imaginary, and both call for the explicit invention of new Maori traditions to displace and rework conceptions of Maoriness that have been largely romanticized or reactionary and dependent upon Pakeha national imaginings. Both films draw upon traditional Maori oral narrative mythology—the story of the *taniwha* in *Once Were Warriors* and the story of Paikea[5] in *Whale Rider*—but both re-inscribe that mythology in ways that require that the Maori take responsibility for their cultural decline and invent new traditions to replace the old, ineffective, corrupted, and inaccessible traditions that are lauded in precolonial mythology.

Once Were Warriors

According to Emiel Martens, "in the postmodern world, *Once Were Warriors* became the most debated novel in New Zealand literary history, the most successful film in New Zealand film history, and the most controversial cultural phenomenon in New Zealand contemporary history" (145). In an interview with Christina Thompson, Alan Duff, author of the novel, stated, "I hope one day they'll say, Alan Duff was the man who started the process of growing Maori New Zealand up!" (8). Duff, the son of a Maori mother and a European father, was a veritable unknown prior to the publication of *Warriors* in 1990. Since that time, he has published two sequels to that work, *What Becomes of the Broken Hearted* (1996) and *Jake's Long Shadow* (2002), along with various other novels and works of non-fiction, most notably *Maori: The Crisis and the Challenge* (1993); he has become a polarizing figure in New Zealand, a fierce advocate of Maori literacy[6] and a strong critic of what he calls the "institutionalized inferiority complex" (qtd. in Thompson 8) from which he feels the Maori suffer. He has been very vocal in his belief that the Maori's blame of the Pakeha and acceptance of their own victim status serve as "an excuse for not overcoming." He says, "all winners have people who run them down and say they can't make it. And you know what winners do? They just try harder" (qtd. in Thompson 8). Such sentiment can be—and has been—interpreted as an overt attack on the Maori characterized by Duff's refusal to acknowledge the structural differences (in terms of socio-economic status, government representation, and educational opportunity) that affect New Zealand's Maori population.

As Duff's first novel, *Once Were Warriors* in many ways functions as Duff's primary—and perhaps only half-realized—attempt to express his specific political ideology. The work is a cacophonous interplay of various voices that are layered, rendered in dialect, and, at times, unidentifiable, often shifting in the span of one sentence from third to first person—for example: "just sat here, a boy and his (good) sister in the foyer of Two Lakes Courthouse, on a Friday morning when his mates (what few he had) were at school, probably laughing at me, I bet" (22). Through these stylistic devices, the novel provides an examination of speech, both Maori and English, and the inarticulate nature, both Duff's and Jake Heke's, of being displaced and marginalized. The text, poly-vocal, violent, and angry, is a study in the bifurcated nature of Maori identity, of existence between European and Polynesian cultures, and, in its overt didacticism, is wildly contradictory. The narrative tells the story of the Heke family, Beth and Jake and their children, as the family deals with poverty, alcoholism, and spousal abuse. Initially, the narrative is focalized through Beth and her struggle to leave the abusive Jake after her daughter Grace commits suicide, but Beth's narrative is largely absent at the end of the novel after she quits drinking, kicks Jake out of the house, and takes on the role of a sort of community mother to the children of Pine Block, the government housing project where she and her family live.

Janet Wilson has claimed that "contemporary Maori literature is about realignment" (267) of the Maori identity, and Duff's novel struggles in its attempt at this task, striking an uncomfortable balance between idealization of Pakeha culture and education, as exemplified by the white Trambert family who live just beyond Pine Block, and disgust with Maori degeneration, as characterized by Jake's Conradesque analysis of his comrades at the bar: "so people going…. Out of their minds, that is. Heads rolling, eyes too, things coming out jumbled, rubbishy, and aggression growing; spit-drops on every spat out word, sentence, a gibberish, a mixed up, fucked-up gibberish from a person sposed to be human" (63). Given its repeated refusals to blame the Pakeha—as Beth states, "oh but I can't blame em half the time when you see all the crime, or too damn much of it, is committed by us" (43)—by both Beth and later Chief Te Tupaea, and its depictions of the Maori as drunk, violent, and uneducated, it is little wonder that the work has been criticized as racist. Wilson asserts that "Duff's essentialist representations of the Maori as violent, racially degenerate, a caste that has lost its warrior-status and sunk into an insensate state, is a crude reduction of contemporary realities" (275). But also inherent in the work is a deep ambivalence about the displacement and destruction of Maori culture that belies an entirely essentialist reading of the text. While Beth bemoans the status of the Maori as a "bookless society" (10), she alternately recognizes "a bookless society's equivalent of several volumes" (121) in the carvings at her family's *marae* where she takes Grace for her funeral. She does note, however, that such volumes are only available to those who "know how to translate" (121) the text. Considering "only four percent of the total Maori population over the age of 16 are fluent speakers of the language" (Lambert 159), such history remains inaccessible to the majority of the Maori. Characters also express a sense of pride and sadness at the loss of their past warrior culture, and, despite the narrative's insistence that the chief—who ultimately comes to share the oral history of the Maori with the residents of Pine Block—is not "into blamin people, the Pakeha, the system, the anything for the obvious Maori problems" (191), one of his earliest lessons is about the Treaty of Waitangi, "an agreement between two peoples to share the land, its resources. *As equals!*…. IT WAS A CONTRACT.…. Which—they [the Pakeha]—broke" (179).

Such ambivalences and contradictions point to the difficulty of imagining and narrating a solution to the issues that plague the Maori in New Zealand. On the one hand, Duff's work calls on the Maori to read, to gain an education (albeit a Western one), but the text also positions Maori history and culture as valuable and powerful, if for no other reason than to situate the contemporary Maori within an historical, lost, warrior past. This past is worth knowing, Duff's novel suggests, but it is impossible to repeat, as evidenced by the novel's treatment of contemporary Maori "warriors," the gang known as the Brown Fists who have their faces tattooed with imitation *moko*, administered by a Pakeha tattoo artist. While the chief tells the people how "*your* warrior ancestor" underwent the *moko* chiseling for months until his face was so swollen that he had to be fed through a funnel (180), Nig Heke's tattoo is merely "a replica of olden-day *moko*, which the tattoist'd copied out of a book from a photograph of a real tattooed Maori head" (181). Within the contemporary moment, *moko* loses all meaning, becomes a copy of a copy, an image created from a photo of a "head," the symbol and all of its cultural significance removed from the body of the warrior it once emblazoned. Just as Beth admires the carvings in the *marae* but realizes that they are meaningless to most contemporary Maori, the description of the modern day *moko* reinforces the narrative's tenuous position that the past cannot be recreated in the present moment. Similarly, the novel's ending reflects a profound ambivalence with regard to the state of contemporary New Zealand: after Nig's funeral, "a sky stayed blue. And that cloud formation had changed shape—Oh, but only if you're looking for that sorta thing" (198). Duff leaves the land without a name; it is neither New Zealand nor Aotearoa, the Island of the Long Cloud. Grace, the sensitive daughter who admires the Tramberts, and Nig, the Brown Fist who embraces contemporary warriordom, both die. Beth takes her children to her family's *urupaa* for burial, but she returns to Pine Block to live among "the People," to care for them, and to teach them their history, yet her voice, so present early in the novel, is silent at the end, and characters even comment on the things "Beth used to say" (192). The final chapters are focalized through Jake, as he finds himself homeless, miserable, and broken. Despite the novel's clear presentation of Beth's transformation as positive and beneficial to her fellow Maori, at the end of the novel, we find her silenced, having faded into the background of the netherworld of government housing, neither in a home she owns (like the Pakeha Tramberts) nor at the *marae* with her "traditional" Maori family.

Lee Tamahori's film adaptation of Duff's novel radically alters Duff's assimilationist story and places Beth's struggle at the forefront of the narrative.

The solution to the problems in contemporary Maori life, the film suggests, will neither be found in assimilation nor in a return to a precolonial ideal. What Beth claims to find at the end of the film is "something better," something she must invent: a Maori family in which the mother is the one who makes the decisions. Tamahori hired Riwia Brown to write the screenplay, something that angered Duff, who had been contracted to write the screenplay and act as consultant: "the scriptwriter, Riwia Brown, is running around the country saying that Alan Duff's book and his characterization is one-dimensional, for God's sake. I don't think the script improved on my original screenplay" (Duff, qtd. in Thompson 13). Maureen Molloy notes that Brown's choice to make Beth the central character imbues Duff's narrative with optimism and hope; however, she claims, "it is a compromised optimism, resting as it does on Grace's suicide" (165). The film alters a few key aspects of the story, removing the white Trambert family and Nig's death from the narrative, as well as identifying Grace's rapist as Bully, thereby removing the possibility that Jake is the perpetrator, as is potentially the case in Duff's novel. Most significant of these changes, however, is Beth's possible return to her family *marae* at the end of the film, a move that contributes to Clelland-Stokes's reading of the film as promoting

> a separatist discourse that extends beyond the widely accepted tenets of bi-culturalism, which, like those of multiculturalism, suggest "unity in diversity." Instead, a distinct binary divide is established between Self and Other, Maori and Pakeha in *Once Were Warriors* with the implicit promotion of a separate and exclusive Maori space within Aotearoa/New Zealand. (188)

Peter Calder claims that the controversy that surrounded Duff's novel was largely dependent on its presentation of Maori misfortune as of a Maori making "and that Maori salvation would come mainly, if not exclusively, from Maori resolve and determination and not from changes in social policy" (185). Conversely, Calder views the film as a "full-steam domestic thriller" with only "incidental" political subtext (185).

The cultural impact of the film was huge, however, both in terms of its financial success and its political repercussions. Along with being the subject of New Zealand's biggest video piracy case, according to Kirsten Moana Thompson, the term "warrior families" entered the national vernacular as a result of the film, and domestic violence was more frequently reported in New Zealand after the film's release (233). Thompson further notes that "the film's harsh unmitigating portrait of domestic violence, parental neglect, poverty, rape, gang membership, and alcoholism also stirred national discussion about the social affects of colonization for the Maori," who, despite representing a mere twelve percent of New Zealand's population, are disproportionally represented in terms of imprisonment, domestic violence, and alcoholism statistics (234). Corrin Columpar disagrees with Calder's claim that the political import of the film was merely incidental, noting that "Tamahori's treatment of the family at the center of his story mandates a political reading that takes into consideration the way in which that family…has been affected by imperialist history and structural racism" (467), and Maureen Molloy reads the film as "narrating the nation, and simultaneously, the feminine" (154).

In the film's opening scene, according to Columpar, Tamahori "draws attention to contemporary cinema's preference for romanticized representations of the pre-colonial or colonial past over depictions of a devastated postcolonial present" (468). The initial shot appears to be of the New Zealand wilderness uninhabited by people, but as the camera pans out, the image is revealed to be of a billboard situated along a busy interstate. In its first moments, the film exposes the iconic tourist image of a pristine and untouched New Zealand landscape as a myth and generates a new image of Maoriland for audiences in New Zealand and abroad; as the camera pans further back, we see Maori teenagers spray painting graffiti beneath the billboard as Beth Heke (Rena Owen) walks past pushing a shopping cart down a cracked cement path toward her home.

Figure 5: Rena Owen as Beth Heke in the film's opening sequence. (Fine Line/Photofest)

While the film works to undermine previous mythological filmic representations of the Maori, its presentation of the urban landscape it depicts has been criticized as equally fictitious. Stephen Turner notes that "the opening sequence seriously distorts the physical environment of Auckland in an effort to make the city look something like South Central Los Angeles" (85). Turner reads this geographic manipulation as an attempt to make the film fit into the American genre of gangster film in order to have it appeal to a wider audience and concludes that "seen in this way, the colonization of the British Empire is merely an earlier phase of globalizing capitalism, now American in effect" (90). Leonie Pihama asserts that *Once Were Warriors* "has the potential to maintain and reproduce the existing negative notions of Maori and how we live, not through its content alone, but because of the context in which it is located," as it is "not located within historical realities of this land" (191). In that Duff's novel works to demonstrate the gulf between Maori and Pakeha that exists as the result of Maori cultural realities both before and after colonization, it serves to situate Aotearoa/New Zealand within a postcolonial framework. Conversely, Pakeha presence is almost entirely absent from the film, and the film provides no postcolonial commentary, with the minor exception of Beth's claim that the two Pakeha police officers who come to claim Boogie are not *taniwhas*, the mythical caretakers about whom Grace writes in her journal.

In that Beth is the film's central character, domestic violence is situated "in the legacy of colonization" (K. Thompson 235). Clelland-Stokes argues that Beth's return to her *marae* and the film's valorization of the country verses the city can be read as "a potentially disempowering message of Maori women's inability to survive in tougher public spaces," and that "no woman-friendly alternative is imagined for Maori society in an urban context" (197). Similarly, Maureen Molloy claims that "this romanticization [of the *marae*] belies the fact that poverty and violence are as much a problem in rural as in urban communities" (166). While I certainly understand and respect these readings, the film ends prior to Beth's return to the marae, and even though she tells her children that "we're going home,"[7] I simultaneously read Beth's statements to Jake that she has found something "better" and that "our people once were warriors… people with spirit" to indicate that a stay at the *marae* may be the place where Beth will go to nurse her wounded spirit, but that there is no way for her to go back to what "once" was.

Prior to this final scene, the film offers ample evidence that that which is external or of the physical world will never provide Beth and her family with a sense of home; therefore, neither her state house nor the *marae* can be the "better" reality that Beth has found. Duff's novel pays particular attention to the concept of mirroring, and characters are constantly looking for external experiences that reflect their own. Furthermore, the reflections that they often find tell them nothing new about their lives: the "same old two-storey houses shared by two families" in Pine Block are "fucking mirrors of each other" (55), while at the bar where Jake goes constantly, the "whole joint is one big mirror of each other" (60), and all the members of the Brown Fists are "fucking ugly mirrors of each other" (75). At her funeral, Trambert claims that Grace is "a mirror, God, a bloodly mirror of my own daughter" (133). Early in Tamahori's film, Beth looks at herself in the mirror in her living room, pulling her hair up and smirking at her reflection. When Jake beats her soon thereafter, he smashes her head into this same mirror, destroying the physical mirror into which Beth looks for meaning and for validation that, despite all her years with Jake, she is still attractive. Furthermore, in that neither the Tramberts nor the chief are present, the film again indicates the absence of external mirrors—either Pakeha or Maori—in which Beth can find a suitable reflection.

While characters in the novel are constantly looking outside for external validation of their feelings and for appropriate models of Maori behavior, however flawed, the film literally smashes all attempts to seek external validation and asks that the characters place the sources of their identity "inside," and the destruction of the mirror early in the film is evidence of this reality; likewise the destruction of the image of a pristine New Zealand via the opening shot of the billboard above the highway reinforces the film's overt insistence on the untrustworthiness an imagined Maoriland(scape). A perfect example of this phenomenon occurs at the end of the film when Boogie compliments Nig on the *moko* that covers only half his face. Nig asks if Boogie would like one as well, and Boogie declines, stating that he wears his "on the inside." Bennett, the child welfare worker who takes Boogie into custody after his court hearing, implants this idea in his charge's mind, telling Boogie that "your mind" will be your weapon, and that he will carry his *taiaha*—the traditional Maori spear—on the "inside." The weapon that, Bennett claims, put the British to shame, is no longer one that can function in the present moment; the Maori must internalize their past as a source of internalized strength and pride. Seeking a reflection, a mirror image of what it means to be Maori, the film suggests, will prove futile.

Maori identity, in the current moment, may be shaped by a past in which the people "once were warriors," but the warrior model, in the present moment, is not the answer. Instead, the film invents a tradition in which the Maori woman is responsible for her family. The home of which Beth speaks, therefore, must be spiritual, dependent upon the internalization of her "warrior" past to enable her to exist in the present, whether at the *marae* or elsewhere. The film ends before we see where Beth goes, either back to her the house she formerly shared with Jake (she says to Jake, "from now on, I make the decisions for my family") or to her tribal *marae*. When her aunt asks her to come to the *marae*, saying "you've got a lot to do back home," Beth states, "and here, too, Auntie." The work that must be done in term of strengthening the spirit, the narrative implies, must be done throughout New Zealand, wherever the Maori live.

I want to end my analysis of this film by looking closely at Grace's story of the *taniwha*, which she tells at the beginning of the film. According to *Explore Te Ara: The Encyclopedia of New Zealand*, the *taniwha* "are supernatural creatures whose forms and characteristics vary according to different tribal traditions." The *taniwha* live in or near water and are alternately viewed as monstrous abductors of women and as protectors. They can be male or female ("Taniwha"). At the beginning of the film, Grace sits beneath the lone tree in her yard, the tree from which she hangs herself later in the film, and tells her younger siblings the story of a female *taniwha* named Rahey who is an *kaitiaka*, or protector. The story is Grace's own, but it is based on traditional Maori legend. Grace is the first character who speaks in the film, and she reads from her journal the story of the *taniwha* who "spent most of her time caring for her greenstone wall. The wall stopped the water from flooding the people who lived by Rahey's lake." The people who live near the lake bring greenstone to help the *taniwha* reinforce her wall, and she, in turn, brings them fish. Immediately after Grace's little brother Huata (Joseph Kairau) asks, "what's a *taniwha*?" and Grace answers, "it's a creature that looks after people," Jake appears in the doorway with a packet of seafood that he has purchased to celebrate quitting his job. Jake is situated as the benevolent *kaitiaka*, the protector who provides fish for his family, but as the film progresses, we learn that he embodies the more malevolent aspect of the creature, as the *taniwha* who abducts the woman from her *iwi* or tribe; "these monsters would inevitably be killed and the women returned to their families" ("Taniwha"). At Grace's funeral, Beth tells her dead daughter a story of a young girl who "fell in love" with a man of whom the old people did not approve. The man, of course, is Jake.

On the one hand, Beth leaves to marry Jake of her own free will. Her experience is like that of Hinemoa, the legendary woman so central to the early Maoriland romance films of Méliès and Tarr, the chosen one of the tribe; Beth even claims to be the "*puhi* of the *marae*, the special one." But it is also easy to read her marriage to Jake as a form of abduction, dependent as it is on the battered woman syndrome she suffers over the course of her eighteen-year relationship with him. After Grace's funeral, Beth tapes her daughter's journal, ripped in half by Jake, back together, and Toot asks that Beth "read me one of G's stories." The youngest daughter Polly (Rachel Morris Jr) says, "yeah, the one about the *taniwha*." As Beth opens the journal to find the story, she finds instead Grace's record of her rape, and it is this story that causes her to load her family into Nig's car and head out to confront Bully and Jake at the pub. Grace's *taniwha* story has been destroyed, ripped in half by her father, just as the mirror into which Beth seeks her reflection is smashed when Jake throws her into it. Beth must rewrite the *taniwha* story based not only on the historical Maori legend that inspired her daughter, but also on the literal story of rape that causes her daughter's suicide, a story that is situated in the present, not the pre-colonial past. The story that she tells Jake at the end of the film is short, simply that "our people once were warriors, but not like you, Jake. They were people with *manna*, pride." She stands before him in black leather and a red shirt, her outfit reminiscent of—but not mirroring—Nig's gang attire. Beth becomes the *taniwha*, the protector of her family, but the film asks that we imagine its ending; Jake, the *taniwha* who abducts the "young girl" has not been slain, nor has the girl returned to the *marae*. Beth's statement that she and her children are "going home," the final statement in the film, asks that we imagine what a re-conceptualized home will look like for this woman.

Whale Rider

As is the case with Duff's novel, Witi Ihimaera's novella *The Whale Rider* (1987)[8] is focalized through a male character. Rawiri, the uncle of Kahutia Te Rangi, the girl who later takes up the mantle of Paikea, the whale rider, narrates the story of his niece's birth and ascent. While the story is ostensibly about Kahutia's attempts to prove herself the legitimate heir to her great-grandfather Koro Apirana's chiefdom—despite the fact that his first words in the novel, just after Kahutia's birth are "a *girl*…I will have nothing to do with her" (13)—the narrative, again like Duff's, is highly didactic, but in ways that are highly contrary to Duff's assimilationist thrust. Ihimaera's work focuses explicitly on the importance of Maori identity and the interdependence of humans, non-human animals, and the environment. Two chapters focus on the racism Rawiri encounters in Papua New Guinea at the hands of his Pakeha friend Jeff's family; in this section of the book, Rawiri indicates that he misses both Kahu and Whangara, and when he returns after a four-year walkabout in Australia and Papua New Guinea, he realizes that Kahu is "the one" for whom Koro searches. Rawiri details the

10,000-year-old legend of Paikea, the ancestral founder of the Ngati Porou confederation:

> In those days man had power over the creatures of land and sea, and it was Kahutia Te Rangi who traveled here on the back of a whale.... To commemorate his voyage, he was given another name, Paikea.... The landscape reminded Paikea of his birthplace back in Hawaiki, so he named his new home Whangara Mai Tawhiti, which we call Whangara for short. (30–31)

Rawiri chronicles the school sessions led by Koro and attended by the village boys, and notes the lessons that are taught in the preservation of oral culture— "remembering long lines of genealogy" (35)—and Maori mythology, of a time when people "had the power to talk to the beasts and creatures of the sea" (36). Kahu is prohibited from attending these lessons because she is a girl and has, according to Koro, "broken the male line of descent in our tribe" (13). Despite the fact that she is excluded from her great-grandfather's search for an appropriate heir, Kahu consistently asserts, in both practical and magical ways, her status as the chosen one, the legitimate chief of her people.

Ihimaera's novel works to codify and preserve the oral legend of Paikea, but it also seeks to inform and shape Paikea's mythology by weaving into it various references to other mythologies, notably those of the Judeo-Christian and Western literary tradition. For example, in a letter that Porourangi, Kahu's father, writes to Rawiri, he claims that Koro "wants to find a young boy...to pull the sword out of the stone, someone who has been marked by the Gods for this task" (71). It is, of course, Kahu who obtains the Maori version of Arthurian sword when she retrieves the carved stone that Koro throws in the ocean to test his male pupils, who are unable to find it. And as Kahu entices the old whale back to the sea late in the novel, Rawiri reminds himself that "Jonah had lived in the belly of his whale" (127). Kahu vanishes for three days, and when she is found, she is in a coma (144); the reference to the death and rebirth of Christ is obvious. But Ihimaera's narrative also seeks to embellish Paikea's story with other Maori myths, particularly the story of Muriwai, the female chief from whom Kahu's great-grandmother, Nanny Flowers, has descended. According to Rawiri, Muriwai

> Had come to New Zealand on the Maataatua canoe. When the canoe approached Whakatane...Muriwai's chiefly brothers, led by Toroa, went to investigate the land. While they were away, however, the sea began to rise and the current carried the canoe so closed to the rocks that Muriwai knew all on board would surely perish. So she chanted special prayers, asking the Gods to give her the

right and open the way for her to take charge. Then she cried, "E-i! Tena, kia whakatane ake au i ahau!" Now I shall make myself a man. (19)

The narrative implies that Flowers is instrumental in Porourangi's decision to name his daughter after the male ancestor Kahutia Te Rangi, an action that causes Koro to chide Flowers, telling her "you've stepped out of line" (19). Women's transgressions in terms of the patriarchal dictates of their tribe or *iwi* are treated within the novel in ways that demonstrate the complexities of power relations between the sexes, particularly in terms of the ways that women's influence is foundational and pronounced. Flowers says early in the work that "rules are made to be broken" (41), and she makes sure that Kahu's birth cord is buried in the earth at the *marae*, linking the girl with her homeland, with the earth itself, and with her ancestors. These references to the destruction of linearity—the line of descent and Flowers's act of stepping out of line—resonate with the destruction of mirrors in *Once Were Warriors*, but this time, it is females who transgress and defy the tendency to ascribe to the mandates of history. Furthermore, this refusal to remain "in line" points to the spiral nature of Maori culture, and to the non-linear nature of mythical time. In her study, *Decolonizing Cultures in the Pacific: Reading History and Trauma in Contemporary Fiction*, Susan Y. Najita describes the spiral as indicative of Maori conceptions of time: "as in Hawaiian notions of time, the Maori past (*mua*) occurs in front and the future (*muri*) occurs behind" (100).

As was the case with Tamahori's adaptation of Duff's novel, Niki Caro's 2002 adaptation of Ihimaera's shifts the perspective, focalizing the narrative through Paikea (Keisha Castle-Hughes)[9] instead of Rawiri (Grant Roa), and, according to Mary M. Wiles, "in the film adaptation, the whale rider's supernatural ability to *interlock* with nature is articulated predominantly through the female voice" (182); in the novel, Kahu's connection to the whales is articulated by the whales themselves, as these animals are given their own concurrent narrative within the work. In terms of criticism, the film adaptations of *Once Were Warriors* and *Whale Rider* are often treated comparatively by critics who note the feminine focus of both, but they are also contrasted in terms of their treatment of and focus on landscape and on Maori cultural identification. Pascale De Souza notes that "the two movies mirror each other in so far as *Whale Rider* portrays a Maori chief struggling to prevent the loss of Maori identity and culture within his rural tribal group while *Once Were Warriors* features a nuclear family struggling to reconcile its urban identity with is rural Maori roots" (15).

Dieter Riemenschneider claims that "temporally and spatially, *Once Were Warriors* and *Whale Rider* mark the conflict between modernity and tradition or between global pressures and local resilience" (140), and Bruce Babington claims that *Once Were Warriors* can be read as "a (dystopic) version of the all-Maori world of *Whale Rider*" (238), noting that in both films, the white characters that are present in the novels are deleted. As is the case with *Once Were Warriors*'s depiction of the urban New Zealand landscape, critics also take *Whale Rider* to task for its depictions of rural New Zealand. Chris Prentice, for example, notes the problematic ways that the film's attention to "the natural" (259) and a "non-materialist authenticity" present a "metropolitan nostalgia for simplicity [that] risks celebrating the poverty of others, reading their old cars, basic houses, and functional clothing as 'lifestyle choices'" (260);[10] furthermore, he asserts that the film fetishizes nature and generates a kind of "sentimental and globally commodified 'environmentalism'" (262). Just as Leonie Pihama claims that *Once Were Warriors* is not "located within historical realities of this land" (191), Prentice asserts that "politics and the broader political context that shape the lives of the Maori community are almost entirely absent from [*Whale Rider*]" (258). Also of some concern to critics is Niki Caro's status as Pakeha and not Maori, a fact with which Caro herself has grappled.

Caro has claimed that the making of the film was a collaborative process, with Witi Ihimaera serving as an associate producer of the film, and that she had the support of the Maori elders for whom she screened the film prior to its release. In an interview with Maria Garcia, Caro says, "I felt a huge responsibility to this project…the privilege of adapting a work by Witi, who is an incredible writer, and then the tremendous responsibility to the community that actually live in the region of the *Whale Rider*, then to Paikea himself, to the legend itself." Caro is also careful to note the universality of the film despite its Maori cast and setting, stating that she was surprised to hear Pakeha audience members say, "that's us. That's who we are. That's what we're proud of" (Caro qtd. in Garcia). In that, as Garcia notes, the subtext of Caro's adaptation is "the rise of a new consciousness, of a…female perspective," the choice of the actor who would portray Paikea was of singular importance to Caro who, in the documentary *Behind the Scenes of Whale Rider*, which is included on the DVD of the film, says that the challenge was "to find the *real* girl" and "not an actor" to play Paikea. Rawiri Paratene, who plays Koro in the film, says in the same documentary that "we just needed one person to play that girl," and Keisha Castle-Hughes was that girl. In Caro's focus on the fact that "Keisha has all the qualities that Pai has in the story" and in terms of Caro's assertion that she was looking for the *real* Paikea, Castle-Hughes, like the character she portrays in the film, becomes the chosen one, chosen for her apparent Maori (mythical) authenticity.[11]

Caro claims that in the film, everything had to be "absolutely real" (*Behind the Scenes*), a claim that speaks to the filmmaker's dedication to rendering the narrative in a way that is authentically Maori (a criteria verified by the Maori elders for whom she screened the film prior to its release) and believable in its rendering of the "marriage of the natural and the supernatural" (Caro, *Behind the Scenes*). But this claim also speaks to the way that fiction can create the reality of that which it represents, despite its attention to an impossible to prove conception of "truth" or "realness/reality." In this case, the narrative rendering of the intersection of the Maori mythic past with the present results in an historical moment during which New Zealand's people—both Maori and Pakeha—identify with the transformative experiences of Koro and Paikea.[12]

In its generation of the reality it hopes to depict, *Whale Rider*, like *Once Were Warriors*, works to smash mirrors, to resist Koro's tendency to look to the past to see the future, and instead depicts the present moment as a translation and reinterpretation of the non-linear, mythic past, influenced by its dictates but also shaped by such variables as globalization, urbanization, and shifting women's roles. These influences, largely absent in the book, are indicated in the film in a variety of ways, particularly in terms of the film's treatment of Koro's tumultuous relationship with his son Porourangi (Cliff Curtis), an artist whose work may be influenced by traditional Maori carving but bears little resemblance to it, and who leaves New Zealand for Germany after his wife's death. The conflict between father and son is based on Koro's perception that Porourangi has abandoned his duty as the next in line for chiefdom, and Porourangi's frustration with his father's inability to see his son as anything other than a failed heir. Porourangi claims, "you don't even know who I am," to which his father replies, "but I know who you're meant to be."

The existence of the gangsters that are so apparent in *Once Were Warriors* is alluded to in the character of the father of one of the boys who trains with Koro; he comes to the school to hear his son's recitation but leaves immediately thereafter, a move that causes his son to cry and Koro to subsequently banish the boy from consideration. The film is full of fathers, like this one and like Porourangi, who leave their rural backgrounds—and their children—to head to the city or to other countries. When Porourangi returns, it is with a pregnant German girlfriend, another affront to his father's insularity and desire for his son to marry a Maori woman, preferably Pai's teacher. Unlike Ihimaera's depiction of him, Caro's Rawiri, once a prize-winning master of the *taiaha*, stays put in Whangara, smoking pot and growing fat, until Pai asks him to teach her his weaponry skills. And early in the film, Nanny Flowers and her friends smoke cigarettes, behavior for which Pai chides them, saying, "Maori women have got to stop smoking. We've got to protect our childbearing properties." The joke, of course, is that Flowers and her friends are well beyond childbearing and Pai is too young to bear children, but the incident highlights a problematic feminist discourse, one alternately dependent on smoking—a transgressive act that the women try to hide from Pai and Koro, the patriarchal authority—and on the assumption that Maori women must have children; the fertility rate for Maori women "in 1995…was twice that of non-Maori women," and Maori women tend to have children at younger ages than their non-Maori counterparts ("Maori Women in Focus" 6).

The film illustrates the ways that gender roles, within the context of contemporary rural Maori culture, are in need of redefinition and revision, and the power struggle inherent in the reshaping of these roles is played out in the interactions between Koro and Paikea. Rawiri, once a promising athlete and cultivator of Maori tradition, has given up, noting that because he is not the firstborn son, his prowess in these areas hardly matters, while Porourangi, the firstborn hope for the future of his people, leaves his rural home for Germany. Koro holds on to a past that is fast becoming obsolete, and he equates the loss of that past with emasculation. In a scene during which Koro is training the village boys to be warriors, Koro's head is positioned in the right part of the frame, while Paikea's face appears in the window behind him as she tries to observe the lesson from which she is excluded because she is a girl. Koro states that if the boys do not learn the chant exactly, they "will suffer…the consequences." Two of the boys look past Koro to Pai, and Koro, following their gaze, turns just as Pai ducks beneath the windowsill. Immediately thereafter, one of the boys asks, "Like what?" in response to Koro's threat of consequences, and Koro answers that "your dick will drop off." The threat that Pai poses to Koro's worldview is apparent from the very beginning of the film, from the moment that Pai's narrative voice begins telling the story, asserting that "there was no happiness when I was born. My twin brother died and took our mother with him." In giving Pai a twin brother, Caro's film engages with the discourse of mirrors that is inherent in both Duff's novel and Tamahori's adaptation of it. Identical twins mirror one another, but because these twins are of different sexes, the reflection is inexact, a dichotomous relationship in which the male child would have been, had he survived, the privileged one of the duality. The last words spoken by Pai's mother are "Paikea, Paikea," and the repetition of the name—perhaps bestowed by the mother on both twins—occurs as the shot shifts from a close-up of the mother's mouth to a close-up of her newborn daughter's. When both mother and brother die, the female baby, the sole surviving Paikea, is left with neither a maternal nor filial mirror; she must *become* a new Paikea, the female chief with no precedent in the context of the film's narrative.

But the new chief that she must become is dependent upon her acquisition of knowledge of the mythic past, and, because she is a girl, information about that past is withheld from her by her grandfather. Early in the film, Pai asks Koro for information about her Maori past, and she wants specific details about when Paikea rode on the back of the whale from Hawaiki. She asks, "Where did the whale come from?" to which Koro replies, "From Hawaiki." She asks, "Where's that?" and he answers, "It's where we lived before we came here, where the ancestors are." In response to her question, "How long ago?" Koro says, "Long time," to which Pai replies, "But how long?" Koro is speaking in terms of mythical, not chronological time, a concept that, up until this point, Pai has been unable to comprehend; hereafter, however, she maintains a sense of mythical time that far surpasses that of her grandfather who, it seems, is capable of explaining the concept but not of realizing its meaning. Koro explains by showing Pai the end of the rope he is using to start a boat motor. He says that all the fibers of the rope are like the ancestors, all woven together and strong, "all the way back to that whale of yours." He wraps the rope around the engine, overlapping it, and providing a visual image that illustrates the cyclical or spiral nature of Maori mythology. When he pulls the rope, however, it breaks, and he proclaims, "Useless bloody rope. I'll get another one." While he is off looking for another rope, Pai ties the two pieces of rope back together, wraps the repaired rope around the engine, and starts it. She calls to Koro, announcing that "It's working!" and he returns to turn off the motor and pronounce, "I don't want you to do that again. It's dangerous." The line (or spiral) of descent from the ancestral Paikea to the present has been broken by the birth of the female Paikea; like Flowers in Ihimaera's book, Pai has "stepped out of line." But Pai is able to build upon her grandfather's knowledge to repair, alter, and make stronger the mythology within which she finds herself. His assertion that such a move is "dangerous" speaks to his rigid belief that the line of chiefs must be unchanging, a male line descended back to the mythical ancestor, despite his earlier illustration—via the rope—of mythical, cyclical, interwoven, and non-linear ancestry.

Visually, the film consistently reinforces Pai's adherence to the circular or spiral notion of time and to a belief in the power of reinterpreted tradition; for example, when her father shows the family a slide show of his art, Pai watches in silence until Porourangi shows a photo of a metallic disk covered with what appear to be round grooves, like the grooves of a record album. Pai remarks, "That's a good one." The piece does not represent the spiral that is prevalent in traditional Maori art—including the *moko*—but it is a kind of interpretation of that familiar cultural image, situated in the context of Porourangi's more global experience. After this piece, the next slide depicts another rounded piece of sculpture, this one shaped like a "u," or unclosed circle. Koro pushes aside the sheet that is serving as a screen for the show, even as this incomplete circle is still being projected; the parallels between the rope that tears when Koro wraps it around the engine and this broken-seeming circle are apparent.

Figure 6: Keisha Castle-Hughes as Paikea, positioned in front of her grandfather Koro (Rawiri Paratene). (Newmarket Films/Photofest)

Later, as Pai is preparing to leave with her father, she rides on the handlebars of Koro's bike as he pedals her in circles. When Porourangi asks if she is ready to leave, she answers, "One more go," and Koro makes one more slow circle around the yard. In this scene, as in the one during which Pai repairs the torn rope, wraps it around the motor, and starts the engine, Pai again seeks to assert her place within mythical time. Pai fully inserts herself in the "line" of chiefs, the line out of which she has stepped, at the film's climax during which the villagers attempt to help a herd of beached whales. Around one of the whales, they tie a rope and work to pull the animal back into the ocean; the rope, of course, breaks.

Pai climbs on the whale's back and rides the animal into the ocean, where her family assumes she drowns. In this instant, Pai has finally taken up a position in the cycle of mythical time, and her grandfather is forced to recognize her rightful place in the (non-linear) line of descent when Nanny Flowers returns his whale tooth to him. Earlier in the film, Koro throws the tooth over the side of the boat and his apprentices try to retrieve it. As is the case with the knife in Ihimaera's book, Pai is the only person who can find the tooth. When Flowers gives him the tooth, he incredulously asks, "which one" of the boys found it. Flowers replies, "What do you mean, 'which one?'"

Throughout the film, Pai's physical positionality with regard to Koro provides an interesting commentary about the way that the new relies upon tradition to bring it to the fore. When she peers in through the window of the Maori school as Koro teaches the boys about their history, Pai is positioned behind her grandfather. But when he pedals her in circles around the yard, she sits in front of him. In the film's final scene, Porourangi's canoe is complete; it is a Maori work of art, but it, like the circular disk, is a reinterpretation that gives rise to a new tradition: the villagers paddle the boat out to sea, and sitting in the center, side by side, are Pai and Koro. Caro's reinvention of the Maoriland romance relies, in many ways, on several conventions of that genre: the absence of Pakeha characters and an idealization of the New Zealand landscape. But this film, like *Once Were Warriors*, challenges conceptions of a unified Maori past and questions the usefulness of traditional beliefs in the present, global context. The film is situated entirely within the rural village of Whangara, but Porourangi's art and his international travels clearly indicate that Maori culture cannot and does not exist in isolation as the idyllic and innocent locale that is part and parcel of the traditional Maoriland script. Pai, like Beth Heke, must internalize her past—and one aspect of that past is the romanticization of the Maori by Pakeha mythmakers. Both women are bolstered and shaped by that past, and by various fictions within it. But they are also able to change it, to step out of line with it and find, in Beth's words, something better.

Notes

1. The legend of Hinemoa is famous in New Zealand. Hinemoa, the daughter of an influential chief is declared *puhi*, destined to marry into another chief's family. Below is a brief synopsis:

> One of the great Maori love stories has a special local connection, because it takes place on Mokoia Island in Lake Rotorua—and it's a true tale at that. Hinemoa, the daughter of an influential chief, lived on the lakeshore. Because of her father's status she was declared *puhi* (singled out to marry into another chief's family), and her tribal elders planned to choose her husband for her when she reached maturity. Although she had many suitors, none gained the approval of her tribe. Tutanekai was the youngest son of a family who lived on Mokoia Island. Each of his older brothers had sought the hand of Hinemoa, but none had been accepted. Tutanekai knew that because of his lowly rank he would never win approval from her family. But he was handsome and an excellent athlete—and eventually Hinemoa noticed him and fell in love.
> From the lakeshore, Hinemoa would hear Tutanekai play his flute, his longing music drifting across the water. Hinemoa's family, suspicious that their daughter would try to reach the island, beached their canoes so that she could not paddle across to Mokoia. The sound of Tutanekai's flute lured Hinemoa to try to swim to the island. After lashing gourds together to help her float, she slipped into the lake; guided by the music, she reached Mokoia. Cold and naked, she submerged herself in a hot pool, where she was discovered by Tutanekai. Enchanted, he slipped her into his home for the rest of the night. When they were discovered, Tutanekai's family feared an outbreak of war with Hinemoa's tribe, but instead the two tribes were peacefully united. ("The Hinemoa Legend")

2. According to Blythe, the terms "Maori" and "Pakeha" entered the vernacular of New Zealand at the time of the signing of the Treaty of Waitangi (5). The implication, of course, is that the Treaty established this binary and codified a discourse of difference.

3. This phenomenon, of the disenfranchised indigenous people's identification with American film mythology, is apparent in the previous chapter on *Tsotsi* as well.

4. Babington notes that the first film made by a New Zealander is George Tarr's 1914 *Hinemoa* (48).

5. According to Edward Shortland's 1882 study *Maori Religion and Mythology*, Paikea is a sea monster or *taniwha* who carries Kahu on his back (83). The two films, therefore, are linked by their incorporation of the *taniwha* mythology.

6. Duff started the Books in Homes Program in 1992 (Martens 23), a program that brings books to underprivileged Maori families to encourage reading.

7. Beth uses the word "home" several times throughout the film to refer to the *marae*. But she also uses the word "home" to refer to the state house. For example, when the family is going to see Boogie only to have the trip interrupted by Jake's overlong stay at the bar, she tells her family that they are "going home" as they head back to the projects.

8. Ihimaera's novel is currently out of print in the United States.

9. The film also changes her name from Kahu to Paikea.

10. Niki Caro stated in an interview with Maria Garcia that on the coast of New Zealand, "there are many Maori communities…and it's like going back to the 1950s or 1960s sometimes." Such an assertion underscores a dualism that equates the urban with the contemporary and the rural (Maori) with the past, a notion typical in the Maoriland romances of New Zealand's early film industry.

11. It is little wonder given the mythic narrative of Castle-Hughes's authenticity—the real Paikea, the genuine Maori savior—that her pregnancy at age 16 generated international controversy.

12. Of course, it is problematic for Pakeha New Zealanders to claim that the characters depicted in the film are "us," and such an assertion in fact points to the way that Caro's film comes dangerously close, at times, to replicating the Maoriland romance.

Four

The New Voy(age)eur: White Women, Black Bodies, and the Spectacle of Sexual Abandon

***

Few of us come to Charlotte Brontë's *Jane Eyre* ignorant of that Other woman to whom Rochester is married, perhaps because no character on the margins of such a revered and much-loved novel is as famous as Bertha Mason Rochester—the "madwoman in the attic," as Gilbert and Gubar successfully branded her.[1] Brontë's quintessential novel of female independence (and subjection) is a story so familiar that it hardly requires summing up. Orphaned, poor, and plain, Jane Eyre struggles against deprivation and hardship to become a governess at Thornfield Hall. She wins the love of Thornfield's Byronic master, Edward Rochester; however, the discovery of a wife still living thwarts their marriage. Jane, proud and resolute, disavows Rochester and leaves Thornfield rather than indulge in an affair so against her nature. After much suffering, she finds herself at the home of St. John Rivers and his sisters. Here, she recovers. With the Rivers, she discovers family connections and an occupation as "a village schoolmistress, free and honest, in a breezy mountain nook in the healthy heart of England" (306). St. John offers Jane romance of a different sort: he wishes her to accompany him to India as a partner in his missionary work. Yet, from across the moors, Jane hears Rochester call her name. She returns to Thornfield to find the grand house a burnt-out shell and its master blind and bent, the victim of his wife's incendiary rage before her suicidal leap from Thornfield's battlements. Jane, desired by St. John, connected to kin, and with an income of her own, is now a more equal partner for Rochester, alone, damaged and dependent, and so: "Reader, I married him," as Jane informs us near the novel's conclusion (382).

Wide Sargasso Sea, Jean Rhys's 1966 "prequel" to *Jane Eyre* in which Antoinette (Bertha) Cosway Mason (Rochester)[2] is reclaimed as the protagonist of her own story, has forced many devotees of *Jane Eyre* to reconsider the pleasures of "the cult text of feminism" (Spivak "3 Women's" 244). Although, like Jane, Antoinette is orphaned and finds herself marginalized by forces over which she has little control, Rhys's novel reveals the economic and social disruptions attendant on imperialism that *Jane Eyre* attempts to conceal. By relocating Antoinette's story to the West Indies of the 1840s *after* the action of Brontë's novel, Rhys is able to investigate the consequences of the Emancipation Act that ended slavery in 1833. Antoinette, a white Creole, is rejected by the island's black population because of her family's former dependence on slaves; as the economic status of the white Creole population declines, they are rejected as well by colonial opportunists who descend on the island to buy the devalued plantations. Both West Indian blacks and British-born whites are skeptical of Creole claims to white racial superiority and national belonging.

Antoinette occupies the interstices of these multiple subject positions, and the first and third sections of the three-part novel are narrated by Antoinette in a deliberately elliptical style that allows for the exploration of her fragmented identity. Rhys establishes from the novel's opening sentences the liminal race and class position from which Antoinette speaks: "They say when trouble comes close ranks and so the white people did. But we were not in their ranks" (9). Disenfranchised, Antoinette is easy prey for Rochester, who narrates the novel's middle section. Rhys respects Brontë's version of Rochester's story: a second son and himself a victim of the laws of primogeniture, Rochester journeys to the West Indies to secure the daughter of a wealthy sugar planter as his bride. Rochester collects his fortune and his wife, but here the narratives diverge. In *Jane Eyre*, Rochester relates the sad fact of Bertha's intemperance and immodesty, a result of a family history of madness. Isolated in the hell of Jamaica, Rochester is saved by a "wind fresh from Europe" and returns to England (Brontë 263). For her own protection, he locks Bertha in Thornfield's third floor.

In *Wide Sargasso Sea*, Rhys rewrites Rochester's hapless journey of self-discovery to reveal his arrogance and his privilege, as they manifest in his reactionary attempts to discipline and domesticate his exotic and, accordingly, unruly new wife. Rather than a marriage that secures Antoinette's position, Rochester's inflexible adherence to standards of Britishness further erode her already shaky sense of identity. In response to Rochester's sexual, ideological, and legal dominance, Antoinette turns to her maid, Christophine, a woman practiced in the occult arts of Obeah, for a potion to secure Rochester's affections and acceptance. Without a fortune, without a family, and without an ideological or epistemological foundation to call her own, Antoinette's attempt to seduce her husband backfires, and Rochester returns to Thornfield with his wife, now a zombie, a hostile hostage who will burn down her captor's house, the symbolic site of British patriarchy and pride.

Wide Sargasso Sea is perhaps so well realized because it foregrounds the imperial imagination of *Jane Eyre* that made Antoinette's imprisonment possible. Jane and Rochester, in the final pages of Brontë's novel, retreat to Ferndean, a natural oasis where their social differences are elided. Yet, even as the novel performs this domestic retrenchment, it reveals the geographies and economies of British imperialism that make it possible. St. John takes up the banner of Christendom to convert the heathens in India, in a climate that overpowers and may soon kill him. Jane's inheritance, the economic sign of her independence, comes from her uncle's business dealings in Madeira. Diana Rivers marries a captain in the Navy; Mary, a clergyman: both men represent institutions emblematic of the nation. The economic, social, and spiritual exploitation of the periphery made the domestic space safe for army, clergy, and family. In "The Governess of Empire," Deidre David explicates the novel's themes of recuperation and recovery that make England a fit place for Jane and Rochester. *Jane Eyre* is a "fantasy of rehabilitated wealth" (84) in which Jane "vanquishes the figure of counterinvasion from the colonies, suffers magnificently in the process, and erases the economic exploitation and sexual debauchery represented by Rochester and his inheritance" (83). Rhys reinscribes the material conditions of Brontë's fantasy by revealing the sexual and epistemological violence appertaining to a similar but less successful recovery project: Rochester's endeavor to renovate his first wife, and correct "the difference between an 'English' core and an 'ethnic' periphery," is disastrous, as Laura Ciolkowski reminds us (347).

I begin with this detailed preface linking *Jane Eyre* to *Wide Sargasso Sea* because these two seminal and symbiotic texts were both recently adapted—again—in 2006. Patsy Stoneman makes a compelling case for tracing the historical and cultural context of each translation of *Jane Eyre*. By studying *Jane Eyre* in her many guises including films and other "derivatives" as they cross-pollinate and reference each other (3–4), Stoneman performs for her analysis of gender what I seek to perform here in an analysis of race and the imperial imagination that circulates in and with *Jane Eyre*. E. Ann Kaplan in her postscript to "Feminism in Brontë's *Jane Eyre* and Its Film Versions," written with Kate Ellis, notes that by the late 1990s no adaptation of *Jane Eyre* had engaged the role of empire and race implicit in the novel, although she anticipates one, given that the scholarly and cultural apparatus exists for its production (204). Susanna White's 2006 Masterpiece Theater version fulfills Kaplan's expectations by forging a relationship between Bertha and Jane that foregrounds their common oppression as women, while also delimiting their relationship by representing Bertha as exotic, promiscuous, and eventually dispensable. Like Stoneman, Kaplan and Ellis provide a model for this type of analysis: they trace the tendency of film adaptations to "liquidate Brontë's ambivalence toward patriarchy," the very ambivalence that allowed readers to question its strictures (195). In the service of a traditional romance, I track a similarly regressive inclination in White's easy resolution of the problems of colonialism.

Both film adaptations of *Wide Sargasso Sea*, John Duigan's 1993 theatrical release and Brendan Maher's 2006 BBC4 telefilm, engage the geopolitics of empire that *Jane Eyre* proposes. By emphasizing that which is most obviously and commercially cinematic—the lush Caribbean landscape, and the uncivilized, dangerous, and erotic inhabitants of Jamaica—both adaptations construct new knowledges about Englishness and the periphery. Each film seeks to recast the story of Antoinette Mason as the story of Edward Rochester and his ill-conceived love affair with an volatile woman who conjures "cinema voodoo": the beating, beckoning drums, sensual dancing, over-ripe physical pleasures, and lax moral standards that invoke western fears of the uncivilized and the occult.

Wide Sargasso Sea is not the only "derivative" of *Jane Eyre* worthy of exploration. In Jacques Tourneur's 1943 horror classic *I Walked with a Zombie*, Betsy Connell, a young nurse from Ottawa, is hired to take care of the catatonic wife of a Byronic sugar planter in the West Indies. A "West Indian version of *Jane Eyre*," as producer Val Lewton initially described the film (qtd. in Bansak 145), *I Walked with a Zombie* asks viewers to imagine an offshoot of Brontë's classic, one that transplants its gothic themes to a foreign locale that Jane only obliquely imagines. Pairing this film with Laurent Cantet's 2005 release *Heading South*, in which women who cannot find partners at home travel South to secure the companionship of Haitian men, allows for an exploration of a complementary dynamic: in these two films, white female travelers from the civilized metropoles of the North head South to gaze at both foreign landscapes and foreign bodies as a means of producing knowledge about the Other. The voy(age)eurs turn their discerning gaze on distant landscapes and foreign bodies, and in "looking at" the South, reveal a complementary politic of exploitation.

The dynamic of viewing the Other, as a tourist, and film viewing of the exotic, as an audience, is theorized by a number of scholars including John Urry in his influential monograph *The Tourist Gaze,* and in "The *Tourist Gaze* Revisited." Like Laura Mulvey, who argued that the camera's gaze is essentially male in its rendering of the female form as an object, Urry argues that the landscape in art provokes the gaze of the tourist who performs an "aesthetic appropriation" of the space.[3] In the "visually built environment" of landscape art and architecture (as in film), the foreign is framed for the visual pleasure of the tourist, relegating social practices and relationships to the background or, indeed, outside the boundaries of the frame (178–179). As Ellen Strain argues, it is not surprising that tourism, cinema and notions of the exotic overlap: cinema from its earliest incarnations relied on "the representation of the exotic to locate or stabilize the new medium while simultaneously promising an authentic experience" (3). The tourists' search for "authenticity," the pleasure of true experience vis-à-vis gazing at the Other, is complicit in myths of the nation. Travel narratives have their source in the colonial acquisition of knowledge and its claims of experiential authority. Kevin Dunn, in "Fear of a Black Planet," has this to say about the "construction and consumption" of Otherness (483): travel narratives seek to fix the peoples and places of the postcolonial world in order to designate where they are geographically, historically, and temporally: "Emplotting Africans within these narratives requires the 'freezing' of African space—in terms of its meaning and boundaries—and an attempt to control African movement" (485).[4] Although Dunn analyzes the travel narratives of contemporary Africa, *Jane Eyre* and *Wide Sargasso Sea* utilize signs of the "exotic" as a visual strategy for negotiating the bodies and economies beyond the borders of the nation. It is an exploration of the dialectic of here-and-there, North and South, that Bertha's cinematic trajectory allows us to navigate.

I begin, then, with an analysis of Bertha's representation in the most recent adaptation of *Jane Eyre* to establish how difference at the edge of empire is coded racially, and how her persistent subjugation within one of the central texts of empire is refashioned for a postcolonial audience. In *Wide Sargasso Sea*, Rochester "looks at" the West Indian woman and his gaze deploys the world of "voodoo," the paradigmatic sign of the erotic, uninhibited, and uncivilized Other, and a visual world that is often foregrounded since it is exhibited "for the titillation of the West" (Olmos/Gebert 7). To shift to another set of narratives—*I Walked with a Zombie* and *Heading South*—in which women cross a similar frontier between metropole and periphery, is not to imply a progressive narrative in which a more liberal feminist ideology is at play. Rather, in this pairing, the films propose alternative dynamics in which women go in search of the exotic, and renegotiate or transcend gendered notions of imperial prerogatives. Still, the economic, cultural, and racial divide between North and South is the field on which romantic explorations and exploitations are worked through. While *Heading South* is not an obvious *Jane Eyre* derivative, it is, much like *I Walked with a Zombie,* a distant relation worthy of analysis.

Jane Eyre

While race and class relations acted out under the mantle of British imperialism are not in the forefront of the numerous *Jane Eyre* translations, film adaptations of *Jane Eyre*, even quite early ones, construct a bond between Jane and Bertha, both physical and figurative, that manages female colonial identity. In the novel, Bertha is often unseen, known only to Jane by a "demoniac laugh—low, suppressed, and deep—uttered, as it seemed, at the very key-hole of my chamber-door" (127). She is frequently mistaken for Grace Poole, the dissolute and hardened servant who watches over her. As many cultural critics have noted, Bertha is a corrective figure in *Jane Eyre,* used to liberate Jane from oppressive patriarchy and restore to Rochester and Jane a better sense of their domestic and imperial prerogatives. Deirdre David reminds us that Jane's intrepid individualism and her spirited defense of her rights as a woman are in the service of empire. Brontë's figurative strategy is to look to the periphery of Empire, and to Bertha—mad, promiscuous, and savage, for subjects and places whose differences could be examples in her attempts to renovate Britain (David 97). Susan L. Meyer identifies Bertha's ambiguous racial identity as the "central locus of Brontë's anxieties about oppression." Nowhere is this more apparent than in Brontë's description of Bertha, when she is revealed to Jane as a threat to her imminent marriage. On the eve before the wedding, Jane relates to Rochester a vision she had of Bertha, who entered her room: "It was a discolored face—it was a savage face. I wish I could forget the roll of red eyes and the fearful blackened inflammation of the lineaments! ...the lips were swelled and dark; the brow furrowed; the black eyebrows wildly raised over the blood shot eyes" (281). Meyer explains the logic of Brontë's approach: As Bertha becomes more "visible" over the course of the novel, she "*become[s]* black...a representative of dangers which threaten the world of the novel" (252).[5] The death of Bertha Mason Rochester restores a civilized order to the novel that is white, feminine, and modest; her death authorizes the fulfillment of Jane Eyre's (and *Jane Eyre's*) objectives.

The 2006 Masterpiece Theater version of *Jane Eyre* visualizes the exotic worlds that provide Jane with her colonial imagination, thus locating the film, like the novel, within the geography of British imperialism. In the opening scene, for example, a young Jane (Georgie Henley) stands in the desert wearing an elegant tunic and gauzy hijab, gazing out over a vast landscape of sand dunes. This is the visual manifestation of the daydream Jane has while reading John Reed's adventure book, *Voyages and Travels*. With Jane, we return to the reality of the hidden alcove in the Reed house and flip through more pages of the book to view additional exotic places. This particular framing of the story explicitly represents the foreign as fantastic, not only in the close-ups of the pictures in the travel book that Jane peruses in secret, but in the silk fabric of the dress she wears in the desert. The motif of the "exotic" circulates within the film to link Jane and Bertha, to develop Bertha as a more complex character, and to establish new notions of Britishness (beyond the scope of the novel itself).

At Thornfield, although she has not yet met Rochester (Toby Stephens), Jane (Ruth Wilson) finds his study door open and peruses his collection of mounted butterflies and stuffed birds, emblematic of Rochester's penchant for trapping beautiful and exotic flora and fauna. In the next scene, Jane is seated outside when she notices a red silk scarf flying from a tower window in the closed wing of the house. This sign draws Jane's attention to one similarly confined, a sympathetic sister whose imprisonment suggests the "trap" of patriarchy, ironically repeated in the film by the pinned and preserved butterflies that Rochester studies. The red flag, like the red dress that connects Antoinette to her Caribbean identity in Rhys's *Wide Sargasso Sea*, symbolizes the captured "Other," the flag of the Caribbean native held unwillingly on British soil. The red flag links Bertha to Jane as women who long for physical and sexual freedom. Among the inhabitants of the mansion, it is Jane alone who notices the flag, and after the fire in Rochester's room during which she realizes her attraction to her master, Jane frequently wears a red scarf around her neck, a visible sign of her sexual awakening.

In the film, unlike the novel, Bertha is established as a distinct presence. In a number of point-of-view shots, Bertha observes the developing relationship between Jane and Rochester. As Jane leaves Thornfield for Gateshead by one road to attend to her Aunt Reed, Blanche and Rochester gallop across the fields in the other direction. In this scene, Bertha's gaze spatially bifurcates Jane and Rochester, the gaze of the woman who ultimately separates the "true" lovers; yet, Bertha, like Jane, must also witness the deceptive relationship Rochester fashions with Blanche. In another scene, Bertha observes Rochester, Jane and Adele as they picnic on the lawn. Adele rehearses a Caribbean song for Rochester, who consents to tell her a story of his travels there. He asks Adele and Jane to imagine a social place where respectable people gather and, as Rochester describes the scene, we are transported to this foreign land where the air is fragrant with the perfume of exotic flowers, and the music is tantalizing. As he describes the beautiful women—seductive, mysterious, and dangerous, Bertha (played by Claudia Coulter, a dark-haired and olive-skinned actress of Argentinian descent) enters the frame. She captivates Rochester, and although Adele and Jane remain ignorant of the encounter, Rochester has lost his bearings until Adele's song snaps him back to the reality of the English countryside and his wife locked in

Thornfield. From the tower, Bertha sadly hums Adele's tune as she looks down on this synthetic family. Through the shifting diagesis of this sound bridge, the film thus provides memories of the Caribbean that are, significantly, shared by Bertha and Rochester.

Whatever narrative authority Bertha might have is compromised in the scene in which Rochester admits to the conditions under which he locked up his intemperate wife. As in the novel and in earlier film versions, Bertha's aggressive sexuality is related by Rochester, who tells his wedding-day audience the story of his voyage to Jamaica, his seduction by Bertha and her family, and their return to England. This crucial scene establishes, at least temporarily, Rochester's control of the narrative. Ellis and Kaplan note a similar reassertion of patriarchal dominance in Robert Stevenson's 1944 film in which Orson Welles exaggerated performance, coupled with Joan Fontaine's portrayal of Jane as reticent and cowed, do much to "liquidate Brontë's ambivalence toward patriarchy" (Kaplan 195). As a result, both audiences—the audience returning from the church to meet Rochester's wife still living, and the film audience—are directed to look at Rochester as he relates the "horror" of his wife's promiscuity. Yet Sandra M. Gilbert notes that it is from Bertha's point-of-view that we watch Welles's *perform* the tragic hero, wild-eyed and cloaked in shadows as he stands at the doorway to Bertha's chamber: "We see the lovers as *she*—raging with pain and desire—sees *them* ("Furious" 370). Another subversive moment occurs in Stevenson's version of this scene: the "voyeuristic fixity of Jane's *gaze* at Rochester, a gaze that…gave Joan Fontaine's otherwise incorrectly timid Jane a compelling epistemological authority" ("Furious" 369–370).

In White's version, the "fiction" of Bertha's sexual excess is validated by a flashback that reveals, quite literally, her ungovernable lust. However, Bertha's point-of-view shots throughout the film have interrupted Rochester's ability to fully characterize her as insane; instead, she has secured the viewer's compassion. Bertha's promiscuity, related as it is by the very person who has a vested interest in her insanity, is contested and perhaps irrelevant since the film simultaneously negotiates the ways in which Jane may express her own sexuality. Rochester and Jane manage to forge a fully clothed yet physical and passionate connection, one that does not go unnoticed by Bertha, who calls Jane a "whore" ("puta") when Jane enters Bertha's chamber in her wedding dress. Rather than Stevenson's shadowy gothic monster, White restores Bertha as a woman who challenges such a hypocritical condemnation of female sexual behavior. As a result, Rochester's final injuries seem a just punishment for wrongs done to the women who are the focus of the film. My question then is how does this twenty-first-century film, one that has recuperated female sexual expression as a sign of independence and refused a representation of Bertha as solely monstrous, eradicate her threat to empire?

In the conclusion of the film, Jane gathers her family to sit for a painting. As everyone takes their places on the lawn in front of a new Rochester family mansion, the revelations of the novel's final chapter are made manifest: Jane and Rochester are happily married, Rochester's recovery is slow but he delights in their children, Adele returns to the family fold, and Diana and Mary are well married. Bertha is, of course, absent; but she is recalled to us by Jane's conscientious inclusion in the portrait of Grace Poole, the lower-class woman who is mistaken for Bertha throughout the film. Bertha's physical exclusion allows the shot to achieve the racial and national homogeneity true to the novel. I might add that there is no obvious reason that the portrait could not include Bertha, for St. John Rivers, although not present either, is "painted into" the picture in a cameo in the frame's upper-left corner. Nor must we rely on notions of fidelity to the novel to explain the ways that White's version strives to manage Britain's imperial legacy and post-imperial imaginary. In Brontë's novel, St. John and Jane learn "Hindostanee" (338) in order to do missionary work in India. White's adaptation, on the other hand, recognizes that Britain's powerful former colony might be a potential audience for the film, and so St. John and Jane learn Xhosa, an African language, in order to do missionary work on "the Cape." As we have demonstrated in earlier chapters, Africa still serves as the "dark continent," a place in the viewer's imagination that might legitimately require aid and intervention.

Bertha is ultimately erased from the film and its production in subtler ways that are important to delineate, especially as they reveal the role that Masterpiece Theater has in articulating the parameters of British imperialism and exporting this image to American audiences.[6] Masterpiece Theater, as many educators realize, is the benchmark for literary adaptations, and the website that promotes the film provides ample teaching tools, including a course syllabus and bibliography. Despite the film's obvious engagement with issues of British imperialism, the history of the "Victorian Governess" is the key theme of the site. Bertha is not included in the website's "Who's Who" section, a genealogy of the major players. Claudia Coulter is not acknowledged in producer Diederick Santer's "Production Notes," which good-naturedly seem to mention every member of the cast and crew. Bertha's ultimate removal from the field of fiction, from the film, and from virtual space speaks to the immobility of the racialized Other, and her exclusion from the historically shifting field of the imperial imagination.

Wide Sargasso Sea

Thus far, I have attempted to read the most recent film version of *Jane Eyre* in such a way that Gayatri Spivak might approve, by "remembering that imperialism, understood as England's social mission, was a crucial part of the cultural representation of England to the English" ("Three Women's" 243). The production of knowledge about the South is central to both *Jane Eyre* and *Wide Sargasso Sea*, *Jane Eyre*'s "reinscription," as Spivak rather disparagingly brands Rhys's accomplishment (244). Rhys, writing within the European narrative tradition, recuperates the "white Creole rather than the native," Spivak argues, and marginalizes, again (and still), the black colonized woman, Christophine (253).

Many critics have responded to Spivak's analysis, most notably Benita Parry, who counters that Christophine does not represent the "limits of the text's discourse," as Spivak characterizes her role in the novel, but instead she is a disruptive voice: "as Obeah woman, Christophine is mistress of another knowledge dangerous to imperialism's official epistemology and the means of native cultural disobedience" (248–249). Laura E. Ciolkowski concurs: *Wide Sargasso Sea* "succeeds in more than simply inserting itself into the literary and cultural frameworks of *Jane Eyre*..."; through its complex narrative strategies and extra-textual narrations, it "inquires into the production of knowledge about Englishness and, in the process, puts Englishness itself into crisis" (339). I pursue my analysis of the film versions of *Wide Sargasso Sea* by delineating the films' recourse to the exotic—the film conventions of drumming, dancing, and display that supplant the social relations drawn forth in the novel by Christophine to emphasize the romance between Rochester and Antoinette. Both adaptations create a liminal space between Rochester's white, British, and normative gaze and the black, West Indian, erotic, and inappropriate bodies that he witnesses, a space that Antoinette—racialized and eroticized—circulates within.

The film adaptations of *Wide Sargasso Sea* maintain the general thematic contours and the main characters of Rhys's novel. Antoinette narrates the opening scenes of Duigan's film, providing details of her childhood on Coulibri, her family's estate that has fallen into disrepair. Her mother's expedient second marriage to James Mason is unsuccessful: a naïve and arrogant Englishman, Mason threatens the remaining servants with economic dislocation, and in revolt, they burn down the estate. As a result, Antoinette's brother dies in the fire, and her mother goes mad. Antoinette's voice-over ends once the film transitions to her life as a young woman, who learns of her stepfather's death and the conditions that Mr. Mason imposed on her inheritance—she must marry someone who can manage her fortune. That someone is Edward Rochester, unnamed in the novel but identified in both films to recognize *Jane Eyre* as the literary antecedent, and ironically, in order to more fully realize the narrative conventions of filmmaking in which the name of the hero is a necessity.

Brendan Maher's recent production of *Wide Sargasso Sea* makes explicit its dependence on *Jane Eyre*. By bifurcating Rhys's concluding chapter that details Antoinette's imprisonment at Thornfield to serve as bookends, Rochester's trip to Jamaica is framed between Antoinette's escape from her jailer and her final act of arson. Maher's adaptation opens with Antoinette in the attic room of the great house. As Grace Poole closes the curtains, she reminds Antoinette, in a snippet of conversation lifted from Rhys's novel, that the outside world is hard for women. Once Grace falls asleep, Antoinette takes her ring of keys, lets herself out of her prison, and proceeds to set the fire that will prove her demise. As she makes her way through the rooms, Antoinette comes across Rochester asleep in a chair and caresses his face. In a brief flashback, she remembers the fervent lovemaking that defined their early relationship. As the fire rages throughout the mansion, she notices a painting on the wall behind her of the Port-au-Prince waterfront done in a "primitive" style. As she gazes at the familiar landscape, the painting of Jamaica and its display in the seat of British Empire dissolves to the dock where Rochester has just "entered the picture." The scene deftly transitions from Antoinette's loving regard of her sleeping captor and her memory of their passionate relationship to Rochester's arrival in Jamaica and the reframing of the film to relate his experience of this foreign land.

Similarly, in the opening title shots of Duigan's earlier film, a motif of colonial entanglements is established: the sargassum, the weedy plants that give the Sargasso Sea its name, form a swirling kaleidoscopic background to the film's credit sequence. The Sargasso Sea, "discovered" by Christopher Columbus, symbolically traps Rochester, the latest voyageur, and frames the film as Rochester's narrative. Over the course of the narrative, the visual motif of floating sargassum recurs to mark Rochester's time on the island and as nightmare visions of his entangling marriage. Maher's version is also quick to document Rochester's discomfort with the climate, the people and his mission, through one highly suggestive metaphor: as Rochester and Mason discuss his upcoming introduction to Antoinette, Rochester picks up a seemingly perfect piece of exotic fruit only to find that it is rotten. He drops it on the floor where it splits open to reveal that there are worms within it. This analogy of the exotic and beautiful native delicacy that hides rot and decay exemplifies Rochester's perceptions of Jamaica and his Creole wife. Everywhere that he sees beauty, it falls away to reveal disarray, decline, and madness. Both films trace Rochester's unsuccessful attempts to integrate Jamaican culture and his alien wife into his usual modes of behavior, a British model to which he demonstrates an increasingly inflexible allegiance.

Rochester's fever upon arrival in Jamaica is the earliest sign that the "overheated" and too-ripe land will produce negative effects; he is plagued for the duration of the narrative by feelings of physical and psychological distress and unease. As the films progress, he is dismayed by Antoinette's revelations about her mother's madness; he is shocked that Daniel, Antoinette's mixed-race half-brother, claims intimate knowledge of the family; he dislikes their summer home and the haughtiness of the servants; and he fears Christophine and her powers. As Rochester's Western presumptions come under attack from these forces, the soundtracks of both films create an aurally "authentic" and exotic spectacle that seeks to reveal or disguise these warring discourses. In two important scenes in Duigan's film, West Indian drumming and dancing mediates the relationships between Rochester, Antoinette, and the exotic forces of the island. During the first love scene between Rochester and Antoinette, Amelie and Hilda are dancing in the yard to the pounding rhythm of drums. Parallel editing establishes the unequal boundary between the yard where the servants spend their time and the house with its luxuries. Shots focus first on the naked torso of one of the drummers and Amelie's perspiring chest, and then shift to Rochester and Antoinette making love inside the house. The crescendo of drumbeats signals both the climax of the dance and the sexual climax of the newly formed couple. In a later scene, Antoinette joins in the servants' dance; like gaming birds, Antoinette and Amelie circle each other, strutting and displaying in a dance of sexual dominance.

This dance constructs an artificial rivalry between Antoinette and Amelie and foreshadows Amelie's eventual seduction by and of Rochester. Rochester, as he rides up to the house from an afternoon at the river, is visibly taken aback by Antoinette, who by dancing in the yard in so uninhibited a manner further compromises his perception of her as a suitable (read white) wife.

These scenes evoke the familiar cinematic tradition of jungle melodramas and exploitative travelogue films in which traditional practices are witnessed, judged, and thereby disciplined. As Clara Henderson reminds us, the beating of drums and the dancing that frequently accompanies it are film conventions that serve to construct the non-European characters as racially inferior and sexually uninhibited, and these norms date from at least the early sound era of filmmaking (10). Maher's version is particularly problematic in this regard.

A soundtrack of beating drums and whispering, disembodied voices frequently accompany unmotivated, sometimes canted shots of the Jamaican landscape, so that the place and people remain strange to the viewer as well. Stewart Copeland, the drummer in the influential pop-rock band, The Police, created the pounding percussive soundtrack for Duigan's film. Copeland's style is influenced by Afro-Cuban, Caribbean, and other "world beat" trends, and West Indian music brought an alternative, non-traditional three-beat rhythm to his drumming (Micallef 33). Copeland's soundtrack and Duigan's direction propose a more nuanced exploration of this landscape. The Jamaican servants who occupy the yard and remain at the margins of the film frame provide sly commentary to counteract Edward's preening self-absorption: the men at their drums meet his judgmental gaze and shrug it off; Amelie and Hilda make fun of his pretensions to superiority; and, Christophine intimidates him.

Figure 7. Amelie (Rowena King) and Antoinette (Karina Lombard). (New Line Cinema/Photofest)

One other scene of an "improper" dance explicates the shifting racial and class tensions between Edward, Antoinette, and the Jamaican community. Like White's decision to cast Claudia Coulter as Bertha in *Jane Eyre*, Duigan cast Karina Lombard, who is part Lakota Indian, as Antoinette, and so similarly invigorates racial difference as a sign of sexual promiscuity. By including a scene in which Rochester rapes his wife, a scene that does not appear as this form of sexual violence in the novel, he investigates a set of racial and sexual dynamics that alter the politics of the novel. Antoinette's rape is an indication that the excesses of the country and culture have further infected Rochester. Although she forgives him, Rochester's shame drives him to seek out Spanish Town's civilizing influences. At a party, discriminating British emigrés insinuate much about his new wife and her familiarity with Obeah practices. Before he can come to her defense,

Mason, Antoinette's stepbrother, pulls him into the dance to "do his duty" by the wallflowers. A tracking shot identifies the line of women for whom no dance partner has been secured; as the camera reaches the end of the row, it stops on a young woman. Then, the camera tracks the black servants in livery who are lined up against the wall. As the camera reaches the last of these expressionless and motionless men, it seeks out again the seated young woman, a mulatta, who gazes with barely disguised interest at one of the servants. The next shot is of Rochester dancing with Fanny Grey (Naomi Watts), a young British woman who considers England "home," even though she has never lived there. To explain this contradiction, Fanny asserts what should be obvious to Rochester: Jamaica is no fit place for a lady. Rochester, annoyed by her faulty logic, silences Fanny by spinning her around the room at an intemperate pace.

The infatuated wallflower accomplishes by her "passing" the most subversive deflation of British racial superiority. The audience is the only witnesses of her transgression, and it is provided *to us* as a way to locate ideologically, again, the racial inbetweenness that the film circulates as a trope. By permitting Edward to recognize the hypocrisy that buttresses the racial and class hierarchies perpetrated by Spanish Town elites, Duigan encourages us to sympathize with the more liberal husband who returns to the summer home to make amends with his wife. As Edward rides up to the door of the summer house, a shot of Hilda and a young boy waltzing awkwardly on the lawn mimics Edward's dance with the exasperating Fanny Grey. Hilda re-enacts the previous scene's metaphoric intent: she pushes her young partner away and accuses him of behaving improperly. Here, in the space outside of the civilized one dominated by the British, we are encouraged by the repetition of the dance to recognize a "not white/not quite" woman engaged in masquerade. In "Of Mimicry and Man," Bhabha recognizes this type of performance as "ironic compromise" (122). Mimicry offers up both a confirmation of the civilizing mission in Hilda's desire for a proper waltz, countered by the match cut, which reveals both similarity and difference, "the sign of the inappropriate, a difference or recalcitrance which...poses an immanent threat to both 'normalized' knowledges and disciplinary powers" (122–123).

Antoinette is the final "improper" woman who we discover in this scene; drunk, loud, and unladylike when Rochester returns, her rape does not subdue her. The knowledge about dominant culture and its conditions represented by and through Antoinette is somewhat different than that gleaned by Rochester in Spanish Town. Although Antoinette has performed, over the course of the film, a complementary interrogation of the stable racial signifiers on which Rochester's understanding of his marriage depends, Rochester's violent act does not result in her incorporation into normative British behavior. Antoinette's unfeminine excesses are both demonized and contained by recourse to Obeah at the end of the film. Even as Rochester accepts the economic and social relations that construct Antoinette's liminal state, once she turns to voodoo in hopes of eliminating the epistemological differences between them, Antoinette becomes, at least in this version, the irreparable woman-in-love, the "madwoman in the attic" who must remain in Rochester's care.

Antoinette's unrestrained behavior and her rejection by Rochester that is its dialectic are similarly linked to notions of colonial control in Maher's 2006 version. After they consummate their marriage, Antoinette tells Edward that *now* she is his wife. Edward declares that he is Christopher Columbus, and Antoinette is his "undiscovered continent." This undiscovered continent, however, has an unnatural landscape and unruly locals: the over-scented air, the buzzing sounds of insects and the clicking of the cicadas, and Christophine's affiliation with Obeah, are all foreign to him, like his increasing sexual desire for Antoinette. In this version, however, whiteness is privileged: Antoinette is played by Rebecca Hall, the daughter of the highly regarded British theater director Peter Hall, and her pale skin is complemented by virginal white dresses that give way to colored silks once she becomes Edward's wife. By eliminating racial difference as it is written on the skin, this version conforms more closely to the novel and Rhys's understanding of Creole culture. However, the despair with which Antoinette wrestles with her social and economic identity as "white nigger" in the novel is nowhere in Maher's film. Maher signifies class difference solely through Antoinette's inappropriate sexual desire, thus reducing social relations to feminine excess and limiting his investigation of the liminal spaces—of Voodoo and the dance—suggested by Duigan.

Duigan's casting of Karina Lombard and the NC-17 rating earned by the film for its sexual explicitness invited a critical response that foregrounds the fraught identification of ethnicity and sexual desire. Lombard, notes one reviewer, has the "requisite exotic looks to be the object of Rochester's obsessive, paranoid desire" (Pawelczak). Margo Hammond identifies the stereotypes invigorated by the juxtaposition of the exotic and the familiar: Lombard plays "the stereotype of the dusky jungle woman, who by her very darkness taps into white fears of wild sensuality," a stereotype, Hammond laments, that "is sadly still with us" (Hammond). Vincent Canby's review of *Wide Sargasso Sea* in the *New York Times* is generally positive but he collapses the racial complexities of both the novel and film: "Miss Lombard, a new actress who is half Lakota Indian, is dark-complexioned and voluptuous in a way that adds an effective if unstated racial dimension to the love story, something not in the Rhys novel. In the film, race is not only a fundamental concern of Jamaican society, but also a metaphor for the power struggle between Antoinette and Edward" (Canby 6). Canby is mistaken: the racial dimension is in the novel, but its use in British culture at this time is to distinguish the class status of the Other as white but "other than" aristocratic and British. We can discover a similar pattern of (mis)identification if we trace Lombard's career. Ella Shohat notes that mainstream films frequently blend or collapse specific ethnic differences and diversity, "obscuring the boundaries among the 'others,' while manifesting a distinguished difference of white ethnicity" (228–229). In a role that reduced ethnicity to generic, predatory sexuality, Lombard was cast as an unnamed Carribean woman who seduces Tom Cruise on a Cayman Island beach in *The Firm* (Pollack 1993). She also played Brad Pitt's wife, a Native American woman, in Edward Zwick's *Legends of the Fall* (1993). Lombard's identity as a "person of color" was central to *Wide Sargasso Sea*'s reception; in 1993, Lombard received an award for her role as Antoinette from First Americans in the Arts, a group that recognizes Native American contributions in the entertainment industry. Ethnic distinction on screen is still so marginal that ethnic presence in and for itself is commended: "After Ellen," a blog that tracks gay representations in the media, applauds Lombard's casting as Marina (a woman of Italian heritage) on the Showtime series "The L Word" because she brought ethnic diversity to the series (Warn).

In both film versions, as in the novel, Antoinette fears Rochester's abandonment and so uses Christophine's potion to secure his love, and, as in the novel, after this event occurs, the point of view is Rochester's, who seems so close to reconciliation with Antoinette but who is poisoned nevertheless. In the 2006 adaptation, Rochester wakes up, sick and naked, and notices the evidence of the previous night's debauchery: Antoinette has bruises on her back. He discovers the poison in the bottom of his wine glass, and writes "poison" with it on Antoinette's dressing table mirror. While Rochester is at the swimming hole desperately trying to wash off the residue of the night before, he has a flashback to their sexual encounter. As he tries to rid himself of this memory, naked on the banks of the river, thrashing at his leg in desperation, the drums on the soundtrack beat furiously. While no Jamaican character is present, the soundtrack reminds us of their "presence," and particularly of the power of Voodoo as Antoinette dispenses it for erotic ends.

Maher's adaptation—and Duigan's, to a lesser extent—elevates Rochester's story to a position of prominence. Rochester's obsession with his position as the second son relocates the film as an investigation of the evils of primogeniture, and his arrogance that manifests as controlling Antoinette is a reaction to his weakness in accepting an arrangement to fulfill his father's ambitions, rather than his own. Antoinette's symbolic role as a zombie is quite diminished in the films, but we can recuperate its possibilities. Sandra Drake reminds us that the zombie symbolizes an alienation both social and individual, and is particularly useful as a way of understanding the "realities of colonialism," the realities of slaves laboring in the plantation system (202). Antoinette is a reminder of the limited social space allowed the Jamaican Creole, and while she sets the torch to Thornfield, the films diminish the socially transformative function that her zombification signified: the power to channel the repressed legacy of slavery to overthrow colonial and patriarchal power. Instead, the films propose that zombie is the final manifestation, or punishment, of an unfeminine excess of desire. Margarite Fernández Olmos and Lizabeth Paravisini-Gebert in "Religious Syncretism and Caribbean Culture," the introduction to their compilation *Sacred Possessions: Vodou, Santería, Obeah, and the Caribbean*, argue that such an hysterical reaction to it "owes much to the role played by Obeah, Vodou, and other African-based religions in inspiring revolts against European colonial powers" (7).

I want to suggest, then, that *Wide Sargasso Sea* reminds us that issues of sexual dominance are worked out in such liminal spaces and that the characters of Rochester and Antoinette draw our attention to these uncomfortable sites of colonial manipulation. In *Wide Sargasso Sea*, we are reminded by Rochester's illness that the Middle Passage takes a physical and mental toll; in *I Walked with a Zombie* and *Heading South* we are presented with other figures who have traversed this geography and who articulate the legacy of slavery. In *I Walked with a Zombie*, and in *Heading South*, voodoo is invoked to better offer a counter-discourse, stories that foreground the violence attendant on Northern economic, social and sexual exploitation of the South.

In his analysis of *I Walked with a Zombie*, J. P. Telotte notes that many scholars have commented on the "mosaic-like structure" of narratives produced by Val Lewton's RKO horror unit. These "vignettes," Telotte says, tell seemingly incomplete stories by tracing only the stories' "borders and possibilities" (18). *I Walked with a Zombie* ostensibly privileges Betsy's voiceover narration, the singular "I" that, like Jane in *Jane Eyre*, authoritatively relates her burgeoning love affair with a much older, already married man, Paul Holland, a plantation owner on the fictional island of San Sebastian. Like Telotte, I recognize that the black descendants of slaves on the plantation also have a voice in the film, one that subsumes and contradicts Betsy's straightforward narration. I want to take the notion of "borders" more literally, however, by recognizing that the natives' alternative discourse polices both the ideological and the physical boundaries of the island. While the Holland family attempts to control native culture and secure it for their own ends, Betsy transgresses the boundaries between the plantation and the voodoo temple to reveal alternative narratives.

Like Rochester in *Wide Sargasso Sea*, Paul Holland is wary of the tropic's exuberant beauty. In the opening scenes of *I Walked with a Zombie*, Betsy and Paul meet on the boat from Antigua to Saint Sebastian; on deck, black men sing at their work, creating a soulful counterpoint to the sounds of the sea. Betsy thinks the water and the night are beautiful. Paul explains that everything is not what it seems, the phosphorescence, for example, is dying plant life: "No beauty," he says, "only death and decay." The film cannily juxtaposes Betsy's empirical observation, Paul's claims to knowledge, and black voices, however muted, to delineate epistemological boundaries. Once they arrive on San Sebastian, Betsy is driven to the Holland Plantation. On the trip, Betsy learns from her driver that the Hollands were responsible for importing the slaves to the island, and that "Ti-Misery," a wooden black man pierced through with arrows propped in the courtyard of the Holland home, is a figurehead from one of the slave boats. Betsy, whose naïveté is provocative, reassures the driver that, "They brought you to a beautiful place." The driver replies, "If you say Miss, if you say." When Betsy re-identifies the masthead as Saint Sebastian, the driver has the same response ("If you say Miss, if you say"). Olmos and Paravisini-Gebert provide a basis for understanding Ti-Misery's dual nature, as representing the intermixing of Western and African-based religions to form the syncretic and original belief systems of the Caribbean—Vodou and Obeah among them (2).For cultures disfigured by European plantation violence, these practices provided "repositories of inner strength and cultural affirmation" (2). Rather than reading the driver's acquiescence to Betsy as submissive, Olmos and Parvisini-Gebert remind us that the "slaves' very survival depended on their ability to manipulate and resist their complete absorption into the core values of the plantation master," perhaps by "mimicking and mocking an oppressive code" (2).Thus, the interplay between the driver and Betsy points to the improbability of Betsy's knowledge and, as Bhabha might suggest, disrupts Betsy's authoritative "knowingness."

Betsy first meets her patient, Jessica Holland (Christine Gordon), when she follows the sound of someone crying into the tower room and discovers her zombified patient, who seems to pursue her. The butler, Clement, assures her it was Alma (Teresa Harris), Mrs. Holland's maid, who was crying at the birth of her sister's child—a tradition, Paul explains, that acknowledges that children born on the island suffer from the memory of slavery. As in *Jane Eyre*, Betsy is misled about the first wife, and she must learn of the cause of Jessica Holland's illness from another source. As Betsy and Wesley Rand, Paul Holland's stepbrother, sit at a sidewalk café in town, Sir Lancelot, a West Indian calypso singer, entertains his audience of locals with the story of the Holland-Rand family. Lancelot's song details the scandal: Wesley and Jessica were having an affair but Paul Holland refused to divorce his wife. When Wesley overhears the song and reacts angrily, Sir Lancelot tells his audience that he'll just slip into the café like a sly fox and make it up to him.[7] Once Wesley passes out, Sir Lancelot takes the opportunity to narrate Betsy's possible assumption of Jessica's position in the family: the nurse is young, he sings, and the brothers are lonely. Sir Lancelot intimidates Betsy in a shot similar in composition to the one in which Jessica intimidated Betsy, creating a visual association that links Jessica to the heritage of slavery when she is mistaken for Alma, and to Sir Lancelot, the narrator of her transgression. Mrs. Rand, Paul and Wesley's mother, intervenes and prevents Betsy from acquiring a more comprehensive knowledge of the island's sexual and social history.

The conflict between Wesley Rand and Paul Holland denotes the conflict between religion and capitalism, the twin forces of European colonial exploitation. Holland is the son of the sugar mill owner and the heir to the plantation; Wesley is Holland's half-brother, the son of Dr. Rand, a missionary. Mrs. Rand amplifies this division: she works in the village pharmacy providing Western medicine to the island people, yet she believes the people too "primitive" to take advantage of it. Unable to control them, she infiltrates the Hounfort, the temple of voodoo beliefs, and participates in voodoo rituals; unable to prevent Jessica from dividing her family, she asks the Hounfort's religious leaders to turn her into a zombie. Like Mrs. Rand and Jessica, Betsy tries to navigate the border between the Hounfort and Fort Hudson. Once Betsy learns that the houngan, the "better doctor" that Alma recommends, can cure mindlessness by speaking with the gods, Betsy is convinced that she must take Jessica to him. Guided by a map drawn in sugar by Alma, and protected by patches Alma affixes to Betsy and Jessica's clothing, they make her way through the cane. The extended tracking shot that documents Betsy and Jessica journey from the Fort to the Hounfort is justly famous. Its main theme, as Chris Fujiwara confirms, is the "crossing of boundaries...marked by a sign," the most important sign is the conch, the only aural marker and one that is used in the Voodoo ceremony (95). Here, Betsy loses her patch, yet Carrefour, the guardian of the crossroads, allows her to pass, perhaps because her search for a cure leads her beyond the borders of traditional medicine. At the Hounfort, women dance in possessed abandon accompanied by the furious pounding of drums, as the Islanders approach the priest to seek guidance from the gods. Once Betsy discovers that Mrs. Rand is the Hounfort's religious force, their journey becomes irrelevant. Yet, the Voodoo practitioners continue to pursue Jessica who is necessary to their rituals.

Jessica's trip to the Hounfort and her subsequent return "home" to Fort Holland changes the dynamic between the two locations, as their imperfect anagram suggests. Her return re-arranges the once-stable relationship between the white landowners, now barricaded on their plantation, and the black natives, brought to the island in slavery but plotting their revenge just outside the Fort's gates. Marcia England identifies the source of horror in *I Walked with a Zombie*: the "invading force...is Voodoo. The plantation home is continually infiltrated with sounds [and] becomes a site of transgression, where religion and science clash and religion wins, where the West and the non-West meet and the non-West dominates" (360). As I have noted in the films discussed in this chapter, and England confirms, it is the ritual drums that signal the infiltration of Voodoo: "Whenever drums are heard within the [Holland] house, the viewer is supposed to be filled with apprehension. The sounds of the Other are invading the home of the self" (360). In the film, in striking imagery, the "Other" physically invades the home. Carrefour comes for Jessica, his shadow against the wall effacing Betsy, who is sleeping in Jessica's room. As Carrefour turns on Paul, Mrs. Rand turns him away and his mission is unsuccessful. Back at the Hounfort, the houngan tries again to lure Jessica to him, and, as she leaves the compound, Wesley opens the gate for her, takes an arrow from San Sebastian and follows her, as if in a trance. The houngan stabs the Voodoo doll representing Jessica with an arrow; Wes, in turn, stabs his zombie lover. To keep Carrefour from her, he carries her into the ocean and they both drown. While Marcia England claims that order is restored at Fort Holland once this conclusion has been reached, two breaks in the logical structure of the film argue against such a precise resolution. First, a hymn-like song accompanies the bodies of Jessica and Paul as fishermen carry them back to the plantation. The song chastises Jessica for her selfishness but asks forgiveness for those already dead and peace and happiness for the living. And, while Carrefour had pursued the adulterers out to sea, the film opens with Betsy and Carrefour walking by the ocean as Betsy says: "I walked with a zombie." She laughs, and reminds herself and us that this seems fantastic. However, this shot seemingly occurs after the action of the film and it frames the rest of the film as a flashback.

I Walked with a Zombie was produced during a rare moment of positive American and Caribbean relations. As Michael Dash has documented in his analysis of imaginative literature and its representation of Haiti, by the 1940s, the "Good Neighbor" policies of Franklin Roosevelt had replaced U.S. military dominance in the region and cultural exchange was more favorable (74). As evidence that Haiti was "no longer hostile and bizarre," but "vital and creative" (76), Haitian art, music, and ceremonial dance was exported to the United States, travel literature promoted the area (77), and Voodoo was "either studied as just another religion or treated as just another factor in Haitian society" (Dash 83). Anti-American sentiment, though, permeated Haitian politics and society, in part because President Lescott's pro-American, anti-peasant policies supported the Catholic Church's anti-Voodoo campaign in the early 1940s (87); and approved a joint venture with a rubber company that would help the American war effort against Japan while ruining peasant crops (91).

While North and South collide in *I Walked with a Zombie*, Betsy's Canadian "neutrality" allows for a more sincere exploration of cultural differences, an interrogation of the binary of "self and other" that zombie films propose, and usually resolve in favor of the industrialized, developed, and dominant nations of the North. In its production as well, *I Walked with a Zombie* subverted the racial prejudices of Hollywood. Robin Wood surmises that Sir Lancelot's intimidation "with the film's at least partial endorsement" of white characters neither "comic nor villainous" was not only rare for the era but preferable to later, more explicitly inclusive films that were "insidiously condescending" (qtd in Fujiwara 92). Tourneur confirmed in an interview that he "refused to caricature blacks" and "always tried to give them a profession, to have them speak normally without drawing any comic effect," a practice that transgressed Hollywood social codes and landed him, as he claimed, on a "sort of gray list" (qtd in Fujiwara 92).

Heading South, because of the complex functions that Voodoo and zombie serve in the film, is part of a visual history that includes *I Walked with a Zombie* but is, in important ways, divorced from it.[8] In *Heading South*, three women— Brenda (Karen Young) a schoolteacher from Savannah, Georgia; Ellen (Charlotte Rampling), a British professor who teaches French at Wellesley; and Sue (Louise Portal), a factory worker from Canada, meet while on vacation at a beach resort in Haiti in the 1970s. These women "of a certain age" are sexual tourists, unable to find appropriate partners at home and willing to exchange gifts and money for a physical and emotional connection with local Haitian men. Legba, a good looking young man, is Ellen and Brenda's object of desire, but it is an objectification that the film does not indulge. Rather, Legba navigates the fraught space between the beach resort and the larger political and social world of Port-au-Prince. As Françoise Lionnet observes in one of the few sustained critiques of the film, *Heading South*, with its complex interrogation of an exploitative tourist economy, would hardly seem to contribute to the now-global array of images that represent Haiti as a place of misery, abject poverty, and rampant crime, fortified by popular culture's "long-standing clichés and distortions" that include the spectacle of zombie (232). Rather, *Heading South* interrogates the "paradoxical object" that is Haiti: both "a commodity with no real value, clad in ridicule or made abject" and "a highly coveted exotic colonial space with magical practices that have inspired artists, writers, and filmmakers…" (232). Lionnet's excellent analysis of the role of Voodoo in *Heading South* is key to understanding the beginning of the film.

The opening sequence of *Heading South* establishes the Voodoo motif to call attention to the political and social contradictions that guide the narrative of the film. Albert (Amboise Lys), the manager of Petite Anse resort, waits at the Port-au-Prince airport for Brenda to arrive. A woman approaches him and asks him to take her daughter. In Haiti, the mother says, such a poor and beautiful girl "doesn't stand a chance," indicating her child standing a little distance away, framed by a door but slightly out of focus. Before the current political upheaval, she explains, her family was secure, but then her husband, a man with a government job, was kidnapped and she never saw him again. Albert naturally refuses. The woman abruptly shifts registers, and warns Albert that it is hard to tell the good masks from the bad, but that everyone wears one. Lionnet notes that the woman serves the function of a Greek chorus, and certainly her abrupt shift to the prophetic draws our attention to the metaphor of identity—good masks, bad masks—as a defining figure for the film (236). Lionnet encourages us to make a number of connections at this juncture of the film: "the mother's expository remarks serve as a warning to the spectators and her allusion to the masks calls attention to several dualities: Western and Haitian, cultural and historical, theatrical and political, while foregrounding questions of appearance and reality, illusion and verisimilitude" (236). Albert gazes after her intensely as she leaves him, one eyebrow raised in bewilderment, but then turns to his task of writing Brenda's name on a blackboard. Dany Laferrière, the Haitian-Canadian writer whose stories the film adapts, confirms in an interview that the film's opening scene references Haitian mythology: to remove your mask is to reveal your "real face…the one who knows it will be able to turn you into his slave" (qtd in Lionnet 237). Lionnet makes explicit the significance of the interaction that has taken place: the "…iconic but nameless, silent, Haitian girl materializes the opposition between word and image, speaking and being, tourists and locals" (237). She provides a heuristic for understanding Legba, "an intermediary between two worlds, as master of the crossroads, as messenger, interpreter, and male double of the girl in the doorway" (237).

Brenda arrives at the airport, and seeing her name, acknowledges Albert. Her appearance at this fraught moment indicates that she is implicated as well in the mother's warning. Like the Haitian girl, she is framed by the doorway and separated from Albert by the waiting room glass, yet the easily erased, and unstable, sign of her name readily identifies her. The totality of the schema of recognition performed in these first moments is rendered ambiguous by the metaphor of good/bad masks. Ironically, while the young local girl has youth and beauty, worthless to her as invitations to violence, Brenda has come to Haiti to recover precisely these intangible attributes that translate into cultural capital in the United States. The film's politics are complicated by its 1970s time frame: Brenda and the women are liberated enough to critique the social conditions that have marginalized them at home. As reviewers have noted, however, Cantet walks a fine line between provocatively juxtaposing two minority groups and compromising the women's feminism. The film explores most revealingly the competition between Ellen and Brenda for the affections of Legba, a young black man whose perambulations around Port-au-Prince serve to expand the scope of the narrative beyond the resort and its petty jealousies. Legba's dependence on and resistance to Brenda allows Cantet to allude to the specter of American imperialism: set in the late-1970s, the film calls to mind the Vietnam War; released in 2006, it also clearly alludes to the war in Iraq. While the women remain mostly shielded from the abject poverty, social disintegration, and political violence unleashed by the regime of Baby Doc Duvalier and his security force, the vicious Tonton Macoute, they are implicated in the politics of the nation when Legba is murdered and their fantasy of liberal and liberating sexuality is shattered.

The film undermines its status as fiction by including documentary-style interviews with the three women, who describe the social and sexual circumstances that have brought them to the island. Brenda, who visited Haiti three years earlier with her ex-husband, remembers their relationship with Legba, then a 15-year-old adolescent, whom they fed and indulged. As she tells the camera with remarkable candor and egotism, Brenda raped Legba during her previous visit when they were alone together after a swim. With Legba, Brenda achieves her first orgasm, and she has returned to the island to reclaim that passionate connection. Ellen, on the other hand, has forged a relationship with Legba over many years. The grande dame of the resort, Ellen is a sharp critic of the preoccupations with love and marriage that she observes among her wealthy but vapid female students at Wellesley. Although she is most capable of articulating the limited relationship options for an educated older woman in America, she can make no common cause with either Brenda or Sue, whom she cattily calls "big-boned." Sue, unaffected and sincere, is the most accommodating of the characters: sanguine about her limited choices in Canada, she is deeply attached to her consort, Neptune. Sue is a detached observer, perhaps not surprising given the geopolitics of Laferrière's work, but in the visual politics of the film, her ultimate inconsequence is signaled by the camera that marginalizes her by choosing to focus on shapelier bodies.

Albert's interview is delivered at a particularly dramatic moment in the story: Brenda, distraught after a date with Legba ends in violence, has demanded that Legba, just returned from his run-in with Tonton Macoute ruffians, be served dinner in the dining room. Unlike the interviews with the women, Albert's monologue is rendered as voice-over, delivered as he prepares food for Brenda. Albert tells the audience that his family fought the Americans during the 1915 occupation, and his father and grandfather both viewed whites—specifically Americans—as vile animals and manifestations of the devil. Albert is faced with a current conjuncture as invasive as an occupation and just as humiliating; he is forced to serve Americans because he needs the American dollars that have so corrupted his country. Albert, too, wears a mask that hides his true identity: the unruffled demeanor that Albert presents to his guests is startlingly contradicted by his hatred for the conditions that have brought them to the resort. Albert's monologue makes us even more aware of Brenda's transgressions: she has upset the race and class dynamics between Albert, his staff and guests, and between the resort and the broader social and political space of Haiti. She has appeared at a public market in Port-au-Prince with Legba; and in her tourist's fascination with the "locals," serves as a reminder that the violent Duvalier regime is backed by American money. Ironically, Brenda, who is from the American South, revokes the separate status enforced by Albert on Legba and the other sex workers. Albert will serve Legba on the beach but not in the dining room, and Brenda is quick to judge Albert's racism and enforce the "lunch counter" equality of the Civil Rights era. While Brenda and Helen's relationship with Legba overturns that most potent of racial taboos—miscegenation—the interview with Albert cuts immediately to a confrontation between Brenda and Ellen, in which Ellen accuses Brenda of upsetting her long-standing relationship with Legba, one that respects the system of established economic and sexual exchange and represses reckless sexual desire and voyeurism.

All of the main characters, except Legba, address the camera in a self-revealing monologue. Critics have addressed the politics of excluding Legba from this engagement with the viewer.[9] Yet while Cantet focuses mainly on the personal lives of the women and the problematic exchange system they have entered into, he frequently leaves them behind to follow Legba in his daily life. In Haitian Voodoo, Legba is invoked at the beginning of every ceremony. He is an emissary between the living and the spirit world, "the guardian of the roads, of all paths or openings" (Dayan 25). In some traditions he is represented as a younger man, and his sign, appropriately, is a carved phallus, but he is also "Papa Legba of the Old Bones," a deity who "lives out the loss suffered by his people....To invoke Legba is to bear the weight of his legacy" (25). In the film, Legba stands sentinel between the resort world and the real world of Haiti. He mediates Brenda's excessive behavior, including her unnatural interest in young boys, which is reaffirmed when she dances too intimately with Legba's brother; Legba steps between them, in part to remove his brother from the system of exchange that Brenda's invitation suggests. At a dance on the resort grounds, Brenda becomes intoxicated by the drums and abandons herself to the pulsing rhythms. Cantet both gestures towards and refuses to exploit the stereotypes of sexual promiscuity that the island drums normally evoke in films in which they signal the exotic. Rather, Legba intervenes and asks the musicians to play something more restrained. Later in the film, Brenda pursues Legba beyond the confines of the resort and ends up at an island club, where she gazes hungrily on a group of men, one of whom asks her to dance. While Cantet recognizes the feminist politics of sexual desire and the necessity of equitable fulfillment, he locates this particular manifestation as part of a global economy of sexual tourism in order to delineate its consequences.

Legba is murdered at the conclusion of *Heading South*. His body washes up on the resort's beach, a testament to the impossibility of separating rich and white from poor and black, Northern privilege from Southern economies based in exploitation and violence. The last shot of the film is particularly telling: rather than return to Georgia, Brenda is standing on the prow of a boat, looking forward to adventures on another island. Like the men in *Jane Eyre* and *Wide Sargasso Sea*, women, too, can be the voy(age)eurs in search of new lands to conquer.

In *Heading South*, Brenda (Karen Young) rediscovers her young lover, Legba (Ménothy Cesar). Legba's prone vulnerability, and Brenda's pursuit of him, compromise any facile appreciation of the resort's landscape. (Shadow Distribution/Photofest)

Notes

1. In *Madwoman in the Attic: The Woman Writer and the Nineteenth-Century Literary Imagination*. Their influential interpretation of *Jane Eyre* establishes the conflict between Jane and Bertha as the novel's central concern.

2. Here I follow Mary Lou Emery's strategy of delineating Rhys's complex renaming of Antoinette to distinguish her multiple identities from Rochester's "renaming" (35).

3. In Laura Mulvey's seminal essay, "Visual Pleasure and Narrative Cinema," she argues that in its perusal of the female body, the camera's gaze is noticeably male. The camera instantiates patriarchy by providing the [male] viewer with the pleasure of looking at the female form, the fetish object of his gaze.

4. In chapter one we discuss representations of Africa across a range of narratives.

5. The scholarly engagement with *Jane Eyre* is extensive. I focus here on those scholars who are in conversation with Gayatri Chakravorty Spivak and her critique of *Jane Eyre* and its "axiomatics of imperialism" (*Critique* 115). See also Jenny Sharpe's chapter on *Jane Eyre* in *Allegories of Empire*.

6. Timothy Brennan in "The Uses of Tradition" makes this point succinctly: "Masterpiece Theater is a cultural colonization in the age of empire—an attempt to fuse together the apparently incompatible national myths of England and the United States, in order to strengthen imperial attitudes in an era of European and North American decline" (103).

7. In African-American folklore, the trickster tale is a story of such doubling.

8. *The Serpent and the Rainbow* (1988) is included in many trajectories of contemporary zombie films, but an engagement with it here is beyond the scope of the project. Wes Craven's adaptation of Wade Davis's "ethnobiology" provides some of the most demeaning images of Haitian culture.

9. See Carina Chocano's movie review of the film in the *Los Angeles Times*. Stephanie Zacharek offers a rationale for Legba's exclusion: Legba is the "true center of the movie: He's a receptacle for hopes and desires that he has no way of fulfilling."

Five

NRI: The Transnational Class and Transnational Class in the Films of Mira Nair

***

It is difficult to reconcile *Amelia*, Mira Nair's pedestrian 2009 biopic of famed aviatrix Amelia Earhart, with her extensive filmography documenting the lives, loves, and losses of the Indian diaspora. A conventional Hollywood production, Amelia harkens back to an American cinematic history at odds with the "accented" or exilic cinema in which Nair usually participates. Yet it is not her only film made in close proximity to mainstream Hollywood. As Jigna Desai notes, *Mississippi Masala*, Nair's 1991 breakout hit, may have been independently financed by "U.S and U.K. sources," but it was distributed by Samuel Goldwyn, a major studio; rising Hollywood star Denzel Washington led the cast, and the film grossed a respectable $7.3 million in the domestic market (74). Nair as well has identified *The Perez Family* (1995) and *Vanity Fair* (2004) as films made in the Hollywood "blockbuster" style (Carnevale). Nair argues that such debates around her mode of production do not account for the complex and diverse ideological functions her films perform for the different audiences she addresses. Interviewed in *Cineaste* on the occasion of *Vanity Fair's* release (2004), Nair claims that her relationship with Hollywood norms and production expectations is oppositional and opportunistic:

> For every sort of Western film I might do, I want to constantly return to putting people who look like us on the screen because there's an enormous validation when you see our stories, our people, our struggles. We all know about how powerful the cultural imperialism of Hollywood is, and how American culture is now commonplace everywhere. It's important to counter it. (qtd. in Badt 15)

Nair, film critics, and cinema scholars have interrogated and defended her participation in, and (re)negotiation of, the social and political space she claims as a filmmaker of the Indian diaspora. Raised in a small town in India, Nair attended

Harvard University, where she studied documentary filmmaking (Badt 10); she divides her time between Kampala, Uganda, and New York City (Badt 11), the home of her production company, Mirabai Films. Alpana Sharma notes in her appreciation of Nair's films that it is her particular investment in Hollywood's global hegemony—a mode of address and a preferred audience that is Western, that has made Nair a "flashpoint" for postcolonial audiences (96). Nair invited criticism for presuming to speak for the subaltern classes that are at the center of her earlier films, many of them documentaries (92). Her first feature film, *Salaam Bombay!* (1988) cast Bombay (now Mumbai) street children as actors in a social drama about the childrens' struggle for emotional and economic security. Her mission to tell stories about marginalized subjects has resulted in complementary and perhaps politically advantageous social projects that Nair readily promotes in interviews. To remedy the appearance of exploiting young children in *Salaam Bombay*, Nair established a trust to assist in their education. In an interview in *Mother Jones*, Nair describes another outreach project, a film school "boot camp" in Uganda that brings together aspiring screenwriters and directors from Africa and South Asia with professional mentors. Her goal, she says, is to "make local cinema. If we don't tell our own stories, no one else will" (qtd. in Rivera). Nair acknowledges that mainstream films have excluded Africans, who remain "nameless and faceless," a problem that her film school is meant to remedy (qtd. in Neill). I want to explore the debates I outline above through three of Nair's films—*Mississippi Masala, Monsoon Wedding* (2001), and *The Namesake* (2006). Together, as a reviewer notes, they make up "a soberly meditative trilogy on the tussle between the noise and music of globalization, and the losses and gains of migration" (Bahri 10). These three films are distinguished by Nair's deliberate ouster of the white racial dominance that has governed Hollywood films, accomplished by foregrounding people of color and pushing whites, quite literally, to the margins of the frame. In these narratives, stories of immigration, home, and belonging are fashioned around diasporic communities in America and abroad. By exploring the multiple discourses that surround the release of these films, accompany their incorporation into film scholarship, and contextualizing their cultural moment of production, I hope to construct a sense of the films' "global imaginary." Particularly, I track the transnational movement of wealth and its attendant status, as it entails a redefinition of class relations across multiple borders. I also account for *Vanity Fair* and *Amelia*, Nair's most distinctively mainstream films. Nair has garnered extensive praise as a "cineaste of uncompromising feminist postcolonial subjectivity in-the-making" (Foster 111).

Yet both *Vanity Fair* and *Amelia* re-inscribe traditional hierarchies of race, class, and gender in the service of constructing a "modern woman." In these films, norms of female sexuality are fluid and shifting yet constrained by the well-worn topos of tradition and modernity. I am particularly interested in the regressive thrust of these two films, and in the critical articulation of Nair's agenda, one that links her identification as a diasporic filmmaker to complex discourses defining feminism in global, universal terms. In a review of *Vanity Fair* in *Rolling Stone*, Peter Travers succinctly states the problem: "The fault here may lie with Indian director Mira Nair (*Monsoon Wedding*), who understandably expands on the novel's India themes but insists on reshaping Becky as a 'modern woman.' The strain shows." Reviewers have also provocatively elided issues of the diaspora: Betsey Sharkey claims that *Amelia* is "exactly the sort of saga Nair loves to tell," noting that "the unconventional woman" is a recurring figure in many Nair films. In this chapter I discuss the films in chronological order: *Mississippi Masala* and *Monsoon Wedding* followed by *Vanity Fair*, *The Namesake* and, finally, *Amelia*. Thus, *Vanity Fair* and *Amelia* are not "addendum" to the films that chronicle the Indian diaspora; rather they bisect Nair's oeuvre, revealing complicated negotiations of minority cultures and feminist fantasies, embedded in the problematics of globalization.

Mississippi Masala: "Passion. Tradition. Mix It Up."

In *Mississippi Masala*, Nair upends standard narratives of immigrant assimilation in America. Played out in the small southern town of Greenwood, Mississippi, the love affair between Mina (Sarita Choudhury), a young Indian woman who has emigrated with her parents, Jay and Kinnu, from Uganda, and Demetrius (Denzel Washington), an African-American man with close ties to family, community, and a business of his own, sparks inter-ethnic tensions. Nair stresses the productivity of the kind of minority contact that she realizes in this film: "I wanted to explore what would happen if a member of one community crossed the border of colour into another…to explore exile, memory, nostalgia, dislocation: this thing we call home" (qtd. in Stuart 212). At the time of its release in 1991, *Mississippi Masala* seemed to offer the possibility of cross-cultural dialogue during a particularly fraught moment in American race relations. Binita Mehta situates the film in the context of the early 1990s, when the Rodney King riots in Los Angeles mobilized multiple identities along race and class lines, and critics and scholars weighed in to speak of multicultural issues (185).

Urmila Seshagiri recognizes *Mississippi Masala* as a defining text that prompted critics and reviewers to portray "the director as an Indian feminist whose films cracked open cultural master-narratives and re-imaged them from previously unconsidered viewpoints" (177). *Mississippi Masala* made Nair "one of the international faces of contemporary cinema, a director whose work describes a new visual language for globalization" (177). *Mississippi Masala* also launched an era of increased visibility for South Asian women filmmakers, who reached larger audiences with films that explore complex racial and cultural relationships across the diaspora—many of them popular with critics and fans for their easier resolutions and exuberant style (178). While the film does not proclaim a utopian global community, it "anticipates the social conditions of the next century," as Andrea Stuart claims in an extended interview with Nair, one that leaves the simple binary of black-white relations behind in order to focus on the complexities of minority relationships (210). With a production cost of $6 million, it was more deliberately mainstream than her successful first feature, *Salaam Bombay!* As Nair acknowledges, *Mississippi Masala* was produced "with a more international audience in mind" (qtd. in Stuart 210). Nair resisted Hollywood pressures to increase the number of whites in the project (211), confessing that she "wanted the white characters to be absent" (qtd. in Stuart 214). Nair reversed the usual Hollywood color palette, and, emulating Spike Lee who revolutionized the photography of black skin, she developed special lighting techniques that lit black skin more appealingly (216).

On the surface, *Mississippi Masala* brings together two seemingly clichéd "American" stories: the immigrant's tale of assimilation and the African-American's tale of discrimination. Yet *Mississippi Masala* maps out multiple, transnational economies of race. Mina Loha and her family are part of the Indian diaspora that emigrated from Uganda to the United States in the 1970s when Idi Amin forced Asians out of the country. In Greenwood, they join an Indian community of small hotel owners who maintain Indian customs and culture, and thus reestablish what Nair identifies as the film's major cross-cultural problematic: the creation of a "little India" in Uganda, and in the American South (Stuart 212). The film makes clear the connections between Amin's condemnation of Indians who maintained their separation from black Africans, even after Uganda's independence, and the white South, with its inherent racism and sharply patrolled color line. In one montage of two-shots, gossiping white storeowners and gossiping Indian hotel owners both confirm that Demetrius's economic advancement is impossible now that he has "forgotten his place" (Seshagiri 190–191).

Demetrius and Mina's relationship mimics, in important ways, the adulterous love connection between her mother, Kinnu, and Okelo, a black Ugandan man who was her father's best friend. While the affair is never made explicit, its dynamics are instructive, in part because Nair frequently relies on tensions in heterosexual relationships to enunciate the dialectic of immigration. When the family leaves Uganda, Kinnu looks lovingly at a photograph of Okelo and Mina before tucking it in her bag; later, Jay, notices that the photograph is the only personal memento that hangs on the wall of the liquor store Kinnu manages. While saying goodbye in Uganda, Kinnu, Okelo, and Mina share an intimate moment until Jay who blames Okelo for supporting Amin's directive and thus condoning his expulsion, tears Mina away from him. Okelo weeps openly as they board the bus that will take them to the airport. On the bus, African soldiers terrorize Kinnu, violently removing the necklace that is a sign of her marriage and thus indicating both her divorce from Africa and the end of her relationship with Okelo. Although there is no indication that Mina is Okelo's child, it is with some irony that Mina reminds her mother that she is a "darky," perhaps too dark to garner a proposal from Harry Patel, the successful Indian with whom her parents hope to arrange a marriage. That skin color constructs national belonging and identification, controls and constrains mobility, is reaffirmed in a later scene in which Demetrius tries to win Jay's acceptance of his relationship with Mina. Jay, after his experience in Uganda and the break with his friend Okelo, believes that people should stay with their own kind; Demetrius, outraged, recognizes the racist rhetoric against which he has struggled all of his life. He points to his cheek and claims a closer connection: "I know that you and your daughter ain't but a few shades from this right here—that I do know."

Many of Nair's later films focus on the love matches between twenty-somethings raised on fantasies of romance but willing to negotiate parental expectations of tradition. Such is not the case in *Mississippi Masala*. While in subsequent films marriages of long standing represent comfortable, middle-class domestic security, Kinnu and Jay do not achieve the possibility of such a future until the end of the film. In part, this is because the film does not offer the economic advancement or possibility of success promised to immigrants by the "American dream," a promise fulfilled for the non-resident Indians (NRIs) who enable the "happy ending" of *Monsoon Wedding* and *The Namesake*. In *Mississippi Masala*, however, the family feels chronically displaced due to its economic dependence on relatives, and incapable of moving forward or "upward" because of Jay's nostalgia for a life left in Uganda. Once a well-to-do lawyer, Jay, who considers himself a Ugandan first and an Indian second, spends his time writing briefs that might restore to him the property he was forced to leave behind. Mina also dreams of their former home, a beautiful, well-appointed estate with a terrace that looks out over lush gardens and distant hills. In contrast, Nair documents the rundown business section of Greenwood, with its decrepit buildings and forlorn streets, and reveals that African Americans are relegated to the minimum-wage working class: Williben (Joe Seneca), Demetrius's father, is a waiter at a white-owned diner; at the grocery store, a black man loads bags into Mina's car. Once Demetrius and Mina realize that they have no economic future in Greenville, they head west.

While the concluding shots of the film seek to recapture the promise of a multicultural American dream by showing Demetrius and Mina embracing in a sunlit cotton field, both wearing ethnic fashions, their departure from family and community forecloses easy resolutions. Contrary to claims that the film imagines a new global order, Jigna Desai argues that the ending refigures a distinctly American notion of "going west" that posits the frontier as a place of possibility: "The film turns to mobility and the heterosexual mixed-race romance as a resolution to displacement and exclusion. It shifts discourses of diaspora from an emphasis on a return to homeland to a refusal and replacement of the homeland with a desire for westward movement and travel; thus, diaspora as exile is rejected in favor of diaspora as the frontier" (73). Invoking a slightly different geopolitical terrain, Urmila Seshagiri locates the failure of the film in its inability to "transcend the geographical and historical boundaries of British colonialism and American slavery...the very hybridity that Mira Nair celebrates through vibrant spectacle finds itself bereft of a 'place' on empire's geographical and political map" (183). Andrea Stuart praises Nair's "positive attitude" towards interracial experiences and downplays Spike Lee's "separatist/nationalist imperative" (214), indicating that competing discourses over race relations in America seek to negotiate the global/local divide through integration narratives, rather than the divisive narratives of Spike Lee. Released in the same year as *Mississippi Masala, Jungle Fever* tells a similar story of an interracial love affair that occasions a social backlash, but Lee's film ends with the separation of the lovers.

Mississippi Masala is Nair's only film to date that integrates the historical memory of American racism, its economic discrimination and class struggle, into a discourse of globalization. It is also her only film in which NRIs cannot transcend the working class; in future films, they will be represented as solidly middle class and thus their mobility to transcend nationally located racisms will be assured. Prateeti Punja Ballal points to Nair's identity as "a Harvard-educated, middle-class, Indian filmmaker" to explain her tendency to thematize "her own middle-class culture as the norm and working-class cultures as Other," thus implicating itself "by using on one level the very strategies of colonial discourse and racism that it seeks to undermine at another.... In both its stereotyping and class biases, a film made by a diasporic Indian woman works within the Western discursive construction of 'Third World women.'" Confirming Nair's complicity with a discourse that constructs Third World women as exotic and thus erotic is Mina's description of her family's migrations, from Africa to England and, finally, to the United States. These geographic dislocations form her "mixed masala" identity; she is like a blend of "hot spices," as she tells Demetrius in the early stages of their courtship. During this "meet cute" conversation, a staple of the romantic comedy genre in which double-entendre inscribes sexual desire, Mina's self-identification as global and exotic shifts easily into the local and erotic register of the discourse of male desire.

Monsoon Wedding: *"The Rain is Coming...and so is the Family."*

Nair has called *Monsoon Wedding* "a love song to my home city" of New Delhi, a personal project in which she deliberately re-created an upper-middle-class Punjabi milieu modeled on the lifestyle of her family (qtd. in Macnab). An elaborate Hindi wedding in Delhi is the event that gathers family together from across the Indian diaspora for the arranged marriage of Aditi Verma (Vasundhara Das) to Hemant Rai (Parvin Dabas), an eligible NRI from Houston, Texas. A modern Indian woman, Aditi is having a secret affair with a married television producer, yet she consents to marry Hemant, if only to start a new life in America. Theirs is not the only relationship to be worked out: Lalit Verma (Naseeruddin Shah), the father of the bride, is having cash flow problems and his son is exhibiting markedly homosexual tendencies. Over the course of the film, it is revealed that Tej Puri (Rajat Kapoor), the family patriarch on whom Verma depends, has molested his niece and must be expelled from the family. In a subplot, the marigold-munching wedding tent builder, P.K. Dubey (Vijay Raaz), falls in love with Alice (Tillotama Shome), the housemaid. Like many of Nair's films about the diaspora, relationships and their complications provide the backdrop for explorations of female sexuality and class relations, set against a modern-traditional dialectic precipitated by India's rapid introduction to global economies.

American reviewers reassured their audiences that they would like *Monsoon Wedding* despite its deviation from standard Hollywood fare. Roger Ebert enthused: this is "one of those joyous films that leaps over national boundaries and celebrates universal human nature...the kind of film where you meet characters you have never been within 10,000 miles of, and feel like you know them at once." Scholar Jenny Sharpe explains that the "crossover success" of *Monsoon Wedding*, "whose characters speak English, Hindi, and Punjabi, lies in the skill with which the film acquaints a Western audience with the sights and sounds of the new global India"

(58). *Monsoon Wedding* was a hit with the Indian urban middle-class as well, an audience that, as Nair has said, she wishes to wean off Bollywood fare and reach with a "different diet" (qtd. in Badt 12). In *Monsoon Wedding*, the family wrestles with the difficult subject of incest, a story not explored in traditional Indian films, even as song-and-dance numbers in *Monsoon Wedding* evoke those Bollywood traditions. For American audiences, Nair's focus is seemingly reversed: to locate sensational subject matter that Hollywood might exploit within an exuberant and exotic mise-en-scène, in the service of introducing American audiences to a more worldly cinema experience. In an interview with *Cineaste*, Nair declares:

> "I'm waiting for [Americans] to get educated about us. It's about time you woke up, baby! You know better than I how insular U.S. audiences are, how unexposed they are to the reality, the beauty, and the refinement of the world. They really don't have a clue. It's the Voice of America mold—they start speaking slower when they meet a foreigner." (qtd in Badt 13)

While it is quite obvious that Nair is invoking the stereotype of a parochial American moviegoer raised on *Rambo*, I want to approach *Monsoon Wedding* by considering that the lively visual style that reviewers and Nair hope might initiate a "homogenous" American audience into the struggle between tradition and modernity in India, also transmits less-progressive ideological claims about women, marriage, and the working classes. Diasporic filmmaking, despite its global distribution, is in tension with the national cinemas that claim it. *Monsoon Wedding* is generally considered alongside American "wedding films," like Robert Altman's *A Wedding* (1978) and Ang Lee's *The Wedding Banquet* (1993) (Sharpe 62). "Imagine an Altman movie done Punjabi style," instructed one reviewer while describing the film's handheld-camera, crammed-frame, and "babble of different languages" aesthetic (Macnab). Simon Featherstone notes that films such as Gurinder Chadha's *Bend it Like Beckham* (2002) and *Bhaji on the Beach* (1993) are considered British comedies (113). They reveal the humor and pathos of (mis)assimilation in Indian diasporic communities. Mainstream Indian cinema has also embraced the diaspora, and specifically the non-resident Indian, as a legitimate subject for more conventional Bollywood fare, most successfully in *Dilwale Dulhania Le Jayenge* (*DDLJ*), Aditya Chopra's 1995 hit (Featherstone 113). Similarly, Jenny Sharpe argues that *Monsoon Wedding* is indebted to the family melodrama genre of Bollywood films, of which *DDLJ* is a particularly success-ful example, and while *DDLJ* was "the first Bollywood film to fuse elements of Eastern and Western cultures" (62) for an Indian audience, Bollywood as a visual style has now "infiltrate[d] a Euro-American consciousness through what can be identified as a new transnational cultural literacy" (59).

Both Sharpe and Featherstone conclude that *Monsoon Wedding* works out the conflicts between traditional Indian values and a more permissive modernity "as it develops through pressures upon female sexuality" (Featherstone 119).[1] In *Monsoon Wedding*, Aditi's consent to the hastily arranged marriage with Hemant seems reckless, especially as she feels the need to test their budding relationship by divulging her affair. As Hemant and Aditi grow to like each other over the course of the film, and as the wedding preparations proceed apace and draw the film towards its inevitable conclusion, a happy union modeled on the older generations that surround them appears possible. *Monsoon Wedding* parallels many contemporary Hollywood romances in which the role of the bride is limited by the conventions of the wedding theme: If Aditi has a career that she enjoys, she willingly relinquishes it; as the film's production notes reveal, Aditi is preoccupied by the expectations of her new life as a Houston housewife (*Monsoon Wedding*). Aditi's transformation from "modern" Indian woman (married within the old-fashioned framework of the arranged marriage) to a traditional wife (within the mobile and seemingly global gendered conventions of Hollywood) relies on the social relations that pertain in the film, revealed by the "double-wedding" theme.

The second marriage in *Monsoon Wedding*, one that requires almost no preparations and to which no family are invited, concludes the love match between the Verma's housemaid, Alice, and Dubey, the wedding tent builder. Dubey falls in love with Alice when he discovers her secretly trying on Aditi's wedding jewelry, and, as she looks at herself in the mirror imagining the affluent bride she might be, Dubey spies on her through a window, imagining that she might be his bride. His marriage proposal is especially poignant. Dubey kneels in the rain outside the kitchen door holding a heart made of carnations, the wedding flower of India, the very carnations that are strewn so lavishly about Verma's wedding tent and that Dubey has been munching on anxiously as he plots his next business venture. In their aspirations to upper-middle-class bride and to technologically fluent worker (that Dubey's manic jumbling of phone and pager parodies), the relationship between Dubey and Alice, and Aditi and Hemat, as Gita Rajan surmises, mirror each other in ways that draw attention to the class divisions that separate the couples, while smoothing over these divisions in the service of representing "a modern, democratic India" (1118).

In the style of her neo-realist first feature *Salaam Bombay!*, Nair uses montages of streetscapes and the cacophony of urban India to more sharply draw this distinction between a traditional, class-bound, and sprawling urban metropolis and the modern, liberal, upper-middle-class, private home. In one scene, Dubey travels through Delhi to the apartment he shares with his mother. The extent of the journey and the number of vehicles that convey him there indicate its far remove from the suburb where he works. This insight into Dubey's life reveals Nair's intent, as she claimed in an interview, to "show along with the upper middle-class—which is my own upbringing—the life of the working class. It's terrible and true that we have thousands of people just serving us and they all have a world, they all have a life, they all have a story" (qtd in Macnab).

Figure 8. Alice (Tillotama Shome) and Dubey (Vijay Raaz) meet in the kitchen. Their romance is revealed in lovely vignettes that play out in "below stairs" spaces as the Verma's wedding preparations occupy the main stage. (IFC Flims/Photofest)

Like *Salaam Bombay!*, there is a similar strategy at work in *Monsoon Wedding* to speak for the disenfranchised and, as Ballal noted earlier in regard to *Mississippi Massala*, to privilege a middle-class perspective. At the close of *Monsoon Wedding*, Lalit invites Dubey and Alice to cross the threshold between the rain-drenched backyard and the wedding tent and join in the wedding celebration, yet as Rajan notes, "the similarity ends there; local relations to labor and production hold this couple firmly down. ...The working-class couple, even with heterosexual privilege, has the right to use only the resources of the nation, while the NRI couple has the potential to access the unlimited resources of America" (1118–1119).

Vanity Fair: *"In a Time of Social Cimbers, Becky Sharp is a Mountaineer"*

Vanity Fair, Thackeray's trenchant satire of Regency mores and manners, is a critique so thorough that, as his subtitle announces, it is "a novel without a hero." Nevertheless, Thackeray unleashed Becky Sharp upon the literary world, the archetype of social climbing and personal ambition. The daughter of an opera singer and an artist, Becky, played by Reese Witherspoon in Nair's adaptation, has neither birth nor wealth but must scheme and flirt her way up the class ranks—and what wretched ranks are these, patrolled by a British aristocracy so venal as to make the attainment of its heights seem meaningless. Orphaned early, Becky works her way through Mrs. Pinkerton's Academy, departs there with her best friend, Amelia Sedley (Romola Garai), and while visiting the Sedley home, captures the heart of Jos, Amelia's brother who is visiting from India. Although Becky is game to see new places, a match between them is vetoed by Amelia's fiancé, George Osborne (Jonathan Rhys Meyers), an arrogant upstart of the rising merchant class. Becky soon takes up her position as governess at the decrepit manor house of Sir Pitt Crawley (Bob Hoskins). Here, she seduces the entire family, including Miss Crawley (Eileen Atkins), Sir Pitt's wealthy, spinster sister, sure to leave her fortune to the second son, Rawdon (James Purefoy). Miss Crawley spirits Becky away to London for her own amusement; Rawdon follows, and they secretly marry, only to discover that Miss Crawley is not as liberal as they had hoped. Cut out of the will, Rawdon relies on gambling to supplement his military career; Waterloo gains him a promotion, yet debt collectors converge and Becky seeks alternatives. Lord Steyne (Gabriel Byrne), a collector of her father's art, offers a way out. Becky toys with the opportunity and pays a high price for her flirtation: her son already sent out of the way at Steyne's request, Rawdon leaves her, Steyne rejects her, and the bottom rung of the ladder is once again her home. Twenty years later, Jos is delighted to discover Becky in Baden Baden, dealing cards at a casino and entertaining customers. Becky, of course, is delighted to discover that Jos is willing to renew an invitation to accompany him to India. Climbing into his carriage, Becky reminds him: "I love to see new places."

Becky's mobility is signified by this motif of opportunistic exploration of undiscovered destinations. Its sign and prop is the monogrammed trunk that Becky drags along behind her, hoists into a tradesman's cart, or has handed into a carriage—the conveyance indicates her progress up (or down) the social ladder. In the final scene, Becky's trunk is tied to the ass of an elephant, an ironic commentary on the vagaries of social climbing, but this four-legged mode of transportation carries her and Jos into India. Becky's journey ends here, happily married to a colonial administrator, seemingly affluent and secure, and impressed with the beauties of the exotic landscape that unfolds under her gaze. The film has provoked a critical investigation of Nair's postcolonial "take" on its subject matter occasioned by her end credit appreciation of Edward Said: "Salaams to Edward W. Said for continuing to inspire." Said influenced Nair's adaptation of the novel: "My conversations with Edward," she said in an interview, "reinforced my desire to link the colonialist experience to the narrative of *Vanity Fair*" (qtd. in Porton). In this section, I explore this critical discussion, one that aligns Becky's mobility as a British, imperial female subject, a position from which she can exploit the benefits that accrue to the colonial traveler, and her instantiation as a "modern woman."

Nair invigorates the British costume drama with the exotic materiality of its far-flung empire, a riot of sights and sounds that literally enriches the mise-en-scène. As one reviewer notes, one of "the film's pleasures turns out to be its (slightly heavy-handed) emphasis on how much Regency England was fascinated by all things Oriental" (Foreman 59). Desa Philadelphia, in a review in *Time* magazine, locates *Vanity Fair* in the tradition of Nair's earlier films: "Audiences have been enthralled by Nair's signature carnivalesque style and her craftiness at tying down epic scenes, like [*Monsoon*] *Wedding's* elaborate, traditional rain-soaked Indian nuptial ceremony." In this $23 million adaptation, Philadelphia states, "Nair's hand creates the movie's personality: she fills the film with vibrant costumes and boisterous energy." Indeed, the film begins with a boots-eye view of the London streets as Lord Steyne, draped in luxurious silks, makes his way to the Sharp studio, literally descending into the bowels of the city, its detritus, both human and animal, giving way before him. Nair describes for Philadelphia the subversive kind of "costume drama" she set out to make: "Early 19th century London was filthy and cacophonous; it had coal and pigs and s____ on the street," says Nair, describing the difference between the conventional London of drawing-room period epics and the street-level disarray that Becky negotiates. "I wanted you to smell the s____, because I couldn't be dragged to see those genteel, hope-the-guy-proposes-to-me kind of movies."

In this basement that Steyne condescends to visit, we meet Becky as a young child, performing a puppet show for the artists' amusement. Steyne has come to buy a portrait of Becky's mother and Becky willingly parts with it, but for a higher price than Steyne expected. Towards the end of the film, she stands in front of the portrait again and reconsiders the bargain, one that Lord Steyne reminds her is no longer negotiable; she has sacrificed her husband and son to his promise to open the doors of society to her. Her conquest of his drawing room is both conventional and provocative: standing by the piano, she delights the audience of society matrons with her voice "like a lark." Later, she performs a Bollywood-style dance number to impress Steyne's royal guest, shocking the same audience of genteel women, but delighting the men with her revealing costume and sensuous performance. As Nair reveals in an interview, this scene, in which the music is Egyptian, "was meant to be a reference to the charades on Bedouin and harem motifs that were performed in the book" (qtd in Porton 16–17). It is Nair's interweaving of Orientalism, as texture and performance, and the occident, as a governing patriarchal orthodoxy to be overthrown, that has galvanized the criticism of the film.

Figure 9. Becky Sharp (Reese Witherspoon) performing an exotic dance at Lord Steyne's party. (Focus Features/Photofest)

Jonathan Foreman's commentary on the film in the National Review is worth quoting at length because its heightened rhetoric reveals that there is much at stake in feminist, postcolonial reinterpretations of British canonical literature. Nair, claims Foreman, imposes "a modern feminist theme" (59) in which Becky is reduced to a "victim of circumstance" (58) and

> trumpets a liberated, "post-colonial" lack of respect for—or even understanding of—a dead white male's English classic, as if Thackeray's perspective on his society were somehow inevitably, cripplingly narrow or politically naïve. Given

that the film's titles include a dedication to the late Edward Said,[2] of *Orientalism* notoriety, perhaps one ought to be grateful that the film's Indian sequences don't show lashed coolies bleeding to produce England's enormous new wealth. (Emphasis added, 59)

Foreman's reaction to the influence of Said on popular culture is not isolated. In an article in the *Times Literary Supplement*, John Sutherland compares Nair's incorporation of a postcolonial perspective in *Vanity Fair* to Patricia Rozema's 1999 revision of Austen's *Mansfield Park*. He begins by correcting Said's description of Joseph Sedley, a description that perhaps influenced Nair. Said writes (in *Culture and Imperialism*):

> Thackeray's Joseph Sedley in Vanity Fair is an Indian nabob whose rambunctious behavior and excessive (perhaps undeserved) wealth is counterpointed with Becky's finally unacceptable deviousness, which in turn is contrasted with Amelia's propriety, suitably rewarded in the end; Joseph [sic] Dobbin is seen at the end of the novel engaged serenely in writing a history of the Punjab. (qtd. in Sutherland 12)

Sutherland notes the many discrepancies between Said's gloss of the novel and Thackeray's description of Joseph Sedley, and he rightly points out that later editions of *Culture and Imperialism* have failed to make the necessary correction that would replace "Joseph" with "William" Dobbin. His critique of both Nair's and Rozema's incorporation of a postcolonial worldview into their adaptations of canonical literature turns on a notion of "purity," his worry that canonical texts are being misinterpreted not only at the sentence level but ideologically as well (12).[3] Like Sutherland, John Wiltshire details the "misreading" of the novel that the film and cultural critics perform, in part due to the "currency" of Said (303). It is worth noting that Said does not make the broad claims that are attributed to him. At the beginning of the chapter "Narrative and Social Space" in *Culture and Imperialism*, Edward Said declares that there is no place better suited to tracing the "allusions to the facts of empire" than in the British novel. Citing examples from Austen, Brontë, Thackeray, and others, Said argues, "Taken together, these *allusions* constitute what I have called a structure of attitude and reference...the right to colonial possessions helps directly to establish social order and moral priorities at home" (emphasis added, 60). Thackeray's *Vanity Fair* is just one example among many of the indirect means by which British imperial presumption insinuates itself into culture, its power circulating through reference and suggestion, discourses that conveniently *mask* the beating of the coolies to which Foreman alludes.[4] Ultimately, Sutherland concludes, canonical texts can weather these kinds of adaptations, and Said, although not correct in the particular, left an important legacy; he is "more often than not, substantially right; or at least on the right track; or at the very least making points that one really ought to consider" (12).

Vanity Fair does reveal its complicity with British colonial structure, even as it interrogates it, in part due to its transformation of Becky into a "modern woman." The representation of India that Becky longs to see is appalling in its banality: according to Foreman, the "'exotic' Indian scenes could come right out of tourist brochures and J. Peterman-style safari catalogues, with red, rugged Rajasthani forts under piercing blue skies, dancing peasants, swaying elephants, and dashing men in riding boots" (59). Karin Luisa Badt, in an appraisal of *Vanity Fair* that precedes her interview with Nair, notes as well that Becky's feminist sensibility is aligned with imperial triumph. Badt reveals that Reese Witherspoon was vocal in the updating of *Vanity Fair* for a "modern feminist account" that applauded Becky's "clever, goal-setting" qualities (11); in a photocall at the Venice film festival, Witherspoon called Becky "an early feminist" ("Mira's Early Feminist"). Yet, as Badt notes, there is no "sense of struggle," and even on its own terms (not Thackeray's), the ending in which Becky triumphantly marries Jos "is too compromised…a colonial image of success that whitewashes the truly difficult politics of English imperialism in India. This lack of political critique is the most significant departure from the novel" (11). Raphael Shargel concurs with Badt, stating that Nair failed in a feminist revision: "Letting the women be whisked away by dashing and adoring lovers reinforces a patriarchal supremacy Thackeray never conceived" (46). By softening the character of Becky and enabling her successful union with Jos, in the manner of a Hollywood romance, Nair ironically confirms rather than undermines the dominance of the British subject. Said might wish it otherwise: "The novelistic hero and heroine exhibit the restlessness and energy characteristic of the enterprising bourgeoisie, and they are permitted adventures in which their experiences reveal to them the limits of what they can aspire to, where they can go, what they can become" (71). Although Nair reveals the grasping of the Osbornes and the inhumanity of both the aristocratic and the emerging middle classes as they bargain for women, it is still Becky's triumphant acquisition of the "beauty" that is India that is ultimately valued in the film.

"Two Worlds. One Journey."

Becky Sharp's trademark catch phrase, "I love to see new places," makes explicit Nair's intent across her oeuvre to introduce seemingly insular audiences to exotic cultures. While *The Namesake* (2006) necessarily reduces the scope of Jhumpa Lahiri's Pulitzer Prize-winning novel on which Nair's adaptation is based, the film retains its focus on the Ganguli family, Indian émigrés to the United States. Their story of assimilation is not unsuccessful, but rather incomplete, fragmentary, and tinged with pathos because they so affectively occupy a diasporic space. As immigrants with strong connections to India and America, they seem permanently lodged between here and there, home and away. In *The Namesake*, the theme of global exploration is reiterated in an invitation from father to son to "see the world," and like *Vanity Fair*, Nair's almost touristic fascination with the oscillation between modernity and tradition, global and local, often minimizes the political and social consequences of the exploration.

Critics praised Nair's ability in *The Namesake* to revitalize the story of immigrant life, a narrative that has, in some estimations, become passé: "In the wake of highly successful films about immigrant life and culture clash (such as the 2002 blockbuster *My Big Fat Greek Wedding*)," writes Deepika Bahri, "this is an unremarkable subject these days, but one rendered poignant by Nair's capacity to imbue its clichéd staples with the depth and ambiguity they deserve but rarely command" (10). Stuart Klawans in *The Nation* concurs: "The narrative (apart from the Gogol business) is perfectly clear about its central concerns: immigration, acculturation, in-betweenness. These are familiar issues, but with her Indian subject matter Nair makes them moving in fresh ways" (44). Parvathi Nayar, in *The Business Times Singapore*, writes that the film will find a ready audience in the diaspora: "*The Namesake* suffers no stereotypes and spins a story of differences and assimilations that can be appreciated by anyone who has lived in a country outside of their own ethnicity." Nair has also promoted the particular yet universal appeal of her stories: "The most specifically told tales become the most universal," Nair said in an interview. "And it was also important that lots of people, both young and old, relate and want to see *The Namesake*" (qtd. in Thompson). The narrative's transnational appeal is a conscious effort, on the part of the filmmaker, to build mutual respect across cultures: *The Namesake* "is meant to be a delicate balance," says the director. "It is very easy to trash this [culture] and lift up that, but that would be too didactic and the world is not like that" (qtd. in Thompson). Nair simultaneously promotes the film's unifying message while distinguishing between her racially diverse films and mainstream films that feature white protagonists. *The Namesake*, like *Mississippi Masala* and

Monsoon Wedding, is a film about brown-skinned people; Nair labels it "a non-Caucasian film on a Caucasian budget" (qtd. in James 12). As one reviewer surmised, *The Namesake* concludes the trilogy that began with *Mississippi Masala* and includes *Monsoon Wedding*: "*The Namesake*...could almost serve as a sequel to *Monsoon Wedding*, showing what happens when the new husband brings his Indian bride back to his adopted country" (Kemp 74). I want to locate *The Namesake* in a chronology of a different sort, as the second film in a trilogy that began with *Vanity Fair* and concludes with *Amelia*, one in which a way of examining and exploring the world is informed by class desire and the means to "see" it.

   The Namesake's central character is Gogol (Kal Penn), the American-born son of Ashoke (Irrfan Khan), an engineering professor, and his wife, Ashima (Tabu). Gogol, who prefers to be called Nick, is named for Nikolai V. Gogol, the Russian writer who Ashoke credits with saving his life: as a young man, Ashoke was reading Gogol's short story "The Overcoat" when the train on which he was traveling derailed. In the film, Ashoke emerges from the wreckage like a phoenix and, with what amounts to a new lease on life, gets married and moves to America. As he tells his son, when presenting a copy of Gogol's stories to him, he feels a certain kinship with this particular author because they both spent much of their adult lives outside their homeland. Gogol, reclining on a bean bag chair and annoyed at his father's interruption, is the stereotypical American teenager: aware of the import of his father's gift and his message—"We all came out of Gogol's overcoat, one day you will understand"—he is too self-involved to pursue this connection to his father. Gogol seems perfectly assimilated in New York City, immune to questions of identity that plague or stage immigrant stories, until his father's sudden death requires him to focus on larger issues of home and belonging.

   As I mentioned earlier in the chapter, it is frequently the already-married, older couple that registers the disruptions of life in the diaspora. The arranged marriage between Ashoke and Ashima reflects traditional Indian values coupled with the humor and resilience necessary for successful immigration: before their first face-to-face introduction, Ashima tries on Ashoke's shoes that are "Made in America," and adjusts to the "feel" of his wingtips. Once in America, her isolation and loneliness, compounded by the cold New York winter, reflects the difficulties of her adjustment. Together, they persevere, move to the suburbs, have children, and become comfortably middle class. Yet they shuttle emotionally and physically between Calcutta (now Kolkata) and New York, a movement that is conveyed visually by "shooting both locations as if they were one," as Nair described the process of organizing Lahiri's novel into a manageable visual narrative (qtd. in James 12). At the level of infrastructure—bridges, trains, airports, and buildings—the two cities seemingly converge by way of these familiar signs of modernity. At street level, however, differences emerge more clearly. In India on a family vacation, Gogol will not ride in a rickshaw drawn by a human being, yet the servant class in *The Namesake*, so integrated in *Monsoon Wedding*, is reduced to a mere caricature. Nick James observes that other distinctions are more cultural: the "criss-crossing of registers between American action and Indian stillness is very effective," he remarks in an interview with Nair; Nair notes that this particular difference is primarily generational: the "stillness of our parents' generation" that cannot find its counterpart in "manic America" (qtd. in James 12).

"Manic America" is where Gogol seems most comfortable and where the majority of his search for identity takes place, an identity largely formed through his relationships with women who are both central and peripheral to the narrative. Nair notes that the film condenses Gogol's many love affairs in the novel to focus on just two: Maxine (Jacinda Barrett), his American girlfriend, and Moushumi (Zuleikha Robinson), "the slick, re-invented immigrant," as Nair labels her (qtd. in James 12). Moushumi enters the story as a bespectacled teenager who visits the Ganguli's and announces her preference for *Bonjour Tristesse* over American television, which she deplores. Gogol is uninterested in Moushumi, in part because he is stoned, and while his aunt circles his head with chili to ward off the "fever" that has made his eyes red, she teases him that he can have fun with whatever girls will have him at Yale, but that he must marry a Bengali. Maxine, his American, post-college girlfriend, feeds Gogol sushi, buys his parents truffles as a hostess gift, and kisses them both in greeting, even after a warning from Gogol that his parents do not display affection. After Ashoke dies, Maxine arrives at his funeral wearing black instead of white, the Indian color of mourning; this gaffe indicates her incompatibility with Gogol. Subsequently, by virtue of her many cultural missteps, Maxine is first rendered almost comically narcissistic and then abruptly discarded by Gogol. Some time later, Gogol and Moushumi meet again, a date arranged by their mothers, and this time the advice of Gogol's aunt—to marry a Bengali—is followed. Their marriage, while seemingly built on the same foundations as the older, traditional marriage of Gogol's parents, is insincere in part because Moushumi cannot shed her life as a European sophisticate still enamored of her French lover to take up the role of a Bengali wife. As Deepika Bahri observes in her review, Moushumi, Aditi in *Monsoon Wedding*, and Mina in *Mississippi Masala*, are the more worldly women of Nair's films, "no longer content to fulfill dutifully their roles as custodians of tradition, these women might all be said to betray a fragile social structure with their promiscuity, but they also demand a reckoning with the diversity of experiences and choices available to them" (14).

At the conclusion of *The Namesake*, Nick/Gogol's two identities seem to be reconciled. Like the image of his father that began the film, he is sitting on a train reading "Gogol's Overcoat" and remembering his father's inducement to "see the world." Without Moushumi or Maxine, he can fashion another trajectory that recaptures a connection to family, one that segues nicely into the final moments of the film in which Ashima relearns the classical music she was passionate about before her marriage, by the banks of the Ganges where her husband's ashes are spread. This return to a more authentic culture, to "home" even as he "sees the world," is a prerogative of the urban upper-middle-class, a lifestyle represented by the elaborate parties, expansive apartments, and country retreats that Maxine, Moushumi, and Gogol have enjoyed throughout the film. The end of the film asks us to believe that Maxine and Moushumi are in some way necessarily discarded, their comfort with their sexuality in the global world order at odds with the nostalgia of the film's conclusion. Deepika Bahri's concern for Moushumi confirms this wistful but perhaps misplaced desire to see "modern" women safely domesticated: "We wonder if she will ever stop to find a home or learn to be faithful to herself or anyone else" (14).

Amelia: *"Defying the Impossible. Living the Dream."*

Of *Amelia*, Mira Nair's 2009 biopic of the famous aviatrix Amelia Earhart, Pete Hammond, "The Awards Insider," writes:

> In some ways *Amelia* is reminiscent of the 1985 Oscar winner, *Out of Africa*, which has the same combination of sweep, adventure and romance this film incorporates. Indeed, if this were 40, or even 20 years ago, Mira Nair's meticulously mounted effort would be deemed a front-runner for awards and a certain thing at the box office. But now we live in a post-*Slumdog* world, and the blueprint for a Best Picture is more likely to favor indie dramas like *Precious* than the old-style craft of an *Amelia*.

Hammond's analysis of Nair's most recent foray into mainstream Hollywood filmmaking is rich with irony. Nair is well known for making highly regarded independent films that, as Hammond imagines it, have only recently superseded more staid Hollywood productions. Nair's films have consistently garnered international acclaim. Her first feature, *Salaam Bombay!* was nominated for the

Best Foreign Language film Academy Award in 1989 and won the coveted Palme d'Ore at Cannes in 1988. *Monsoon Wedding* was nominated for a Golden Globe for Best Foreign Language film. She was the first female director to win the Golden Lion, the highest honor at the 2001 Venice Film Festival. The elision of Nair's independent, award-winning film history is symptomatic of a discursive ability of Hollywood odds-makers to shape mainstream film culture. Yet Hammond's review is trenchant in ways that are worth investigating: specifically, I want to acknowledge Earhart's feminist desire to "see the world," as completing a cycle (begun with *The Namesake* and *Vanity Fair*) that privileges a very Western narrative of discovery and subsumes historical and social struggle—much like *Out of Africa* (1985), the colonial fantasy of which Hammond approves.

Amelia is a major Hollywood production. Its $40 million budget was financed by Fox Searchlight, the independent film arm of 20th Century Fox, and by Gateway computer co-founder Ted Waitt, an Earhart enthusiast, who formed Avalon Pictures, a production company and a subsidiary of his private investment firm, to make the film. *Amelia* is the company's first film. The film also features established A-list stars: two-time Academy Award winner Hilary Swank as Amelia Earhart; Richard Gere as her husband, the publisher George Putnam; and, Ewan McGregor as her lover, Gene Vidal. Nair's feminist sensibilities made her a natural fit for the project, according to the director and her fans: "The more I read about [Amelia], the more I thought she is like I was.... Beyond the enigma of how she died, I'm hoping that people will see themselves in her decisions to set aside her fears and live her life to the fullest" (qtd. in Carr). Elgen M. Long, a devoted Earhart memorabilia collector and amateur historian, served as a consultant to the film. Long makes explicit the connections between Earhart and Nair, two pioneering professionals: "Amelia is responsible for so many things that we take for granted these days in terms of what has happened in aviation and in the rights of women," Mr. Long said. "I was thrilled that Mira directed the film because she is something of a pioneer in a man's field, and I think a lot of the insights into Amelia's character came to her quite naturally" (qtd. in Carr).

Amelia hues closely to Earhart's biography: the jaunty adventuress, convincingly played by Swank whose lean boyish physique and angular features seemed to embody the aviation pioneer's tomboyish appeal, defies convention and takes to the air, determined to make a place for herself in the record books. A free-spirited, independent woman, Earhart certainly earned her feminist credentials. Fearing that marriage would ground her soaring aspirations, she negotiated an open relationship with her husband, publisher George Putnam, and she was a proponent of female pilots' participation in the burgeoning public aviation industry. Yet the film is incredibly dull. It begins with Earhart embarking on the final and fatal journey that ended in her disappearance in 1937 at the age of 39, when she and her navigator were unable to locate tiny Howland Island, a necessary pit stop but a mere speck of land in the vast Pacific. As she flies around the world, flashbacks (indicated by shots of gauzy clouds and blue sky) propel us through her life: from a youngster in the Kansas wheat fields dreaming of the freedom of the skies to an unconventional young woman who learned to fly; her affair with Gene Vidal (Ewan McGregor) and the toll it took on her marriage; and Putnam's creative "branding" of his wife that made her hawk a line of luggage, among other consumer wares, to keep her in planes.

While it is refreshing and rare for Hollywood to represent a woman enjoying this kind of freedom—to fly, to beat men's records, to work on planes, and to have affairs—all while Putnam seems to keep the home fires burning, Nair's Earhart is so thoroughly modern that historical specificity is elided. Although there is a moonlit flight with Eleanor Roosevelt, one of Earhart's most ardent supporters, and a deft use of archival footage, there is very little social or material history in which to ground Earhart's independence. The removal of historical referent was deliberate. Cinematographer Stuart Dryburgh explains that he and Nair chose a visual style that transcended historical specificity: "Amelia was, after all, a thoroughly modern woman," Dryburgh said in an interview. "The idea was not to go for a period look, but to let the people, landscapes, and aircraft really speak for themselves" (qtd. in Pais). Dryburgh's sweeping vistas of Victoria Falls and the African veldt with its migrating herds of animals—the landscape that "speaks for itself"—most clearly signals the reduction of personal and political struggle to aesthetics and represents the film's most defining homage to *Out of Africa*, the story of Danish Baroness Karen Blixen's life in colonial Kenya and her love affair with big-game hunter Denis Finch-Hatton, based in part on Blixen's own stories of her adventures. Rob Nixon articulates the political and historical conditions of which *Out of Africa* was a symptom. *Out of Africa*, like *The Jewel in the Crown* and *A Passage to India*, reclaimed India and then Africa for the British empire (albeit the "empire of the imagination"), in part as backlash against the postcolonial "redressing of history" by Aimé Césaire, Frantz Fanon, and others that documented the human cost of empire (Nixon 217). Nixon notes that Sidney Pollack's *Out of Africa*, which won seven Oscars in 1986, is a distinctly American revision of British imperial nostalgia. America, claims Nixon, has "stepped into Britain's imperial shoes and is walking abroad more confidently than ever," although it "still lacks a strong national image of empire and is borrowing from a presently enfeebled Britain the glorious style that once went with possession of the earth" (217). Although Finch-Hatton mocks Blixen's penchant for treating the Africans who work on her estate as possessions, Nixon reminds us that Blixen practiced "a species of philanthropic feudalism, with her at the center exercising noblesse oblige and anticipating a deferential loyalty in return" (219). It is the exploitation of resources (on Finch-Hatton's safari, on Blixen's plantation) that are masked by the panoramic flyover. The edenic landscape that Blixen and Finch Hatton witnessed from Finch Hatton's plane conceals the very serious social and economic fragmentation happening on the ground (221).

Like *Out of Africa, Amelia* also adopts the gaze of the surveyor, or the armchair tourist. *New Yorker* critic David Denby correctly identifies *National Geographic* as *Amelia*'s nearest ideological and visual relation:

> Again and again, as Earhart soars around the world, Stuart Dryburgh's cinematography captures the landscapes below, filled with scampering animals and native children. The over-all visual style is pretty, even luscious, in a familiar, *National Geographic* sort of way.

Figure 10:. Amelia Earhart (Hilary Swank) touches down in Africa. (Fox Searchlight/Photofest)

National Geographic has had a profound influence on how Americans see the world and thus on how Americans see themselves. In *Reading National Geographic*, Catherine A. Lutz and Jane L. Collins define the magazine's distinct worldview: to present geographic knowledge about the world to a curious middle-class American audience in a style that is positive and appreciative, while simultaneously presenting the members of the Third World as "Other" yet familiar. David Jansson succinctly summarizes their analysis of the non-Western peoples that the magazine casts in variously limited ways, as pilgrims on the road to civilization, or "occupants of an unchanging mythic past" (354–355). Similarly, in *Amelia*, the landscape, its features, and its peoples are exotic and striking; the earth is revealed as a magnificent pattern of ocean, land and light, and on the ground, native children surround Earhart during a pit stop.

Earhart, eager to document each step on her journey, carries with her a small movie camera to record the world that she, the explorer, discovers.

It might appear that *Amelia* is an anomaly in Nair's film canon. It features few actors of color, restores a particularly regressive colonial perspective to the world's screens, and looses Nair's "unconventional woman" from the bonds of histories and cultures that have traditionally been her focus. Although the film was panned by critics and proved a "financial and creative disaster" for Fox Searchlight (Horn), and we can perhaps understand that the "lure" of Hollywood, especially in its mainstream, big-budget guise, proved compelling for Nair, we should delineate as well the consequences of Hollywood's hegemony. Stephen Prince reminds us that Hollywood frequently entices international filmmakers and co-opts their unique stories (4). With its focus on special effects and spectacles that demand a global audience to recoup production costs, "Hollywood exports a model of film that contains an implicit threat to the diversity of international film culture" (5). Thus, Hollywood reduces the pool of filmmakers, like Mira Nair, who might investigate the more diverse cultures at the edges of Hollywood's empire.

Notes

1. Sharpe argues that Nair has created a new model for Bollywood-style family melodramas in which "heteronormative female sexual desire" is permitted. Sharpe also has reservations about Alice's role in the film, noting that dividing "Indian femininity along class lines leads one to question the gender politics of her feminist intervention" (64).

2. Said died September 2003.

3. Patricia Rozema's revision of Austen's *Mansfield Park* was recognized by some critics for its timely reappraisal of the colonial conditions of British wealth: Embeth Davidtz's "cold-blooded performance as Mary" Roger Ebert notes, "strips bare the pretense and exposes the family for what it is—a business, its fortune is based on slave plantations in the Caribbean" ("Mansfield Park").

4. In the conclusion, we perform an analysis of recent films and other cultural products utilizing a methodology derived from Said: an analysis of "First World" representations of the Third World as allusions to a structure of dominance.

Six

NRI: The Transnational Class and Transnational Class in the Films of Deepa Mehta

***

> "As a product of these considerations, I have put together the
> sentence 'White men are saving brown women
> from brown men.'"
> *(Spivak 92)*

The above quote from Gayatri Spivak's famous and perhaps over-cited essay "Can the Subaltern Speak?" has particular resonance in the post-*Slumdog Millionaire* (2008) world, noted by Pete Hammond in his review of Nair's *Amelia* discussed in the previous chapter, in terms of my reading of the discourses surrounding the production and release of Deepa Mehta's "elemental" trilogy *Fire* (1996), *Earth* (1999), and *Water* (2005). It is my intention to demonstrate how, in terms of the cultural discourses that it generated, British director Danny Boyle's Oscar-winning *Slumdog* effectively served to enact Spivak's sentence with regard to a usurping of the subaltern female voices of Mehta's characters. According to Rahul Gairola, Spivak's essay "questions whether Indian women imbibed with the non-secular ideologies of Hinduism have a say in their own existence...and what agency these women secure in the perpetual resurrection of the very roles that construct their gendered domination" (307).

Spivak formulates her sentence, that white men are saving brown women from brown men, as a way of engaging with the linguistic and social complexities of nineteenth-century British legislation that outlawed the practice of *sati*, or widow immolation. In the context of *sati*, the meaning of Spivak's sentence can be understood to demonstrate the ways that the subaltern woman is doubly silenced, once by the "brown men" who dictate that she throw herself on her husband's funeral pyre, and secondly by the "white men" who rescue her from this fate. At no point in this transaction—white men vying against brown men to save brown women—is the agency of the woman considered, and the larger point of Spivak's argument is that, within Western codification, the "voice" of the subaltern woman does not achieve the status of dialogic utterance. The act of "saving" becomes an act of "speaking for." She concludes her essay with a brief narrative of the contemporary suicide of a young Bengali woman whose actions constitute a failed speech act; despite the fact that the woman waited until she was menstruating before killing herself—an act that situated her death outside of patriarchal discourse—her suicide was still read, by her family and community, as evidence of "illicit love" and unplanned pregnancy.

Deepa Mehta's films explore questions of female agency and female choice for Indian women, particularly those, like the women Spivak's essay explores, "imbibed with the non-secular ideologies of Hinduism." Mehta's work challenges the historical scriptedness of mythological and political female response. As Tutun Mukherjee notes, Mehta's trilogy

> binds the elemental with the feminine and probes the way women are preyed upon and shackled by social institutions, pulverized and bartered by patriarchy. The trilogy represents in its totality a powerful and significant cultural challenge to the dominating masculine values and practices of oppression, subjugation and exploitation of women. (36)

Because of Mehta's obvious feminist focus in her work, the fact that her films turn a critical eye towards the intersections between politics, religion, and patriarchy, and because of Mehta's status as a non-resident Indian (NRI)—born in 1950 in Amristar, Punjab, India, she immigrated to Canada in 1973—she and her work have been subjected to a range of harsh criticisms from Hindu nationalists, Indian politicians, and members of the Indian diaspora, and the protest against Mehta and her work within India has, at times, turned violent. According to Shohini Chandhuri, Mehta is a filmmaker who attempts

> to confront aspects of Indian reality left out of the domestic popular cinema. Her high media profile and "crossover" success has often bred accusations that she packages themes and aesthetics in a deliberate attempt to stir up controversy for publicity and produce an exotic, commodified "India" for Western audience. (8)

I want to examine the various discourses that surround Mehta's project in *Fire, Earth,* and *Water*—and Mehta's own agency in the construction of those discourses—in order to demonstrate the ways that her provocative feminist narratives strive to articulate the liminal, in Homi Bhabha's sense, a space that is at once co-opted by various audiences as alternatively transnational, universal, or inauthentic. Furthermore, I want to look at how the discourse generated by *Slumdog Millionaire*—a film that had its own share of controversies—factors into and, perhaps, alters a reading of the various voicings and silencings that Mehta's work interrogates.

Of Mehta's life, particularly her status as a non-resident Indian, Jacqueline Levitin claims, "born into a family relocated because of partition, Mehta was already transnational by birth. Following her new husband Paul Saltzman [whom she later divorced] to Canada in 1973 was a second dislocation" (282). Mehta began documentary filmmaking after receiving a philosophy master's degree from Delhi University. She made her first feature *Sam & Me* in 1991, and the film received honorable mention at Cannes. She later worked with George Lucas on two episodes of the *Young Indiana Jones Chronicles*, and her second feature, *Camilla* (1994), starring Jessica Tandy and Bridget Fonda, was released worldwide (McKibbens 148). The elemental trilogy, which constitutes her most highly regarded and controversial work, followed. Mehta has claimed that despite the fact that she has lived in Canada the majority of her life, she has "never felt Canadian" (Ramchandani) and claims instead an Indian identity, noting in an interview with Salman Rushdie, "I feel very strongly about being an Indian, even though I'm considered an NRI" (Charlie Rose);[1] her most esteemed works focus on the plight of Indian women and were filmed in India (or, in the case of *Water*, in Sri Lanka).

But her status as an NRI has been the source of much of the criticism leveled against her, particularly in terms of her supposed "motive" for depicting India in a "negative" light and in terms of her authority—as an outsider—to speak any kind of supposed "truth" about India. As Jigna Desai aptly states, "as a diasporic cultural producer, Mehta is caught in the neither-nor of diasporic (dis)placement; however, her cosmopolitan transnationalism also provides her citizenship (cultural and state) within the postcolonial nation-state" (185). The complexities of this diasporic positioning with regard to Mehta's work are myriad. On the one hand, Mehta has had trouble getting funding to film in Canada because of criteria that determine that much assistance to film production and distribution in Canada is allocated to Canadian citizens; because of these factors, Mehta has claimed that her films are not sufficiently Canadian to qualify for funding (Levitin 275). On the other hand, "Mehta as a diasporic intellectual playing native informant is interrogated by South Asians…in regard to her alienation from, and lack of intimacy with, her homeland" (Desai 185).

If moving away from India has made her "fearless" (Levitin 281) in her artistic approach and has given her the critical distance necessary to explore various instances of female silencing in India, it has also made various contingencies fearful of the voicings her films enact. The neither/nor of the diasporic position plays itself out in (appropriately) three ways with regards to Mehta's trilogy, dependent upon her audience. First, her academic critics, in India and the West, tend to read Mehta as transnational in her focus, noting that her films, such as *Fire*, recognize "the fluidity of culture" (Levitin 273) as opposed to its fixity. Second, the Hindu right, particularly Shiv Sena and conservative Indian politicians[2] read Mehta as inauthentic and, therefore, incapable of accurately depicting India. This discourse is most visible in the controversies that erupted around *Fire* and *Water*. The first film, *Fire*, "elicited a particularly violent reaction from Hindu fundamentalists…. They stormed theaters that were showing the film, set posters on fire, and threatened patrons"; furthermore, Shiv Sena leaders "claimed that the film was an affront to 'Indian' values and that they were defending India from 'alien' influences such as same-sex desire" (Barron 65). According to Gayatri Gopinath, "both the mainstream media and the extremist Hindu nationalist movement use the charge of authenticity…to disavow both [*Fire*'s] queer and diasporic origins" ("Transnational" 150). When Mehta attempted to film *Water* in Varanasi, protestors stormed the set and destroyed it. A statement released to the press by a protestor claims that destroying the set was not enough, that "the people involved with the film should have been beaten black and blue…. The West…is only interested in our snake charmers and child brides. And people like Deepa Mehta pander to them" (McKibbins 150).

Finally, and perhaps in response to the two readings above, Mehta herself, as well as some of her critics, have read her work as universal as opposed to invested with any national identity. Of *Fire*, Mehta claims she wanted the "emotional content to be universal" (qtd. in Margetts),[3] and in his review of *Earth*, Roger Ebert, who, as noted in the previous chapter, also touted the universality of Nair's *Monsoon Wedding*, claims that the film is "effective because it doesn't require much history from its viewers, explains what needs to be known, and has a universal message." Within the context of Mehta's status as a transnational filmmaker, then, there appears to be a necessary tension between the need to be "authentically" Indian and "universally" acceptable, and it would seem—given the overwhelming amount of activist outcry that sought to silence various aspect of the trilogy—neither position is attainable, at least not for a NRI female filmmaker who identifies as a privileged Indian and seeks to depict subaltern female voices. To be authentic would mean to be male, to be Hindu, and to live in India; to be universal would be to undermine the specific religious, gendered, political, and national frameworks that Mehta's work so assiduously interrogates. In order to see more clearly how this discourse plays out in Mehta's work, it is necessary to look more closely at the content of her films and at the various controversies that surround them. Mehta's trilogy constitutes, in my reading, a backwards-looking lens, beginning with *Fire*, set in New Delhi in the 1990s, moving with *Earth* to Lahore in 1947, and ending with *Water* in Varanasi in 1938, through which to view various "truths" about Indian women's lives at various real locations and at various real points in India's history.

None of Mehta's films, however, makes any claim to be documentary in nature; the truths that they seek to explore are staged in the context of various fictions with regard to location, language, and history. For example, *Fire* was filmed entirely in English as opposed to Hindi; *Water*, set in Varanasi, was filmed in Sri Lanka with a Sri Lankan lake standing in for the Ganges, and Sarala, the Sri Lankan child who plays the film's lead Chuhiya did not speak Hindi or English when she was chosen for the role. In terms of *Earth*, the film challenges the historical colonial narrative that indicates that partition was a bloodless event (Herman 108) as well as the historical Hindu-dominated Indian congress narrative that, as partition drew closer and more real, focused on "images of Mother India and the motherland—bodies imagined as whole, pure, fertile, and newly freed—and...refocused on independence and decolonization, as opposed to the partition through which independence would be accomplished" (Herman 116).

Furthermore, the events depicted in Mehta's films are conveyed via the medium of melodrama, a mode of presentation that is not only part and parcel of Bollywood filmmaking[4] but also serves as a conscious affront to realistic narrative. While melodrama is often treated in a dismissive manner, due in particular to its gender-specific valences, such readings also miss the political power of the genre. As Chandhuri notes, "melodrama can...be a strategy to channel the power of emotions in order to raise awareness of social issues and reach larger audiences. Melodrama often controversially dramatizes social problems and injustices and...can generate popular debate" (16). Such debate is dialogic, inviting various perspectives to enter the discussion that Mehta's films clearly generate. In all three films, there is a conscious and explicit sense that what is at stake is not the presentation of a master narrative of "truth," but the dialogic unearthing and exploration of various *versions* of history—political or mythological—and that Mehta's work moves backwards in time to situate history as story, to locate and unearth the spaces in which various voices (always female) have been excluded from a position of storytelling.

***

Fire, the first film in the trilogy, is also the most contemporary, set in the 1990s in New Delhi. More scholarship has been written about *Fire* than either *Earth* or *Water*, and this may be in part because the film has been around longer and, therefore, scholars have had more time to focus on it as a subject of inquiry. However, nearly all of the scholarship on *Fire* focuses, to varying degrees, on the film's controversial nature, and much of this scholarship seeks to situate the film within the heated rhetoric that characterized its release.[5] As a result, very little has been written about the artistic or aesthetic aspects of the film. I bring this up not to say that one way of viewing the work—aesthetic or political—is better than the other but to note the marked differences in terms of reading criticism about *Fire* as compared with *Earth*, about which there was much less controversy. In the case of *Fire*, it seems, it is impossible to read the film without reading the incendiary discourses—religious, sexual, and political—as inherently productive of its meaning.

Fire depicts a same-sex relationship[6] between two Hindu middle-class sisters-in-law, Sita (Nandita Das) and Radha (Shabana Azmi), who share a home. Sita's new husband Jatin (Javed Jaffrey) loves a Chinese-Indian woman who refuses to marry him, and the two continue their relationship after Jatin's marriage to Sita. Radha and her husband Ashok (Kulbhushan Kharbanda) have been married much longer, but Ashok has taken a vow of celibacy in response to the teaching of a swami who preaches that desire is evil. Therefore, both women are effectively denied—by their husbands—heterosexual relationships that one would expect to be normative within the institution of Hindu marriage. In response to their alienation from avenues of patriarchially maintained "appropriate" desire, Sita and Radha not only fall in love, but maintain a relationship within the predominantly homosocial space of the household, which they share with Jatin and Radha's voiceless mother Biji (Kushal Rekhi) and the family servant Mundu (Ranjit Chowdhry), who eventually outs Sita and Radha's relationship to Ashok. After Ashok catches the women in bed together, Radha tells him that she is leaving him for Sita, and Ashok, enraged, first attempts to seduce/rape Radha and then pushes her into the stove, where her sari catches on fire. Ashok picks up Biji and leaves Radha to her fate. In the end, Radha passes through the flames to return to Sita.

As I have already mentioned, fundamentalist reaction to *Fire* was overwhelmingly negative; Shiv Sena members stormed theaters that screened the film, set posters on fire, and threatened moviegoers and theater employees, and when "Mehta appeared to talk about the film at the International Film Festival of India, a man in the audience stood up and announced, 'I am going to shoot you, madam!'" (Coleman 20). Of the reactions to her film, Mehta says, "it was amazing that a film which explores choices, desires, and the psyche of people who are victims of tradition would cause such an uproar. But perhaps I was naïve" ("Controversy"). The reasons for the outrage are essentially twofold: the film's depiction of same-sex female desire, and the use of the names "Sita" and "Radha" for the film's female protagonists. As Barron notes, "naming the characters 'Radha' and 'Sita' intensified responses to the film.... Radha and Sita are the two main female characters in Hindu mythology; Sita in particular represents the ideal Indian woman for many Hindus" (66). Furthermore, the film's depiction of same-sex desire is inherently linked to Hinduism via this act of naming: "in naming both characters after goddesses, the film does more than make reference to Hindu mythological texts. It actually positions same-sex desire in the context of Hindu religious traditions" (Arora 234).

As Arora notes, the question of the origin of same-sex (specifically female) desire was of great significance within the context of *Fire's* reception, by both Hindu nationalists and Indian feminists alike, who had to engage with the idea that female sexuality—lesbianism in particular—is a Western import, or with the counterargument, which labeled "homophobia an import [from Britain]" and posited "homosexuality in the context of Indian traditions" (Arora 238). Neither approach, it seems, is particularly useful in terms of getting at how same-sex desire functions in the film as a nameless act that constitutes choice: as Sita says to Radha, "there is no word in our language to describe what we are to each other." We can read this utterance as meaning that within a Hindu tradition, there is no such thing as "lesbianism," or we can read this relationship as one that fails to conform to the imposition of language and naming that typically delineates the boundaries of love. As Gopinath states, "the film makes explicit the ways in which not all female same-sex desire culminates in an autonomous 'lesbianism' and not all 'lesbianism' is at odds with domestic marital arrangements" (482).[7] At stake, then, within the various debates in which one can situate *Fire*, is the element of naming—of speaking of or for—female desire.

With this point in mind, I would like to return to the controversy surrounding Mehta's decision to name her characters after significant figures in Hindu mythology. Within the *Ramayana*, a Hindu sacred text written between 500 BC and 200 AD, Sita, the wife of Ram (one incarnation of Vishnu) must walk through fire to prove her chastity to her husband after she is abducted by Ravana. Even through Sita survives the trial by fire, Ram banishes her to the forest, where she is swallowed up by the earth, leaving Ram to realize—too late—that his wife was chaste. Radha, according to Barron, is the "consort of the god Krishna...a slightly less charged but equally significant mythic figure; Radha and Krishna represent perfect and transcendent, albeit extramarital, love" (67). Barron notes that *Fire* incorporates three different dramatic and televised versions of Sita's trial by fire throughout the film in order to remind us "that many variations of the story exist" (77). Such a claim brings me back to my earlier assertion that Mehta's project, here as elsewhere, is to situate history as a story that exists in dialogue with others, and to locate the omissions of female agency within the construction and dissemination of mythological and political narratives. By rewriting the stories of Sita and Radha, by allowing them to choose to create new roles and new modes of desire for these mythical women, Mehta situates a female-authored story in the midst of discourses—political, religious, and sexual—that have, at least in India, been the purview of men.

That Mehta so deliberately names her heroines is significant; that she leaves unnamed the relationship they experience is more so: despite all the controversy surrounding the Western or non-Western nature of lesbianism, Mehta never ascribes "lesbianism" to the relationship of Sita and Radha, thereby refusing to position their relationship as something so easily (or contentiously) codified. Biji, the women's mother-in-law, is silent, we learn, the victim of "a major stroke," who rings a bell in order to get the attention of her family. As Mundu says of her, "no talking, but much listening." And much watching. She knows the nature of Sita and Radha's relationship, but she cannot speak to tell her sons of their wives' transgressions—and perhaps, even if she could speak, she would not be able to name the relationship, as no word for it exists. It seems impossible for me to read Biji as other than Spivak's voiceless woman, unable to articulate her own desires, forced to ring a bell, forced to watch as Mundu masturbates at one point in the film and as Sita and Radha dance together before her in another.

Biji upholds the patriarchy that caters to male sexuality, in all of the various forms in which it is manifest in *Fire*: Jatin's extramarital affair, Ashok's celibacy, and Mundu's autoeroticism. She may wish to protest, but she remains silent, crippled, and unable to enact her own will; her character functions as a manifestation of the stifling aspects of Indian womanhood that Sita and Radha choose to cast off, and her story—one scripted for her by the transcribers of Indian history and Hindu mythology—is that which Deepa Mehta revises. When Ashok picks up Biji and walks out of his house with her as Radha's sari burns, he takes with him womanhood in its "appropriate" Hindu manifestation: silent, compliant, non-resistant. We might also note that Biji, old and frail, embodies notions of womanhood that are dying out and being replaced by womanhood as constituted and mythologized by women; after all, in Mehta's telling, Radha survives her trial by fire and is reunited, in the end, with Sita.

***

The various controversies that surrounded *Fire*'s release were almost entirely absent—at least in India—from *Earth*, Mehta's second film in the trilogy; in Pakistan, however, the film, which deals with the 1947 partition of Indian into India and Pakistan, was banned (Herman 112). Jeannette Herman notes

> The reception of the film across its various locations varied from deeply affected and enthusiastic to unmoved and critical. Though some critical South Asian viewers have attributed the more enthusiastic responses to the film's catering to Western audiences poorly informed about the history of partition...the reception does not divide easily along national, regional, or cultural lines. (112)

The primary criticism of *Earth* is its supposed catering to a Western viewership, not the incendiary premises that underscore the other two films in the trilogy, despite the fact that *Earth* depicts graphic incidents of Hindu/Muslim violence. Bridget Kulla notes that in *Earth*, "Mehta shows how partition divided a people as well as the land, with women becoming the targets for the hatred that was produced. The film's subject matter—the victimization and violence towards women during the forging of a new nation—is one that is rarely addressed on a popular level." I contend, however, that the reason the film has not proven as controversial is that it does not explicitly address violence done to women during partition,[8] but instead produces a male-articulated dialogue beneath which violence against women *can* be read, but is not explicitly stated. I read *Earth*, based on Bapsi Sidhwa's semi-autobiographical novel *Cracking India* (1991),[9] as a film that depicts the very polyphonic male dialogism that both *Fire* and *Water*, because of their more feminist foci, instigated: in *Earth*, various voices—significantly all of which are male—present partition from various subject positions of Hindu, Muslim, and Sikh. What begins as "just a discussion among friends" ultimately turns violent, and, despite the fact that men are those who engage in the discussion, women are the ultimate victims. Female perspectives are present in the film, but those perspectives are not political—at least not in the way that they occupy political territory in Mehta's other two films. Lenny's mother, a Parsee, proclaims that "the Parsees aren't taking sides," and Lenny's Hindu ayah Shanta tells her male suitors that if they do not stop talking about the conflict between Hindus and Muslims, she will no longer come with Lenny to the park where they all congregate. The film is focalized through eight-year-old Lenny, but aside from two instances of narration—the adult Lenny speaking at the beginning and end of the film—we see Lenny's perspective via her physical response to the events taking place around her. In the context of partition as it is depicted in *Earth*, women become objects caught up in the violent politics of partition and the riots that followed, but their voices are almost entirely absent from the debate surrounding those events.

The reasons why Mehta might have, with *Earth*, shied away from speaking the subaltern female voice seem obvious: given the vociferous response that *Fire* engendered, Mehta might have wanted to avoid controversy. Sidhwa's narrative is much more explicitly focused on the violence that was done to women during partition, so Mehta clearly stepped back a bit from engaging with this issue in as explicit a way as she might have, had her experience with *Fire* been different. *Earth*, like *Fire*, also depicts the silencing of a Hindu female perspective, this time the voice of the ayah Shanta—played by Nandita Das who also plays Sita in *Fire*—who cares for Lenny (Maia Sethna), the story's young female Parsee narrator. In Sidhwa's novel as well as in Mehta's film adaptation of the novel,[10] Lenny observes partition from her neutral position as a member of the Parsee community in Lahore and serves as witness to the ways that partition fractures relationships on a personal level, within the context of a single household, that serves as a microcosm for the dividing of India into India and Pakistan. It is Lenny's position of neutrality that distances her from her filmic "sisters," Sita in *Fire* and Chuhiya in *Water*, both of whom actively confront injustices they experience. Of this difference, Hopgood notes,

> all three films…share the device of a naïve innocent girl as a figure of social critique. In *Fire* and *Water*, this figure openly questions and challenges tradition, while in *Earth* she is witness…a powerless observer who stands in for the audience. (146)

By creating a neutral protagonist who witnesses rather than challenges, Mehta generates in *Earth* a less incendiary narrative than in either *Fire* or *Water*. Furthermore, the characters that initially form a multifarious ethnic and religious community—made up of Hindus, Parsees, Muslims, and Sikhs—within the context of *Earth* are divided against one another during partition. The film is likewise multilingual; the dialogue is spoken in Hindi, Urdu, Gujarati, Punjabi, and English, and these languages, like the characters who speak them, engage in dialogue about religion, nation, and gender—the very discourses invoked previously by *Fire*.

Of Sidhwa's novel, Ambreen Hai notes the complex and often symbolic role that Lenny's ayah Shanta plays within the text. In terms of the construction of national narrative, Shanta,

> the female domestic servant who is abducted, gang-raped, and forced into prostitution by an erstwhile Muslim admirer, and who becomes the sole representative figure of female violation in this text...functions...as the center of fascination for the upper-class child narrator—beautiful, desired (before Independence) by men of all religious and class backgrounds.... But the ayah's sexuality also has other functions that become more problematic for the text: in the second half, in a strange conflation of political and sexual violation, the ayah's ethnic, gendered, and class position enables her body to become the displaced figure for a nation that is brutalized and ravaged for telling a story otherwise too traumatic to be told. (390-91)

In the novel, the story that Ayah's[11] body tells is the story of the violence done to women during the partition riots, and that story, like the story of Sita's trial by fire, is one that has more than one face: according to Herman, the official 1948 figure for the number of women abducted and raped during the riots is 12,500; more recent estimates, however, range between 88,000 and 125,000 (139). During the riots as well as during the recovery operations aimed at finding abducted women that followed, "the treatment of women's bodies and the meanings assigned to them...make literal the nationalist move of locating national definitions and national virtue in Indian women's bodies" (Herman 140). While Lenny's family locates Ayah at the end of Sidhwa's novel, her location in Mehta's adaptation remains unknown, her history a silence that haunts both the adult Lenny and the history of partition. Mehta's decision to change Sidhwa's ending and render Shanta absent at the end of the film allows for Lenny's adult articulation, via a voiceover, to indicate not only the loss of Shanta but also the loss of a "large part" of herself as well.

In its closing scene, we see an adult Lenny, played in a brief cameo by Babsi Sidwa, 50 years after partition. The film flashes to the present from the scene in which Ice Candy Man/Dil Navaz (Aamir Khan) has coerced Lenny into telling him that Shanta is hiding in Lenny's family's house. Navaz tells the Muslim mob of Shanta's location, even as Lenny realizes what has happened and yells to Ice Candy Man that she has lied, that Shanta has gone to Amristad. As men drag

Shanta from the house, the scene shifts to the present, to Lenny's contemporary question about partition, "Was it all worth it?" By allowing the adult Lenny to ask this question, Mehta places the female voice—at the very end of the film—in dialogic engagement with the men whose voices debated the pros and cons of partition throughout the film. Lenny's question invites a response not only from these men, but also from viewers of the film, and the response must be, in large part, dependent upon various sets of memories and constructed narratives—like this one, based to some extent on Sidhwa's childhood memories—of the experience of partition. Herman notes that *Earth* "raises questions about the capacity of acts of memory to transform past traumas, about the purposes and potentials of different forms of memory for collective engagement with histories of material and symbolic violence" (109).

Lenny's question, "was it all worth it," may well be Mehta's: was it worth it to downplay the female perspective in *Earth*? It is noteworthy that in *Earth* the history that Mehta remembers is *not* explicitly the violence done to women: as I have indicated, while Sidhwa's novel deals specifically with Ayah's rape and subsequent prostitution, that particular partition story is absent from Mehta's film. Instead, the film ends with the following postscript: "Over one million people were killed during India's division. Seven million Muslims and five million Hindus and Sikhs were uprooted in the largest and most terrible exchange in population known to history." Nowhere in this text is any mention the status of the thousands of women who experienced sex-specific violence during partition—the reality of which, while made very explicit in Sidhwa's novel, is merely alluded to in the film: the body of the woman, Shanta, like that of Biji, is literally removed from the frame, co-opted and spoken for, during this particular moment in India's history, by the discourses of male power.

***

While *Earth*'s story is dependent upon relationships between men and women, and while those relationships are often shown in a predominantly positive light—perhaps another reason why the film engendered less controversy than the other two—*Water*, like *Fire*, is a story of Hindu women without men, in this case, women (and female children) who are forced, because of their status as widows, to live a cloistered life of poverty far removed from the male gaze. What *Water* and *Fire* have in common, then, is their situatedness within homosocial female spaces—the middle-class home of *Fire* and the widow house of *Water*—from which men are visibly, socially, politically, and religiously excluded. With regard to the discourse surrounding the reception of Mehta's films, Mehta herself has become increasingly codified as a figure who instigates controversy and disseminates a particular—many claim, negative—view of India to the rest of the world. By the time we get to *Water*, Mehta herself can be read as a character in the narrative of the NRI female filmmaker and an active agent in the history that her films seek to portray; she is the Indian woman whose perspective heretofore has been subject to various silencings, co-optings, and denouncements. With *Water*, we can read Mehta as a conscious player in the discourse that that film engendered, a woman able to perform an expected role that allowed her to capitalize on the controversy that has historically surrounded her work. In this section, I read Mehta not as "shocked" by the protests over *Water*—as she has said she was over those that erupted over *Fire*[12]—but as actively engaged in the production of the discourse that ensued. The naïvety that Mehta claims underscored the surprise she felt when *Fire* was met with such vitriol has given way to wisdom and a shrewd sense of the politics of *being* Deepa Mehta and a realization, I feel, of the value of performing that role. My reading of Mehta as a participant in the construction of her image is not meant to undermine the value of her work or to indicate that the protests that took place at the instigation of *Water*'s filming were not legitimate. What I hope to show, however, is how, via the historical progression from *Fire* to *Water*, Mehta has been able to gain agency in the conscious construction of the discourse surrounding both her image and her work.

Of *Water*, Kulla claims "at last [Mehta's] voice has been forcefully silenced." This assertion was made after Mehta was forced, in the wake of violent protests, to stop filming the third and final part of her trilogy. According to Fincina Hopgood, the controversy surrounding *Water* is, as I have already noted, "not without precedent in Mehta's career, although it is by far the most violent and devastating response to her filmmaking" (144), and this violence speaks to the vehemence of the fundamentalist Hindu protests with which the final film in the trilogy was met. After protestors destroyed sets in Varanasi—Hinduism's holiest city where widow houses still exist—where Mehta first tried to film *Water*, Mehta ceased work on this picture, noting that she was too angry to continue work on the project: "I was very angry at what had happened, and I said to myself that I would not make *Water* until I stopped being angry. But I knew I would make it" (qtd. in McKibbins 151). In 2000, "filming…was interrupted by violent protests from Hindu fundamentalists, who destroyed the sets and threatened the safety of the director and her cast. The fundamentalists alleged Mehta's film denigrated their religion and the sacred river of the Ganges" (Hopgood 142); furthermore, protestors threatened to set themselves on fire if the filming were to continue (Coleman 19). On the day that filming was set to begin, approximately 2,000 protesters stormed the ghats and destroyed the film's main set. As a result, Mehta delayed filming for four years, and eventually "filmed *Water* in a 45-day shoot in Sri Lanka under the working title *River Moon*, to avoid attention and troubles" (Hopgood 150). *Water*, once it finally reached the light of day, was nominated for an Oscar for Best Foreign Language Film in 2005 (Mukherjee 35). In a short documentary, "The Making of Water," that is included on the DVD version of the film, Mehta claims that the reason protests began even before the first day of filming was because rumors that the film was anti-Hindu had begun to circulate as a result of a leaked earlier version of the script.

Of the controversy, Jacqueline Levitin asks, "why such opposition in a city that, although indeed holy, is host to production companies shooting action films and love stories almost daily?" (271), and she then provides a compelling answer:

> The filmmaker has become embroiled in the decades-old polarization between left and right, secular and theocratic in India, a battle that extends beyond India's borders via the non-resident players of the South Asian diaspora. For detractors and defenders, Mehta may be simply a pawn in the current chapter of this civil conflict. But through her filmmaking, and in the international responses she has rallied to her defense, she has also *taken a role*, both national and international, in this conflict. (271, my emphasis)

What is interesting to me in this reading of Mehta's position with regard to the opposition that surrounded the film is Levitin's recognition of Mehta's status as an actor—taking up and performing a specific role—in the current narrative moment, a "chapter" in the history of the battle between the secular and theocratic components and contingencies in India. It may have been possible, in the wake of the uproar over the screening of *Fire*, to read Mehta as merely a "pawn" in this battle, but with *Water*, her ability to utilize controversy in a way that was ultimately beneficial to her career is a palpable reality; having already experienced a fundamentalist backlash with the first film in the trilogy, the outcry against the final film could hardly have come as a much of a surprise—even as the intensity of fundamentalist reaction to *Water* could not have been anticipated. It also seems that the actions on behalf of opposition to Mehta's film were likewise scripted, as discussion of the fundamentalist protests focuses on the way both the Indian government and various protestors were involved in the "staging" of their discord. According to Richard Phillips and Waruna Alahakoon, "*behind the scenes*, in fact, the state government and senior figures in the central government...encouraged the provocations" (my emphasis), and "police officers made no attempt to arrest any of those responsible." Furthermore, "a Shiva Sena member tied rocks to his body and jumped into the river in protest. According to press reports the man, who is known for staging suicide protests, leapt into the river three times before he was able to attract media attention."

Whereas the controversy that surrounded *Fire* erupted after the film had already been made, violent reaction to *Water* began prior to filming. Therefore, the enactment of protest and its subsequent effects on filming are caught up in the dissemination of a narrative of exiled widows during Gandhi's rise to power—and it is quite possible to read *Water* as Mehta's metafictional commentary on her own displacements: the film is haunted by a desire, by protagonist and filmmaker, to return to a now inaccessible "home." The story of the controversy, of Mehta's being forced to film in Sri Lanka as opposed to India, is almost the larger story, and Mehta's daughter even wrote a book, *Shooting Water* (2006), about the experience. As Hopgood notes, "the story of *Water's* production is as compelling as the film itself. Indeed, the saga of the film's survival threatens to overshadow the finished product" (142). In terms of the historical status of Hindu widows in India, Mukherjee claims that when a woman is widowed, "she begins to be regarded as a disruptor of the social order...because a woman is not regarded as an independent being. As a widow, she is reduced to a void, a zero. The question arises about where to place her" (36). In the context of this essay's preceding discussion of Mehta, the issues that affect the status and placement of widows—issues of determining an appropriate "home" for them or for women in general, a concept that all of Mehta's films interrogate—Mukherjee's analysis resonates with Mehta herself, a disruptor of the social order, a transnational filmmaker who, as a result of the fact that she immigrated to Canada and because her films place her at odds with many Indians, is unable to successfully claim a specific placement, an unequivocal home. In *Water*, Chuhiya (Sarala Kariyawasam) continually tells the other widows that she will not be staying, that she will be going home soon. When, near the end of the film, Shakuntala (Seema Biswas) tells her that she is never going home, Chuhiya answers, "I know." Given the difficulties that Mehta experienced in terms of filming her trilogy—and of being forced to film *Water* outside of India—Chuhiya's statement is, perhaps, also Mehta's, the admission of a filmmaker whose project continually displaces her.

As was the case with *Earth*, *Water* is also focalized through the eyes of a child, this time seven-year-old Chuhiya, who becomes a widow without even realizing that she had been married. Unlike Lenny, however, Chuhiya actively questions the injustices of her situation, as do two other widows, Kalyani (Lisa

Ray), who falls in love with an idealistic disciple of Gandhi named Narayan (John Abraham), and Shakuntala, who finally breaks with tradition and rescues Chuhiya from a life of inevitable prostitution. The film opens with an excerpt from the Laws of Manu from the *Dharamshastras*: "A widow should be long suffering until death, self-restrained and chaste. A virtuous wife who remains chaste when her husband has died goes to heaven. A woman who is unfaithful to her husband is reborn in the womb of a jackal." The film traces the stories of three such widows as they seek to make sense of their alienation and as they come to the conscious realization that, as Narayan tells Shakuntala after Kalyani commits suicide, "disguised as religion, [the reason why widows are banished is] all about money." Kalyani's suicide by drowning, committed after she realizes, on the way to meet Narayan's parents, that Narayan's father has engaged her in prostitution, harkens back to Sita's trial by fire and to Spivak's discussion of both the British outlawing of the practice of *sati* and her analysis of the suicide of a young woman who killed herself while menstruating in order to assure that no one would read her death as the result of an illicit pregnancy.

Figure 11: Lisa Ray as Kalyani and Sarala as Chuhiya. (Fox Searchlight/Photofest)

Kalyani's suicide functions, within the context of Mehta's film as well as in the context of my analysis of the discourse surrounding Mehta's project with the elemental trilogy, to overdetermine the ways that various voicings and silencings—of Indian women, Mehta's fictional representations, and Mehta herself—are co-opted and imbricated in the stories that make up the political and mythological narratives that Mehta both deconstructs and rewrites. In Mukherjee's reading, in its depiction of this suicide, *Water* "succeeds in making apparent the helplessness of a woman trapped within the social grid when she had neither the means nor the opportunities of standing by herself in defiance of society" (45). But we must also consider Kalyani's suicide in the context of Mehta's backwards-looking lens; despite the fact that the film closes with the statement that "there are over 34 million widows in India according to the 2001 Census," and "many continue to live in conditions of social, economic, and cultural deprivation as prescribed 2000 years ago by the Sacred Texts of Manu," we have seen, in the two films that precede *Water*, the ways that history and story alter a reading of Hindu women's choice as being limited to suicide or alienation. It is easy to read a kind of progression in women's ability to choose from Kalyani, who takes her own life, to Shanta, who fights against the men who abduct her, to Sita and Radha who save each other from immolation and male domination.

***

I would like to return now to my initial premise in this chapter, that, despite the overwhelming success of Mehta's elemental trilogy, after the success of *Slumdog Millionaire* (*SM*)—which won eight Academy Awards including Best Picture in 2008—we find ourselves in a contemporary moment during which India is, once again, spoken for and about by white British men: the film was directed by Danny Boyle[13] and produced by another British man, Christian Colson. The screenplay was adapted from Indian novelist Vikas Swarup's 2005 novel *Q & A* by Simon Beaufoy, an Englishman best known for having written *The Full Monty* (1997). Simon Beaufoy has spoken specifically of the role of the white filmmaker in India as the liberator of Indian narrative:

> Bollywood cinema is always about beautiful, rich people marrying well and doing dances in front of the Matterhorn to fabulous music, and suddenly a film comes along which shows the slums. It has really disturbed the status quo, sparking an argument not just about whether outsiders should make a film about slum dwellers but whether a film should show slums at all. Indian film directors have been very warm and generous. They believe it will allow them to do things in future that were unacceptable before. (qtd. in Rose)

This satement seems particularly arrogant given the extent to which Mehta's work has interrogated that which is "unacceptable" in India as well as the ways that Mira Nair's 1988 film *Saalam Bombay!* depicted street children and the slums of Bombay, and such sentiment speaks to the ways that white male filmmakers such as Boyle, Beaufoy, and Colson feel entitled to speak for India despite their supposed recognition of the problems that such a stance raises. For example, to do a just reading of Danny Boyle as a filmmaker worthy of postcolonial critique would require another chapter, but Boyle's work almost always engages with the politics of colonization. From his exploration of heroin-addicted DIY Scottish stoners in *Trainspotting* (1996)—during which Renton pontificates, "most people hate the English, but I don't. They're just wankers. We, on the other hand, were colonized by wankers. We can't even find a decent culture to be colonized by"—to *Sunshine* (2007), a sci-fi thriller with overtones of *Heart of Darkness*, to *Slumdog Millionaire* (2008), set in Mumbai, Boyle has, sometimes overtly, sometimes tacitly, engaged with both colonial politics and locales. Boyle's creation of a "gameshow Bollywood picaresque" (Tyree 34), which follows the life of slum-dweller Jamal Malik (Dev Patel) as he gleans, over the course of his childhood, information that will allow him to succeed on *Who Wants To Be a Millionaire?*, raises complex issues with regard to much of what I have already discussed in terms of Mehta: the authority of the outsider filmmaker to speak "truth" about India, and the role of intentionality in terms of the presentation of negative images of India. With regard to the role of women, Boyle's film, focalized through Jamal, is a fairy-tale story of the rescue of the female protagonist Latika (Freida Pinto) from the clutches of men—one of whom is Jamal's brother Salim (Madhur Mittal)—who exploit her, sell her into prostitution, and physically abuse her.

Like *Earth* and *Water*, *SM* is largely focalized through the eyes of a child, but in this instance, the child is male. The film is a "touchy-feely feature replete with platitudes about eternal love that indulges in backroom police torture, child prostitution, begging rackets, and anti-Muslim massacres" (Tyree 34), and such a disparate union of love story and violence creates a film that, according to J. M. Tyree, "wants to have it both ways by allowing images of actual horror into a Bollywood-like dream and then letting us off the hook by suggesting not only that true love conquers all, but also that personal decency results in a million dollar payday" (36). The film's narrative operates under the assumption that Jamal is able to win the money and rescue the girl—despite overwhelming poverty, abuse, and lack of formal education—because "it is written," a statement that appears on screen as the film opens. Starting with this statement, *SM*, in terms of both its content and the discourse that it generated, can be read as a counter-narrative to Mehta's filmic depictions of female choice and agency; Mehta's work challenges the idea that just because something "is written"—as is the case with Hindu proscriptions for widows in the Laws of Manu or the story of Sita's trial by fire in the *Ramayana* or the official 1948 figure for the number of women abducted and raped during the partition riots—it must be the truth. *SM*, in its generation of an implausible predestined triumph, one dependent on Jamal's ability to win money in the context of a British-imported game show, posits a rags-to-riches, individualistic, Western-style Cinderella story as unalterable myth, written and codified *nowhere* except within the context of the film itself. Therefore, the film, as source for *where* "it is written," becomes a prophetic text that silences female characters and female filmmakers.

It is not surprising that *SM* generated controversy, particularly in that it coined the derogatory term "slumdog" and in that Boyle has been plagued with accusations that he underpaid his child stars. While Boyle asserted that he made the film to showcase Mumbai and to honor its "lust for life," he has also noted that he was ignorant about India prior to making the film: "I knew nothing about India.... I love [starting] off naked. I learned as I went along. That sense of discovery hopefully comes through in the film. To me, that's exciting" (qtd. in Aaron). Boyle's status as an outsider has worked in two conflicting ways for him with regard to this film. On the one hand, he has been able to generate a narrative that, according to Arindham Chowdry, would have been "trashed like an old hat" had it been made by an Indian filmmaker ("The *Slumdog* Controversy"), but on the other, "*Times of London* political and national affairs columnist Alice Miles called Slumdog 'vile...poverty porn' that invites the audience to enjoy the misery it depicts," and "Amitabh Bachchan...formerly a presenter on India's *Who Wants To Be A Millionaire?*,...has criticized the drama's 'Western' qualities" (Quill). Despite the criticism that the film engendered, it nonetheless garnered a huge following, both in India and abroad, and has earned nearly four times as much as the highest grossing Bollywood film of all time.[14] The success of the film marks a new era in the politics of transnational filmmaking and demonstrates the potential not only for the cultural colonization of India by the West, but a willingness on the part of Indians to buy into—in both the literal and figurative sense—Western interpretations of Indian culture. Sudesh Mishra cites the example of Mumbai-based billionaire Anil Ambani who, in 2008, purchased 200 movie theaters in the U.S. and linked up with

Nicolas Cage's Saturn Productions, George Clooney's Smokehouse Productions, Tom Hanks's Playtone Productions, Brad Pitt's Plan B Entertainment, and Jim Carrey's JC 23 Entertainment, with the intention of coproducing films in Hollywood. In a deal worth 1.5 billion dollars, Ambani has audaciously teamed up with Steven Spielberg to establish a film studio in Hollywood with the aim of shooting thirty or so films in the next five years. Such transnational collaborations, targeting an international viewing population stratified and differentiated according to class, language, life style, and cinematic expectation, are bound to impinge on the form and content of future films, whether produced in Mumbai or Los Angeles. (326)

I quote Mishra at some length because the above information points to the power of male-owned Hollywood production companies to generate, disseminate, and market "India." That Ambani brokered this deal during the same year that *SM* demonstrated the money-making power of such collaborative endeavors seems not coincidental; that the India that is marketed through such venues will continue to be largely male-authored seems a certainty.

The Hollywood machine, like *SM*'s assertion that Jamal (and therefore the film) will succeed because "it is written," is a self-perpetuating truism. Of *SM*'s success, Arun Gupta notes that "Hollywood's goal…is not to succeed as a creative fount but as a profit hub," and that the Academy lavished *SM* with Oscars not because of the quality of the film but because of its box-office success: "what Hollywood is really celebrating is its ability to mine other cultures for raw material, manufacture a bland product with wide appeal, and use its marketing juggernaut to rack up enormous profits." Gupta reads Boyle's film as a textbook example of Orientalism à la Edward Said, "a 'semi-mythical construct' of the Orient,…a 'Western style for dominating, restructuring and having authority over the Orient' (as Edward Said defines it). It's the cultural logic of the imperialist conquest of the East." One of the mythical constructs that *SM* offers is in its presentation of Latika as part damsel in distress and part child bride/prostitute—a hybridity that plays on two familiar (to a Western audience) ideas of femininity. First, Latika continually needs to be rescued from various men and is, therefore, devoid of any agency in terms of deciding her own destiny; she is, in fact, Jamal's "destiny," as he asserts during the film. Latika functions, in typical Hollywood fashion, as the impetus for all the male action that takes place in the film; Jamal even claims that he agrees to appear on *Who Wants To Be a Millionaire?* because he thinks Latika might be watching. Furthermore, Latika come to the train station to meet Jamal at the end of the film, but the two are only able to escape together *after* he wins the money. Therefore, she is a late capitalist-era fairy-tale princess, rescued by her prince, destined to live happily ever after. The second, perhaps competing, idea of femininity is of Latika, as both a child and young woman, as a victim of the sex trade—an idea that is a part of a highly visible mainstream Western media discourse about non-Western cultures' treatment of women. Latika, like Spivak's subaltern woman, is doubly victimized as a player in two narratives of female helplessness: the Western-styled princess and the third-world prostitute.

Figure 12: Dev Patel as Jamal and Freida Pinto as Latika. (Warner Bros./Photofest)

It is worth noting here, as I did in the context of Mehta's films, that *SM* makes no claim to truth; the film is highly fanciful and improbable. If we can read Mehta's narratives as dialogic stories invested in the deconstruction and restitution of political and mythological history, then perhaps we should afford Boyle the same courtesy, and I might be willing to do so, if it were not for the question of Loveleen Tandan, the Indian woman who started out as casting director but was promoted, by Boyle, to co-director (in India) of *SM*. Given that the entire movie was filmed in India, Tandan's designation as co-director in India *only* seems odd. According to Aaron Tristin, many of the film's cultural decisions were made by Tandan, who worked closely on the film's direction. However, "the absence of nominations for Tandan for any directing awards, and the fact that she apparently wasn't invited to be present at the ceremonies…has raised questions about the proper acknowledgement of women and people of color in filmmaking" (Aaron). Tandan has said that she is embarrassed by the suggestion that she should have been recognized alongside Boyle, but regardless of this stance and Boyle's assertion that he hopes Tandan's work on *SM* will push her to do more directing, Tandan's official omission from award-based public recognition is telling. Boyle may have "saved" Tandan, by providing her with an opportunity to work as a director, but her absence from consideration for the awards associated with this film undermines her contributions and voicings—Tandan was even responsible for talking Boyle into letting the child actors speak Hindi instead of English.

At this point, I would like to return to Spivak's sentence: "White men are saving brown women from brown men." As I have already noted, Spivak constructed this sentence in order to examine the discourse surrounding the British outlawing of the practice of *sati* or widow immolation, but in Boyle's project with *Slumdog Millionaire*, I see this sentence carried out. In the context of the predestined mythology of Boyle's film, Latika is saved from numerous "brown men" because "it is written" (and therefore unalterable) by Boyle and Beaufoy; despite the fact that she is saved, within the context of the filmic narrative, by Jamal, within the discourse of appropriate Indian femininity, Boyle and Beaufoy silence her (as a stand-in for Mehta's Sita, Radha, Shanta, and Kulyani)—as they do Loveleen Tandan—by refusing to allow her to disrupt the narrative of white male transcendence.

Notes

1. Rushdie responded, "join the club." In the same interview, Mehta makes a counter claim, asserting, "if I think of myself as an Indian filmmaker, it cuts me off from the rest of the world."

2. According to Fincina Hopgood, "a Hindu who lives in Toronto, Mehta's uncompromising examination of her home country's traditions and history has resulted in her being branded a troublemaker by conservative politicians in India, such as provincial finance minister Harish Chandra Srivastava" who has claimed that Mehta is always up to "mischief" (144).

3. Barron notes that many people who supported *Fire* did so from a perspective that "the film is not about lesbianism but is instead a 'universal' story" (69). The claim of universalism is problematic, here as elsewhere, in that it erases the specificities that the film addresses: queerness, femaleness, Indianness.

4. Mehta's work contains elements of the Bollywood tradition, even as she incorporates those elements in a way that allows her a broader viewership. Of Bollywood film, Jigna Desai claims that "most commercial Indian films are often characterized as unappealing to Western viewers…because of their content and aesthetic forms that derive from diverse Indian sources including Pari theater and Hindu performances. These three-hour films are often identifiable by their all-encompassing forms that include elements of comedy, (melo)drama, action, romance, and music that do not fit Western aesthetic expectations" (41).

5. Alexandra Lynn Barron, Gayatri Gopinath, and Kulvinder Arora all examine the controversy surrounding *Fire* in great detail.

6. I do not feel comfortable referring to Sita and Radha's relationship as "lesbian," as this label forecloses the meaning of a relationship that these characters claim has no name.

7. Jigna Desai supports this reading as well, claiming that *Fire* "does not present the relationship between Radha and Sita as some form of lesbianism imported from the West, nor does it assert some traditional Indian same-sex relationship traceable to the kama sutra" (164).

8. The film does, however, allude to this violence: Ice Candy Man's sisters are murdered and Shanta is abducted, at the behest of Ice Candy Man after he sees her making love with Masseur, by a group of Muslim men at the end of the film.

9. Sidhwa's novel was originally titled *Ice Candy Man* when it was released in India 1989.

10. Sidhwa helped Mehta with the adaptation of the novel, and she appears in the film as the grown-up Lenny (Herman 110).

11. In the novel, this character is referred to by her title, "Ayah," and not her name, "Shanta." In the film, she is called Ayah by Lenny and Shanta by other characters.

12. In a segment on the controversy surrounding *Fire* called "Firestorm" that is included on the DVD, Mehta says, "nothing had prepared me for the way the Shiv Sena attached *Fire*."

13. Loveleen Tandan is credited as co-director.

14. According to Arun Gupta, "showing the muscle of Hollywood, *Slumdog* has grossed more than $200 million worldwide, far outstripping the most successful Bollywood film ever, *Sholay*, which has grossed $60 million (inflation adjusted) since its 1975 premiere."

Conclusion

Intercultural Film in 2009: The Year of South Africa and Pandora

***

As we mention in our introduction, the impetus behind the writing of this book was the dissemination of a discourse analysis assignment that we gave to a group of graduate students in our Postcolonial Film seminar in 2006. In terms of this assignment, students were to examine how we, as Westerners, come to know, understand, and, in many ways, own a concept of "Africa" in the contemporary moment and to discuss how our understandings of this entity are the products of various—often problematic—political and commercial interests emanating from within and outside of imagined and real Africas. We based the assignment on our and our students' readings of two 2006 films, *Blood Diamond* and *The Last King of Scotland*, and the 2006 *Vanity Fair* "Africa" issue. In 2006, our awareness of the multitude of discourses and counter-discourses with regard to the construction of Africa was somewhat nascent. Since that time, however, we have felt overwhelmed by the sheer amount of material that popular culture continues to offer us as we have worked through this project, from white American celebrities' persistent adoption of African children,[1] to the media brouhaha over the fact that, in 2008, Sarah Palin thought that Africa was a country and not a continent (Graham), to HBO's production of a series based on Alexander McCall Smith's *No. 1 Ladies' Detective Agency*, to *The Onion's* Sunday, November 22, 2009, weekly satirical report that "a brutal coalition of Hollywood A-listers took control of the entire continent" after becoming distressed with the ineffectual nature of their humanitarian efforts: "stars including Brad Pitt and Gwyneth Paltrow[2] led a rag-tag army of fans, extras, and paparazzi to a bloody overthrow of all 53 sovereign countries." Such instances serve to illuminate the obvious fact that—whether we realize it is a continent or not—Africa, as an idea and as a physical location, is very much a part of the mainstream American imagination.

While our study begins with an analysis of the role of the white man in Africa as that trope is played out in *Blood Diamond* and *Last King of Scotland*, we move away from imagined Africas in subsequent chapters to explore other locales—

India, New Zealand, and the Caribbean—but throughout our study, we train a consistent eye on the fact that the discourses that shape our understandings of other cultures are mythic, changeable narratives, subject to political, social, global, and economic pressures. In our analysis of *The Last King of Scotland* and *Blood Diamond*, our focus was consistent with the mandate that we assigned our students. In this chapter, we paid particular attention to the way that both films perpetuate Conrad's legacy as defined by Chinua Achebe in his 1975 "An Image of Africa" speech; through a dismissal of specific cultures and histories via the phrase "this is Africa," both films render Africa as a monolithic entity that functions as background for the coming to consciousness of the white man. In both films, Africa is depicted as absolute Other to both the United States and the United Kingdom, a space rife with violence, plagued by inept leadership, and in need of Western salvation. Similarly, *Tsotsi*, as both a novel and a film, is a story imagined by white South African men, Athol Fugard and Gavin Hood. But we provide a reading of both film and novel as discourses of witness; therefore, the narrative of the black South African man, Tsotsi/David, the film's protagonist, is rendered via the gaze instead of the voice—or its omission. In this case, the white narrative resists a sense of "speaking for" the other, and such a position inherently generates ambiguity with regard to how to depict that which lies outside the realm of the personal experiences of both author and director. As a result of this ambiguity, both Fugard and Hood generate multiple and dialogic endings to their apartheid and post-apartheid era tellings of this particular story.

We leave Africa for New Zealand in our analysis of *Once Were Warriors* and *Whale Rider*, two films that we read as contemporary reinventions of the trope of the Maoriland romance genre that was part and parcel of New Zealand's filmic imaginary Maori culture early in the twentieth century. We read both films in the context of the novels—both written by Maori men—that preceded them in order to examine the ways that women, Riwia Brown, the screenwriter for *Once Were Warriors*, and Niki Caro, the director of *Whale Rider*, generate more female-centric narratives of Maori nation-building that are both overtly aware of the role that myth plays in the maintenance of tradition and simultaneously able to challenge and reshape myth in the construction of the contemporary Maori nation. The role that women play in the construction of national narrative is further examined and critiqued in our analysis of white female objectification and sexualization of the bodies and identities of the colonial Other, both male and female, in the Caribbean. In this part of our study, we posit an analysis that situates the tension between travel, tourism, and the exotic within the realm of the female gaze in order to explore the way various film adaptations of *Jane*

Eyre and *Heading South* generate a problematic discourse of female complicity with and ineffectual aversion to the colonial project. Finally, in our analysis of non-resident Indian filmmakers Mira Nair and Deepa Mehta, we examine the discourse that surrounded the production and release of films that sought to tell stories of India but were created by transnational female filmmakers. We examine the possibility that in the current post-*Slumdog Millionaire* moment, white male narrative works to silence the subaltern female voice.

***

To conclude, then, we arrive in the present discursive moment, a period in intercultural film history marked by a particular focus on South Africa, as evidenced by three 2009 releases, Steve Jacob's adaptation of J. M. Coetzee's 1999 Booker Prize winning novel *Disgrace*,[3] Johannesburg native Neill Blomkamp's sciencefiction thriller, *District 9*, and Clint Eastwood's *Invictus*, the adaptation of John Carlin's 2008 *Playing the Enemy: Nelson Mandela and the Game that Made a Nation*. All three were filmed and set in post-apartheid South Africa, and they are all political narratives, to varying degrees: *Disgrace*, true to Coetzee's novel, offers an ambiguously bleak view of the post-apartheid South African world—a world in the throes of sexual violence and AIDS—of the late 1990s. Conversely, *Invictus* offers an inspirational look at the period just prior, the mid-1990s, and Nelson Mandela's ascension to occupy the role of the first black democratically elected president of that country, a period, we are led to believe, during which the scars from hundreds of years of racial oppression can be healed by a game of rugby. *District 9* provides social commentary about the present twenty-first century South African moment, marked as it is by increasing xenophobia. The film, a full-fledged science fiction thriller about the relocation of an alien species that arrived in Johannesburg nearly two decades earlier, uses archival news footage of black South Africans speaking against the influx of displaced and economically dispossessed Zimbabweans that has taken place during the past decade.

A brief look at this trinity of narratives is revelatory in terms of how we have, heretofore, mapped a theory of the intercultural as a space, both transnational and specific, delineated by a concern with the liminal and perhaps preoccupied with the concept of truth. *Disgrace*, based on a novel by a white South African man, was directed by a white American man, and produced—after considerable financial difficulty—by Screen Australia. The film's director, Steven Jacobs, speaks in an interview with Anders Wotzke about the difficulty of getting funding to film in South Africa:

We tried for quite a few years to actually get funding from South Africa, but it was unsuccessful.... It's just unfortunate that there is not one dollar of South African money in the film, and when we didn't get the rebate from [the Australian] government, that was a further disappointment.... It's considered an Australian film, which we went through the taxation department to get that classification. Screen Australia also thought it deserved funding, because it was going to show off the abilities of many Australians behind the camera and a few in front of it.

The film chronicles the journey of David Lurie (John Malkovich), a white English professor at Cape Town University, who engages in a sexual relationship with a colored student named Melanie (Antoinette Engel) and loses his position as a result of her complaint against him. After this disgrace, David, unrepentant for his actions, travels to the Eastern Cape to visit his lesbian daughter Lucy (Jessica Haines), who shares her smallholding with Petrus (Eriq Ebouaney), a black man who helps her care for the dogs she kennels. When Lucy is raped and David set on fire by men who are somehow connected to Petrus, David is forced to confront the shifting power differential in the "new" South Africa.

Coetzee's novel was roundly criticized by the African National Congress for its depiction of the rape of a white woman by three black South African men. Rachel Donadio, in a 2007 *New York Times* essay chronicling Coetzee's move from South Africa to Australia, notes the South African controversy surrounding the novel:

In public hearings on racism in the media held by the government's Human Rights Commission, the African National Congress accused Coetzee of representing "as brutally as he can the white people's perception of the post-apartheid black man," and of implying that in the new regime whites would "lose their cards, their weapons, their property, their rights, their dignity," while "the white women will have to sleep with the barbaric black men."

Literary criticism of the novel has taken a wide range of forms, from exploring Coetzee's allegorization of the Truth and Reconciliation Commission, to the role of animals in David's transformation (or lack thereof), to the nature of secular confession, to name a few.[4] Coetzee's work, in *Disgrace* and elsewhere, offers no easy answers to South Africa's various dilemmas; his characters, consistent outsiders, are seldom likable, and their stories constitute exercises in self-reflexivity, explorations of the nature of truth telling, and critiques of the concept of a master narrative of history—for both character and writer. Coetzee, as a writer who always avoids taking an overtly political stance, is often posited as the Other of Nadine Gordimer, South Africa's other white Nobel Prize-winning novelist; while Gordimer's work always interrogates the political, Coetzee is a writer who refuses to "appropriately" engage with South Africa's most pressing issues and whose narrative endings tend toward ambivalence. While various factions have called on Coetzee to take a side, the dialogic nature of his work is what makes it so provocative.

While Coetzee's novel is narrated through the free indirect discourse of a third-person narrator and focalized through the character of David Lurie, the film is, of course, focalized through the viewer. Therefore, the narrative perspective that generates ambiguity with regard to Melanie and David's "affair" in the novel is completely absent from the film: her utter disgust is palpable, visible on her face and apparent in her feeble attempts to refuse his advances. While the film stays extremely close to the novel, this shift in perspective allows for the audience to see the various other characters not simply from David's perspective—although the camera does focus on David watching Melanie at various points—and the effect allows these other characters, players in the drama of David Lurie in Coetzee's novel, to be more fully realized. As Stephen Holden notes, the film is "a hard-headed allegorical meditation on the bestial side of human nature and its reflection in a poisoned social climate in the throes of change," and "is all the more devastating for being so coolly dispassionate." As a film, *Disgrace* rips to shreds both the buddy film genre and the salvation narrative of the white man in Africa. The alliance that David forms with Petrus is not one of friendship, and Petrus is as morally complicated as is David; he is not the noble and gentle Other, but a man situated, like the rest of the characters, within the confines of a post-apartheid historical moment in which power is being renegotiated and old structures demolished. And David is not a white savior of any kind; in a narrative in which the battle for South African sovereignty is played out on the proving ground of the racialized female bodies of both Melanie and Lucy, Lurie remains unable to save himself, his career, his daughter, or even the dogs he helps to euthanize. The film, like the novel that preceded it, refuses to offer any solution to the various crises that mark the contemporary South African moment, and it resists the enactment or generation of a national mythology of either despair or triumph. In its refusal to take a side, then, *Disgrace*, instead of telling its audience how it should feel, opens up a space for active engagement with South African history.

Like *Disgrace*, Neill Blomkamp's *District 9* is similarly transnational in that it was filmed in South Africa but produced by New Zealand filmmaker Peter Jackson.

Made for "roughly $30 million, which is about how much money Jackson spent on the Orc makeup for *Return of the King*" (Douthat 50), *District 9* grossed five times as much as *Tsotsi* in South Africa. The film, Blomkamp's first, is, ostensibly, the least political of the three, focusing on the plight of both a displaced group of aliens—called "prawns" by the resident South Africans—and of Wikus Van De Merwe (the heretofore unknown Sharlto Copley), the white yes-man whose work for Multinational United (MNU) sends him into the prawn slums of District 9 to deliver eviction notices and search for alien weapons. During the course of his machinations, the utterly unlikable Wikus, who at first seems to be imitating Steve Carell's character on the sitcom *The Office*, is contaminated with alien DNA, which causes him to begin to turn into a prawn. When MNU captures and tries to dissect him, Wikus flees and is able to escape with the help of Christopher Johnson, an alien who, along with his son, has readied an underground spacecraft to return to his home planet and who tells Wikus that he can procure the antidote for his condition. On the one hand, the film plays out the familiar conventions of the buddy movie à la *Blood Diamond* in which a morally bankrupt white man befriends a noble and benevolent non-white man whose friendship enables him to get in touch with the better angels of his being. On the other, the film makes no claim of appealing to our higher moral functions, concerning itself instead with the conventions of the science fiction and action genres, dependent as they are on bloody violence and acts of outrageous heroism. In fact, the film's lack of an overt political narrative was a problem for many viewers and critics. Joshua Clover, who notes that the film is "fab genre fare," claims that *District 9* tests "the limits of allegory," and that it is not about apartheid but "perhaps concerns superfluous populations in general." Clover states that the film's lapse into the action idiom has "annoyed numerous commentators, drawn by the promise of nuance and liberal position-taking, disappointed by the formulaic banality of mere genre fare."

But despite its status as "mere genre fare," the film drew protests from Nigerians who were displeased at the film's portrayal of them as gangsters and cannibals. Of this reaction and of claims that the film is mere fluff, Blomkamp claims:

> For the most part, *District 9* is absolute popcorn...compared to how serious those real-life topics are. The topics in the film are on my mind all the time and they're very interesting to me. The bottom line is *District 9* touches on one percent of those topics in terms of how severe they could be portrayed, and I knew that when I made it. But people got the messages. Xenophobia, racism

allegories—they got all of it. I don't think the film was misunderstood. Not everybody loved it. Nigerians weren't happy. They were pissed. And I suppose that's fair enough because I directly named them and they don't come off well in the film. But that was part of the whole satirical nature of the film. (Boucher)

District 9 subtly undermines the notion that politics must be of preeminent concern in South African narrative, but the metaphorical care it takes in its presentation of the very real and often dire circumstances in which black Africans find themselves is significant. Lucius Shepard notes that reviewing such a movie is a challenge because it will mean to American audiences something quite different than it will mean "to audiences cognizant of the fact that the nation has undergone a decline under the leadership of President Zuma" (189). Certainly the film will mean different things to its various international audiences, but one symbol can, we think, be read consistently across cultures. The ship that breaks down over Johannesburg hangs in the air above the city for over two decades. It is a colossal and seemingly permanent presence, evidence of a technologically savvy and significant culture, rendered meaningless within the South African moment into which it has descended. The ship remains unviable in the present, a visible artifact of a now inaccessible past. It is a silent testament to the loss of African cultural identity and heritage in the face of empire, and one could almost forget it was there if one never bothered to look up. The ship, then, is the legacy of not only apartheid, now in the past but still hanging over the entire country, but a testament to the persistence of memory of various African histories.

Figure 13: Sharlto Copley as Wikus Van De Merwe (foreground), with the "prawn" spaceship overhead. (TriStar/Photofest)

Clint Eastwood's *Invictus*, produced by Morgan Freeman, retells the historical story of South Africa's 1995 World Cup win over New Zealand. Nelson Mandela (Freeman), newly elected, decides that it is in the country's best interest for the Afrikaaner rugby team the Springboks—all white except for one member—to win the World Cup, so he befriends Springbok captain François Pienaar (Matt Damon) and encourages him, via the presentation of British poet William Ernest Henley's 1875 poem "Invictus," to accomplish this seemingly impossible task. The Springboks are a symbol of the old apartheid order and are universally hated by black South Africans who, as Mandela notes, always cheer for the opposing team. Over the course of the film, Pienaar comes to understand that his country has changed and that the Springboks—and Pienaar himself—must change as well. And many changes, within Pienaar and his fellow Afrikaaner countrymen as well as within the black South African population, occur over the course of the film: the Springboks learn the new South African national anthem, and Pienaar, after a visit to Mandela's jail cell on Robben Island, says, "I was thinking how a man could spend thirty years in prison, and come out and forgive the men who did it to him." When the Springboks win, black and white South Africans embrace and dance in the streets, the racial inequalities that have marked hundreds of years temporarily forgiven in the shared triumph of this symbolic moment. Eastwood's film relies on sentiment and strong performances by both Damon, who spent a great deal of time with Pienaar in order to get into character, and Freeman, who has claimed that "he was chosen by Mandela, who, in essence, told him over a decade ago that if there was to be a film made about him, he would like the actor to portray him" (Misani 17).

Despite its Oscar-worthy pedigree, this story—the only "true" story told by any of these three films—rings much more false than the other two, perhaps in large part because it was released after them but is set in a period that predates them; *Invictus* exists in a singular moment, at once very much a part of South African history and simultaneously outside of it, that requires its audience to disregard the more contemporary and stark South African realities presented in *Disgrace* and *District 9*. For anyone familiar with South African history, *Invictus* can feel very much like a work of mourning rather than inspiration, a testament to a hope that remains unfulfilled. As famous South African author and political dissident Breyten Breytenbach states in an interview, "the victory and ensuing celebration certainly make for uplifting cinema material, but the political significance was short-lived. The poor were still poor, and getting poorer and more desperate by the day; the rich, if they could, took their money elsewhere" (qtd. in Thompson).[5] And in its invocation of the promise for the first democratically elected black president, American viewers may be tempted to draw historically inappropriate comparisons between their country's recent presidential election and Mandela's.

While A. O. Scott praises Freeman's depiction of Mandela, "played with gravity, grace, and a crucial spark of mischief," as someone who "knows that score-settling would be a disastrous course for a new and fragile democracy" (1), Brian Moore notes the film's tendency to omit the various controversies surrounding the South African win, most notably "the indirect claims by New Zealand that [its] players were poisoned and their sleep was deliberately interrupted before the final." Furthermore, Moore notes that the Springboks only "gradually won the backing of the black population. It was not there in 1994 nor when the tournament started." Finally, the film's main narrative arc, so clearly aimed at an American audience, is of Pienaar's transformation and development; this is not Mandela's story, as is made immediately clear by the film's publicity posters that feature Freeman's Mandela in shadow with his back turned toward the audience, his body enlarged to serve as a background for the illuminated and forward-facing Damon, the white man enlightened by the nobility of this most revered South African Other. As Nadine Gordimer has stated—and has been referenced elsewhere in this study—fiction is often truer than the so-called truth, and in the case of these three films about South Africa, the truths told by the fictions of *Disgrace* and *District 9* resonate more clearly and more pronouncedly than those expressed in *Invictus*, a narrative that seeks to capitalize on an instant of South African myth making that is rendered obsolete in the present.

Figure 14: Poster for *Invictus*, with Morgan Freeman as Nelson Mandela (background) and Matt Damon as François Pienaar. (Photofest/Warner Bros. Pictures)

***

We would be remiss if we ended our study without some mention of the phenomenon that is James Cameron's 2009 blockbuster *Avatar*, because to do so would be to overlook the ways that this film functions as an imaginary colonial narrative, one completely removed from—yet utterly entrenched in—the various postcolonial mythologies that we have so assiduously worked to explicate throughout this study. Cameron's CGI *Avatar*, which cost several hundred million dollars to make, is the highest grossing film in history, recently outpacing Cameron's 1997 feature *Titanic*. Since its December 2009 release, the film has become a cultural phenomenon, fueling such circumstances as an *Avatar* depression syndrome supposedly caused by moviegoers' realization that the world in which they live is not nearly as beautiful as Pandora (Piazza), to actual death: a 42-year-old Taiwanese man died of a stroke that was apparently brought on by the over-stimulation caused by watching the 3-D version of the movie (Sacks). The film, set in 2154, is the story of Jake Sully (Sam Worthington), a crippled marine who travels to the planet of Pandora, the home of the humanoid Na'vi, a ten-foot-tall, blue race of people, who hunt, gather, and literally hug trees. Sully, via control of a Na'vi avatar, gathers information about the Na'vi, the indigenous residents of Pandora, a planet rich in unobtainium, a mineral that can potentially save earth from the environmental destruction wreaked on the planet, which is now all but uninhabitable, by human beings. Sully begins his infiltration of the Na'vi with Colonel Miles Quaritch's (Stephen Lang) promise that, should Sully successfully complete his mission, his legs will be restored. Of course, once Sully begins to interact with the Na'vi, he becomes conflicted with regard to the ethics of his mission, especially after falling in love with Neytiri (Zoe Saldana), the beautiful daughter of the tribe's chief. The film concludes in an epic battle of good (Na'vi) versus evil (humans), and, amazingly, the technologically advanced humans prove no match for the mystical Na'vi who fly through the air on their Mountain Banshees and shoot arrows. At the end of the film, Sully's paraplegic human form is consumed by a tree and he is reborn, to live life among the Na'vi, as his avatar.

Suffice it to say that *Avatar*'s CGI effects are seamless and that the world of Pandora is an impressively realized fantasy. The nearly three-hour narrative, however, is not only formulaic and predictable, but the dialogue, in typical James Cameron fashion, is atrocious. But what is most stunning is the way that Cameron's expensive film invokes, in the cheapest and most misguided ways possible, an imaginary colonial mythology that runs completely counter to the discourses generated and enacted by the body of film we examine in this study. In Pandora and the Na'vi, we have a shoddy amalgamation, dependent upon base Western-authored cultural stereotypes, of various indigenous populations; there are elements of a Western idea of Native American identity—indeed the Pocahontas story is enacted almost verbatim in Sully's initial encounter with Neytiri's father—of African ancestor worship, and of Maori ornamentation, all of which are underscored by a seemingly innate Na'vi environmental ethos that is positioned as oppositional to the "civilizing" technology of the humans. Furthermore, *Avatar* constitutes the myth of the white savior writ large. As David Brooks discusses in his review of the film, "a racial fantasy par excellence" containing peace-loving natives "compiled from a mélange of Native American, African, Vietnamese, Iraqi and other cultural fragments," the white messiah fable is

> a pretty serviceable formula [that] gives movies a little socially conscious allure. Audiences like it because it is so environmentally sensitive. Academy Award voters like it because it is so multiculturally aware. Critics like it because the formula inevitably involves the loincloth-clad good guys sticking it to the military-industrial complex.

In *Avatar* we see, within the context of a major commercial success, the familiar and, we would like to believe, outdated tropes of both the white man going native and of serving as the salvation to a culture over which he gains immediate mastery. In *Avatar*'s treatment of these tropes, there is no self-awareness.

In creating a completely fictional culture and landscape to colonize, Cameron is still utilizing familiar and highly essentializing notions of real peoples and cultures in order to generate a composite Other; one can assume that, in the global era, it is no longer acceptable to assign Otherness to extant peoples, that now we must, in order to avoid charges of racism, create them. But these Others, as we indicate above, have too much in common with the historical stereotypes Westerners hold about multiple groups of colonized, exploited, and displaced peoples. And this film, so didactic in its apparent message of environmentalism and care for the planet, is propped up by the likes of McDonald's, a corporation long known and chastised for its unsustainable business practices.[6] As Achebe reads Conrad as a racist despite *Heart of Darkness*'s attention to the injustices done to native peoples as a result of the colonial project, one can similarly call Cameron's supposed environmental ethos into question. David Brooks notes that the narrative of the white man as savior rests on the stereotype that white people are rationalist and technocratic while colonial victims are spiritual and athletic. It rests on the assumption that nonwhites need the White Messiah to lead their crusades. It rests on the assumption that illiteracy is the path to grace. It also creates a sort of two-edged cultural imperialism. Natives can either have their history shaped by cruel imperialists or benevolent ones, but either way, they are going to be supporting actors in our journey to self-admiration.

It may seem unfair to come down so hard on *Avatar*, a fantasy that, like Blomkamp's *District 9*, is genre fare and "popcorn," an item meant only for indulgent and non-politically motivated consumption. Yet in the global world that has produced such nuanced intercultural films as those explored in our study, films that, regardless of their overall success, interrogate the malleability of colonialist and national mythology and seek to make sense of real instances of silencing and exploitation, we cannot turn a blind eye to the problematic national imaginings that Cameron's film puts forth. We hope that having read this study, our audience will engage in similarly sustained and unflinching critiques of filmic manifestations of empire and the Other, in whatever form they appear on the screen in the future.

Notes

1. Particularly the high-profile adoption of Madonna of Malawian children and Angelina Jolie of an Ethiopian child.

2. Paltrow's and other celebrity participation in Iman's "I am African" Keep a Child Alive campaign has generated significant backlash. Stars, many of them white and from the United States, appear wearing supposed war paint above the statement "I am African." The most notable parody of this campaign is a photo of an African woman pictured above the slogan "I am Gwyneth Paltrow." The image is available here: http://gawker.com/193729/gwyneths-african-ad-inspires-imitators

3. *Disgrace* premiered at the Toronto International Film Festival in 2008, but it was not released in Australia, the country that funded its filming, or the United States, until 2009.

4. For more on Coetzee, see Laura Wright, *Writing "Out of All the Camps": J. M. Coetzee's Narratives of Displacement*, New York: Routledge, 2006.

5.. In the same interview, Breytenbach eloquently characterizes South Africa as follows:

> For the vast majority life in South Africa is short, brutal, brutish, and desperate. That for the cadres it is a pig's trough. That for some Whites it is still a paradise of cocktails and well-watered lawns at the same time it is a place of cynicism and fear to flee from if they can, and where racism is resurgent. That for most Coloreds it is a place of confusion, sometimes of posturing, often of bitterness.

> That for foreign Africans it is mostly hell. A place where, it is predicted, two or more out of every five children in 15 years' time will be AIDS orphans. Where life expectancy has dropped by nearly seven years. Where Indians have collectively become the richest community. Where language policies are no longer a question of "race," but of class. Where the wine is good and nature spectacular. Where people are immensely hospitable.

> Where you will be killed for a cell phone and count yourself lucky not to have been tortured. Where everybody is a believer, and even robbers pray for success before going out on a killing spree. Where capital punishment has been

abolished and, wherever possible, criminals are executed on the street in cold blood. Where the president is a crook, but also a great dancer. Where history has not yet been written once and for all. Where the struggle continues.

6. We should note that *Newsweek* listed McDonald's at number 22 in its 2009 Green Rankings list of America's 500 largest corporations. *Newsweek* includes these company remarks:

> Leader among its peers in extending environmental concerns throughout its supply chain. Buys fish from sustainably managed fisheries and has policy in place (since 1989) not to buy from cattle suppliers who destroy rainforests. After criticism from Greenpeace, also agreed not to purchase soybeans that had been grown on recently deforested land in the Amazon. Also working to end use of antibiotics in food products, reduce pesticides, find more humane slaughtering methods and eliminate Styrofoam in packaging.

Bibliography

❧❦❧

Aaron, Tristin. "Loveleen Tandan, *Slumdog Millionaire*'s Co-Director." *Women's Media Center Majority Post*. 30 Jan. 2009. Web.

Achebe, Chinua. *Things Fall Apart*. New York: Houghton Mifflin, 1996. Print.

Appadurai, Arjun. "Disjuncture and Difference in the Global Cultural Economy." *Public Culture* 2.2 (1990): 1-24. Rpt. in *Colonial Discourse and Post-Colonial Theory: A Reader*. Ed. Patrick Williams and Laura Chrisman. New York: Columbia UP, 1994. 324-339. Print.

Archibald, David. "Violence and Redemption: An Interview with Gavin Hood." *Cineaste* 31.2 (2006): 44–47. Print.

Arendt, Paul. "Movies: Blood Diamond (2007)." Rev. of *Blood Diamond*, dir. Edward Zwick. BBC. British Broadcasting Co, 26 Jan. 2007. Web. 30 Dec. 2007.

Armes, Roy. *Postcolonial Images: Studies in North African Film*. Bloomington: Indiana UP, 2005. Print.

Arora, Kulvinder. "The Mythology of Female Sexuality: Alternative Narratives of Belonging." *Women: A Cultural Review* 17.2 (2006): 220–50. Print.

"*Avatar* Rules Box Office for Sixth Weekend." *Reuters.com*. Thomson Reuters, 24 Jan. 2010. Web. 4 June 2010.

Babington, Bruce. *A History of the New Zealand Fiction Feature Film*. Manchester: Manchester UP, 2007. Print.

Badt, Karin Luisa. "I Want My Films to Explode with Life: An Interview Mira Nair." *Cineaste* Winter 2004: 10-15. Print.

Bahri, Deepika. "The Namesake." *Film Quarterly* 61.1 (2007): 10–15. Print.

Ballal, Prateeti Punja. "Illiberal Masala: The Diasporic Distortions of Mira Nair and Dinesh D'Souza." *Weber: The Contemporary West*. 15.1 (Winter 1998)

Bansak, Edmund G. *Fearing the Dark: The Val Lewton Career*. Jefferson: McFarland & Co, 1995. Print.

Barnard, Rita. *Apartheid and Beyond: South African Writers and the Politics of Place.* Oxford: Oxford UP, 2007. Print.

Barron, Alexandra Lynn. "Fire's Queer Anti-Communalism." *Meridians: Feminism, Race, Transnationalism* 8.2 (2008): 64–93. Print.

Bascom, William R. *African Dilemma Tales.* Chicago: Aldine, 1975. Print.

Beardsworth, Liz. "Review of *Tsotsi.*" *Empire Magazine* 1 April 2006. Web.

Beaufoy, Simon, adapt. *Q & A* [*Slumdog Millionaire*]. By Vikas Swarup. Dir. Danny Boyle. Fox Searchlight, 2008. Film.

Benson, Mary. *A Far Cry: The Making of a South African.* London: Penguin, 1990. Print.

Bhabha, Homi. *The Location of Culture.* London: Routledge, 1994. Print.

Blythe, Martin. *Naming the Other: Images of the Maori in New Zealand Film and Television.* Metuchen: Scarecrow Press, 1994. Print.

Bono, ed. *Africa Issue.* Special issue of *Vanity Fair* July 2007. Print.

Boucher, Geoff. "Interview with Neill Blomkamp." *Los Angeles Times*, 30 Dec. 2009. Web. 11 Jan. 2010.

Bove, Paul. "Discourse." *Critical Terms for Literary Study.* Ed. Frank Lentricchia and Thomas McLaughlin. Chicago: U of Chicago P, 1990. 50-65. Print.

Brennan, Timothy. "Masterpiece Theatre and the Uses of Tradition." *Social Text* 12 (1985): 102–112. Print.

Brontë, Charlotte. *Jane Eyre.* 1847. Ed. Richard J. Dunn. New York: Norton, 2001. Print.

Brooks, David. "The Messiah Complex." *New York Times*, 7 Jan. 2010. Web. 25 Jan. 2010.

Budde, Robert. "The 'Valuable Deformity': Calipers and the Failed Trope of Postcolonial Debt in Deepa Mehta's *Earth.*" *Canadian Journal of Film Studies* 17.1 (2008): 44–51. Print.

Calder, Peter. "Would-be Warriors: New Zealand Film Since *The Piano.*" *Film in Aotearoa New Zealand.* Eds. Jonathan Dennis and Jan Bieringa. Wellington: Victoria UP, 1992. 183–190. Print.

Cameron, Kenneth M. *Africa on Film: Beyond Black and White.* New York: Continuum, 2004. Print.

Canby, Vincent. "Mrs. Rochester No. 1, Long before 'Jane Eyre.'" Rev. of *Wide Sargasso Sea*, dir. John Duigan. *New York Times.* 16 April 1993. Web. 3 June 1010.

Cancel, Robert. "'Come Back South Africa': Cinematic Representations of Apartheid over Three Eras of Resistance." *Focus on African Films*. Ed. Françoise Pfaff. Bloomington: Indiana UP, 2004. 15–32. Print.

Carnevale, Rob. "Amelia - Mira Nair interview." indieLONDON.co.uk. IndieLondon, n.d. Web. 23 January 2010.

Chaudhuri, Shohini. "Snake Charmers and Child Brides: Deepa Mehta's Water, 'Exotic' Representation, and the Cross-Cultural Spectatorship of South Asian Migrant Cinema." *South Asian Popular Culture* 7.1 (2009: 7–20). Print.

Chocano, Carina. "Heading South." *Los Angeles Times*, 21 July 2006 Web. 20 March 2010.

Ciolkowski, Laura E. "Navigating the Wide Sargasso Sea: Colonial History, English Fiction, and British Empire." *Twentieth-Century Literature* 43:3 (1997): 339-359. Print.

Clelland-Stokes, Sacha. *Representing Aboriginality*. Skjern: Intervention Press, 2007. Print.

Clingman, Stephen. *Novels of Nadine Gordimer: History from the Inside*. Amherst: U of Massachusetts P, 1992. Print.

Clover, Joshua. "Allegory Bomb." *Film Quarterly* 63.2 (2010): 8–9. Print.

Codell, Julie. *Genre, Gender, Race and World Cinema*. Malden: Wiley-Blackwell, 2006. Print.

Coetzee, J. M. "Confession and Double Thoughts: Tolstoy, Rousseau, Dostoevsky." *Doubling the Point: Essays and Interviews*. Ed. David Attwell. Cambridge : Harvard UP, 1992. 251–293. Print.

---. *Disgrace*. New York: Penguin, 1999. Print.

Cohen, Derek. "Beneath the Underworld: Athol Fugard's *Tsotsi*." *World Literature Written in English* 23.3 (1984): 273–284. Print.

Coleman, Sarah. "Shaking the Tree." *The Independent Film and Video Monthly* 29.2 (2006): 19–21. Print.

Colley, Linda. "Britishness and Otherness: An Argument." *The Journal of British Studies* 31.4 (1992): 309-329. Print.

Collier, Aldore. "Forest Whitaker's Big Step." *Ebony* Feb. 2007: 150. *LexisNexis Academic*. Web. 5 Jan. 2009.

Columpar, Corinn. "'Taking Care of Her Green Stone Wall': The Experience of Space in *Once Were Warriors*." *Quarterly Review of Film and Video* 24 (2007): 463–474. Print.

Dargis, Manohla. "Blood Diamond (2006): Diamonds and the Devil, Amid the Anguish of Africa." Rev. of *Blood Diamond*, dir. Edward Zwick. *New York Times*, 8 Dec. 2006. Web. 30 Dec. 2006.

Dark of the Sun (The Mercenaries). Dir. Jack Cardiff. MGM, 1968. Film.

Dash, J. Michael. *Haiti and the United States: National Stereotypes and the Literary Imagination*. New York: St. Martin's, 1997. Print.

David, Dierdre. *Rule Britannia: Women, Empire, and Victorian Writing*. Ithaca: Cornell UP, 1995. Print.

Dayan, Joan. "Vodoun, or the Voice of the Gods." *Sacred Possessions: Vodou, Santería, Obeah, and the Caribbean*. Ed. Margarite Fernandez Olmos and Lizabeth Paravisini-Gebert. New Brunswick: Rutgers UP, 1997. 13-36. Print.

Desai, Jigna. *Beyond Bollywood: The Cultural Politics of South Asian Diasporic Film*. New York: Routledge, 2004. Print.

DeSouza, Pascale. "Maoritanga in *Whale Rider* and *Once Were Warriors*: A Problematic Rebirth through Female Leaders." *Studies in Australian Cinema* 1.1 (2007): 15–27. Print.

Donadio, Rachel. "Out of South Africa." Sunday Book Review *New York Times*. 16 Dec. 2007. Web. 11 Jan. 2010.

Donahue, Francis. "Apartheid's Dramatic Legacy: Athol Fugard." *The Midwest Quarterly* 36.3 (1995): 323–330. Print.

Douthat, Ross. "Inner Space." *National Review* 7 Sept. 2009: 50. Print.

Dovey, Lindiwe. "Redeeming Features: From *Tsotsi* (1980) to *Tsotsi* (2006)." *Journal of African Cultural Studies* 19.2 (2007): 143–167. Print.

Drake, Sandra. "Race and Caribbean Culture as Thematics of Liberation in Jean Rhys's *Wide Sargasso Sea*." *Wide Sargasso Sea*. Ed. Judith L.Raiskin New York: Norton, 1999. 193-206. Print.

Dube, Reena. *Satyajit Ray's The Chess Players and Postcolonial Film Theory: Postcolonialism and Film Theory*. New York: Palgrave Macmillan, 2005. Print.

Duff, Alan. *Jake's Long Shadow*. New York: Vintage, 2002. Print.

---. *Maori: The Crisis and the Challenge*. Auckland: Harper Collins, 1993. Print.

---. *Once Were Warriors*. Auckland: Tandem, 1990. Print.

---. *What Becomes of the Broken Hearted*. New York: Vintage, 1997. Print.

Dunn, Kevin C. "Fear of a Black Planet: Anarchy Anxieties and Postcolonial Travel to Africa." *Third World Quarterly* 25.3 (2004): 483-499. Print.

Eagan, Daniel. "*Tsotsi* Review." *Film Studies International* 1 March 2006. Web.

Earth. Dir. Deepa Mehta. Zeitgeist Films, 1998. DVD.

Ebert, Roger. "Earth." Rev. of *Earth*, dir. Deepa Mehta. *rogerebert.com*. Chicago Sun Times,15 Oct. 1999. Web. 1 Jan. 2010.

Ebert, Roger. "Mansfield Park." Rev. of *Mansfield Park*, dir. Patricia Rozema. *rogerebert.com*. Chicago Sun Times, 24 Nov. 1999. Web. 8 June 2010.

Ellapen, Jordache Abner. "The Cinematic Township: Cinematic Representations of the 'Township Space' and Who Can Claim the Rights to Representation in Post-Apartheid South African Cinema." *Journal of African Cultural Studies* 19.1 (2007): 113–137. Print.

Ellis, Kate and E. Ann Kaplan. "Feminism in Brontë's *Jane Eyre* and its Film Versions." *Nineteenth-century Women at the Movies: Adapting Classic Women's Fiction to Film*. Ed. Barbara Tepa Lupack. Bowling Green: Bowling Green UP, 1999. 192-206. Print.

England, Marcia. "Breached Bodies and Home Invasions: Horrific Representations of the Feminized Body and Home." *Gender, Place and Culture* 13.4 (2006): 353-363. Print.

Ezra, Elizabeth and Terry Rowden, eds. *Transnational Cinema: The Film Reader*. New York and London: Routledge, 2006. Print.

Featherstone, Simon. *Postcolonial Cultures*. Jackson: UP of Mississippi, 2005. Print.

Fire. Dir. Deepa Mehta. Zeitgeist Films, 1996. DVD.

Forché, Carolyn. "Twentieth-Century Poetry of Witness." *American Poetry Review* 22.2 (1993): 9-16. Print.

Foreman, Joel and David R. Shumway. "Cultural Studies: Reading Visual Texts." *Cultural Studies in the English Classroom*. Ed. James A. Berlin and Michael J. Vivion. Portsmouth, NH: Boynton/Cook Heineman, 1992. 244–61. Print.

Foreman, Jonathan. "A Flat Sharp." *National Review* 27 Sept. 2004: 58-59. Print.

Fugard, Athol. *Notebooks: 1960-1977*. New York: Knopf, 1984. Print.

--. *Tsotsi*. Jackson, TN: Grove Press, 2006. Print.

Fujiwara, Chris. *Jacques Tourneur: The Cinema of Nightfall*. Jefferson: McFarland, 1998. Print.

Gabriel, Teshome H. "Towards a Critical Theory of Third World Film." *Colonial Discourse and Post-Colonial Theory: A Reader*. Ed. Patrick Williams and Laura Chrisman. New York: Columbia UP, 1994. 340-58. Print.

Gairola, Rahul. "Burning with Shame: Desire and South Asian Patriarchy, from Gayatri Spivak's 'Can the Subaltern Speak?' to Deepa Mehta's *Fire*." *Comparative Literature* 54.4 (2002): 307–24. Print.

Gamm, Kate. *Teaching World Cinema*. London: British Film Institute, 2008. Print.

Garcia, Maria. "Whale Tale: New Zealand's Niki Caro Brings Maori Legend to Life." *Film Journal International* 106.6 (2003): 16–18. Print.

Ghosh, Bishnupriya and Brinda Bose, eds. *Interventions: Feminist Dialogues on Third World Women's Literature and Film*. New York and London: Routledge, 1997. Print.

Gilbert, Sandra M. "*Jane Eyre* and the Secrets of Furious Lovemaking." *Novel* 31.3 (1998): 351-372. Print.

Gillespie, Eleanor Ringle. "*Tsotsi* Yields an Emotionally Charged Performance." *Atlanta Journal Constitution* 23 March 2006. Web. 1 Dec. 2009.

Givhan, Robin. "Dressing Up in the Latest Fashionable Cause?" *Washingtonpost. com*. 3 Nov. 2006. Web. 3 June 2010.

Glaser,Clive. *Bo-Tsotsi: The Youth Gangs of Soweto*, 1935–1976. Portsmouth: NH Heinemann, 2000. Print.

Goodhew, David. *Respectability and Resistance: A History of Sophiatown*. Westport and London: Praeger, 2004. Print.

Gopinath, Gayatri. "Local Sites/Global Contexts: The Transnational Trajectories of Deepa Mehta's *Fire*." *Queer Globalizations: Citizenship and the Afterlife of Colonialism*. Ed. Arnaldo Cruz-Malavé and Martin F. Manalansan. New York: New York UP, 2002. 149–61. Print.

---. "Nostalgia, Desire, Diaspora: South Asian Sexualities in Motion." *Positions: East Asian Cultures Critique* 5.2 (1997): 476–89. Print.

Gordimer, Nadine. *July's People*. New York: Penguin, 1982. Print

---. "Living in the Interregnum." *The Essential Gesture: Writing, Politics and Places*. Ed. Stephen Clingman. New York: Penguin, 1989. 261–84. Print.

Graham, Nicholas. "Palin Didn't Know Africa is a Continent, Says Fox News Reporter." *Huffington Post*. 5 Nov. 2008. Web. 11 Jan. 2010.

Gray, Stephen. "The Coming into Print of Athol Fugard's *Tsotsi*." *The Journal of Commonwealth Literature* 16.1 (1981): 56–63. Print.

Gugler, Josef. *African Film: Re-Imagining a Continent*. Bloomington: Indiana UP, 2003. Print.

Guneratne, Anthony R. and Wimal Dissanayake. *Rethinking Third Cinema*. New York: Routledge, 2003. Print.

Gupta, Arun. "Slumdog Colonialism: Hollywood Mines Another Culture for Raw Material, Celebrates a Box-office Bonanza." *The Indypendent*. 20 March 2009. Web. 9 Jan. 2010.

Hai, Ambreen. "Border Work, Border Trouble: Postcolonial Feminism and the Ayah in Bapsi Sidwa's *Cracking India.*" *Modern Fiction Studies* 46.2 (2000): 379–426. Print.

Hammond, Pete. "The Truth about Amelia" *Notes on a Season.* Los Angeles Times. 14 Oct. 2009. Web. 8 June 2010.

Haraway, Donna. *The Companion Species Manifesto: Dogs, People, and Significant Otherness.* Chicago: Prickly Paradigm Press, 2003. Print.

Harrow, Kenneth W. *Postcolonial African Cinema: From Political Engagement to Postmodernism.* Bloomington: Indiana UP, 2007. Print.

Hay, Rod. "Out of the Ghetto: Tsotsi and South African Cinema." *Screen Education* 44 (2006): 70–75. Print.

Henderson, Clara. "'When Hearts Beat Like Native Drums:' Music and the Sexual Dimensions of the Notions of 'Savage" and 'Civilized' in *Tarzan and His Mate*, 1934." *Africa Today* 48.4 (2001): 91-124. Print.

Herman, Jeanette. "Memory and Melodrama: The Transnational Politics of Deepa Mehta's *Earth.*" *Camera Obscura* 58.20 (2005): 107–47. Print.

Heron, Barbara. *Desire for Development: Whiteness, Gender, and the Helping Imperative.* Waterloo: Wilfrid Laurier UP, 2007. Print.

Hill, John, ed. *World Cinema: Critical Approaches.* Oxford: Oxford UP, 2000. Print.

"The Hinemoa Legend." *Fodors.* n.d. Web. 9 October 2009.

Hobsbawm, Eric and Terence Ranger. *The Invention of Tradition.* Cambridge: Cambridge UP, 1983. Print.

Hogg, David. "Unpublished Fugard Novel." *Contrast* 12.1 (1978): 60–78. Print.

Hood, Gavin. "A Note from Filmmaker Gavin Hood." *Tsotsi Final Production Notes.* 2 January 2009. Web.

Holden, Stephen. "In South Africa, Harsh Losses of Privilege." Rev. of *Disgrace*, dir. Steve Jacobs. *New York Times.*18 Sept. 2009. Web. 11 Jan. 2010.

Hopgood, Fincina. "The Politics of Melodrama in Deepa Mehta's *Water.*" *Metro Magazine* 149 (2006): 142–7. Print.

Hornbuckle, Del. "Blood Diamond…TIA (This is Africa)." Rev. of *Blood Diamond*, dir. Edward Zwick. *Pambazuka News.* Fahamu, 17 Jan. 2007. Web. 8 June 2010.

Hough, Barrie. "Fugard's *Tsotsi*: The Missing Novel." *English in Africa* 5.2 (1978): 74–80. Print.

Ignatieff, Michael. Introduction. *Truth and Lies: Stories from the Truth and Reconciliation Commission in South Africa.* By Jillian Edelstein. New York: New Press, 2002. 15-21. Print.

Ihimaera, Witi. *The Whale Rider*. Orlando: Harcourt, 1987. Print.

James, Nick. "Out of Gogol's Overcoat." *Sight & Sound* Apr. 2007: 12. Print.

Jansson, David R. "American National Identity and the Progress of the New South in *National Geographic Magazine*." *Geographical Review* 93.3 (2003): 350-369. Print.

Kaplan, Amy. "'Left Alone with America': The Absence of Empire in the Study of American Culture." *Cultures of United States Imperialism*. Ed. Amy Kaplan and Donald E. Pease. Durham: Duke UP, 1993

Kemp, Philip. "The Namesake." *Sight & Sound* Apr. 2007: 74-75. Print.

Klawans, Stuart. "The Things They Carried." Rev. of *The Host*, dir. Bong Joon-ho, *The Wind that Shakes the Barley*, dir. Ken Loach, and *The Name sake*, dir. Mira Nair. *The Nation* 26 Mar. 2007: 42-44. Print.

Kulla, Bridget. "Why Has *Water* Evaporated? The Controversy over Indian Filmmaker Deepa Mehta." *Off Our Backs* March/April 2002. Web. 1 Dec. 2009.

Lambert, Iain B. M. "Representing Maori Speech in Alan Duff's *Once Were Warriors*." *Language and Literature* 17.2 (2008): 155-65. Print.

Lee, Nathan. "Say It with Diamonds?" Rev. of *Blood Diamond*, dir. Edward Zwick. *The Village Voice*. 28 Nov. 2006. Web. 30 Dec. 2010.

Levitin, Jacqueline. "Deepa Mehta as Transnational Filmmaker, or You Can't Go Home Again." *North of Everything: English-Canadian Cinema Since 1980*. Ed. William Beard and Jerry White. Edmonton: U of Alberta P, 2002. 270–93. Print.

---. "An Introduction to Deepa Mehta: Making Films in Canada and India." *Women Filmmakers: Refocusing*. Ed. Jacqueline Levitin, Judith Plessis, and Valerie Raoul. Vancouver: U of British Columbia P, 2002. 273–83. Print.

Lindfors, Bernth. "Hottentot, Bushman, Kaffir: The Making of Racist Stereo types in 19th-Century Britain." *Encounter Images in the Meetings Between Africa and Europe*. Ed. Mai Palmberg. Uppsala: The Nordic Africa Institute, 2001. 54-75. Print.

Lionnet, Françoise. "Postcolonialism, Language and the Visual: By Way of Haiti." *Journal of Postcolonial Writing* 44.3 (2008): 227-239. Print.

Lutz, Catherine A. and Jane L. Collins. *Reading National Geographic*. Chicago: UP of Chicago, 1993. Print.

Macnab, Geoffrey. "The Weather Woman." The *Guardian.co*. 14 Sept. 2001. Web. 13 Dec. 2009.

"Madonna Wins Adoption Appeal in Malawi." *CNN.com*. 12 June 2009. Web. 3 June 2010.

Maingard, Jacqueline. "South African Cinema: Histories and Futures." *Screen* 48.4 (2007): 511–515. Print.

---. *South African National Cinema*. London and New York: Routledge, 2007. Print.

"Making Tsotsi." *Tsotsi: The Official Film Site*. 6 June 2009. Web.

"Maori Women in Focus." Ministry of Women's Affairs. April 1999. Web. 25 June 2007.

Marchetti, Gina. "Action-Adventure as Ideology." *Cultural Politics in Contem porary America*. Ed. Ian Angus and Sut Jhally. New York: Routledge, 1989. 182-197. Print.

Margetts, Jayne. "Deepa's Doctine." *Celluloid Interview*. 4 February 2010. Web.

Marks, Laura. *The Skin of the Film: Intercultural Cinema, Embodiment, and the Senses*. Durham: Duke UP, 1999. Print.

Martens, Emiel. *Once Were Warriors: The Aftermath*. Amsterdam: Aksant 2007. Print.

Martin, Helen and Sam Edwards. *New Zealand Film*, 1912–1996. Auckland: Oxford UP, 1997. Print.

McGinn, Daniel. "The Greenest Big Companies in America." *Newsweek*. 21 Sept. 2009. Web. 11 Jan. 2010.

McKibbins, Adrienne. "Meeting Mehta: A Conversation with the Director of *Water*." *Metro Magazine* 149 (2006): 148–52. Print.

Meyer, Susan L. "Colonialism and the Figurative Strategy of *Jane Eyre*." *Victorian Studies* 33.2 (1990): 247–268. Print.

Micellef, Ken and Donnie Marshall. *Classic Rock Drummers*. New York: Backbeat Books, 2007. Print.

Misani. "Invictus Scores Victorious Points." Rev. of *Invictus*, dir. Clint Eastwood. *New York Amsterdam News*. 10 Dec. 2009: 17. Print.

Mishra, Sudesh. "News from the Crypt: India, Modernity, and the West." *New Literary History* 40 (2009): 315–344. Print.

"Mission and Vision Statement." *Diamond Empowerment Fund*. Simmons Jewelry Co. n.d. Web. 20 March 2010.

Modisane, Bloke. *Blame Me on History*. New York: Dutton, 1963. Print.

Mohney, Chris. "Gwyneth's African Ad Inspires Imitators." *Gawker.com*. Gawker Media, 11 Aug. 2006. Web. 3 June 2010.

Molamu, Louis. *Tsotsi-taal: A Dictionary of the Language of Sophiatown*. Pretoria: U of South Africa, 2003. Print.

Molloy, Maureen. "Death and the Maiden: The Feminine and the Nation in Recent New Zealand Films." *Signs: Journal of Women and Society* 25.1 (1999): 153–170. Print.

Moore, Brian. "Invictus's Long Walk to Telling the Truth about 1995 Rugby World Cup." *Telegraph.co.uk.* 11 Jan. 2010. Web.

Mukherjee, Tutun. "Deepa Mehta's Film Water: The Power of the Dialectical Image." *Canadian Journal of Film Studies* 17.2 (2008): 35–47. Print.

Mulvey, Laura. "Visual Pleasure and Narrative Cinema." *Visual and Other Pleasures.* Bloomington: Indiana UP, 1989. Print.

Munro, Margaret. "The Fertility of Despair: Fugard's Bitter Aloes." *Meanjin* 40 (1981): 472–479. Print.

Murray, Rebecca. "Writer/Director Gavin Hood Discusses His Film, *Tsotsi.*" *About.com* 2010 Web. 4 Feb. 2009.

Naficy, Hamid. *An Accented Cinema: Exilic and Diasporic Filmmaking.* Princeton: Princeton UP, 2001. Print.

Najita, Susan Y. *Decolonizing Cultures in the Pacific: Reading History and Trauma in Contemporary Fiction.* New York and London: Routledge, 2006. Print.

Nayar, Parvathi. "A Subtle Tale of Two Cities." *The Business Times.* Singapore Press Holdings, 7 Sept. 2007. Web.

Ohlson, Thomas and Stephen John Stedman. *The New Is Not Yet Born: Conflict Resolution in Southern Africa.* Washington, D.C.: Brookings Institution, 1994. Print.

Olmos, Margarite Fernandez and Lizabeth Paravisini-Gebert. "Introduction: Religious Syncretism and Caribbean Culture." *Sacred Possessions: Vodou, Santería, Obeah, and the Caribbean.* Ed. Margarite Fernande Olmos and Lizabeth Paravisini-Gebert. New Brunswick: Rutgers UP, 1997. 1–12. Print.

Once Were Warriors. Dir. Lee Tamahori. Fine Line Cinema, 1994. DVD.

Outwater A, Abrahams N, and Campbell JC. "Women in South Africa: Intentional Violence and HIV/AIDS: Intersections and Prevention." *Journal of Black Studies* 35 (2005):135–154. Print.

Pais, Arthur J. "Mira Nair on the Making of *Amelia.*" *FilmContact.com.* N.p. 21 Oct. 2009. Web. 9 June 2010.

Parkhurst, Carolyn. *The Dogs of Babel.* New York: Back Bay, 2004.

Phillips, Richard and Waruna Alahakoon. "Hindu Chauvinists Block Filming of Deepa Mehta's *Water.*" *World Socialists Web Site.* International Committee of the Fourth International, 12 Feb. 2000. Web. 8 Jan. 2010.

Piazza, Jo. "Audiences Experience *Avatar* Blues." *CNN.com.* 11 Jan. 2010. Web. 25 Jan. 2010.

Pieterse, Jan Nederveen. *White on Black: Images of Africa and Blacks in Western Popular Culture.* New Haven: Yale UP, 1992. Print.

Pihama, Leonie. "Repositioning Maori Representation: Contextualizing *Once Were Warriors.*" *Film in Aotearoa New Zealand.* Ed. Jonathan Dennis and Jan Bieringa. Wellington: Victoria UP, 1992. 191–193. Print.

Porton, Richard. "Visualizing *Vanity Fair:* Nair Directs Witherspoon in 19th-Century Classic." *Film Journal International* 107.9 (2004): 16-17. Print.

Post, Robert M. "Journey toward the Light: Athol Fugard's *Tsotsi.*" *CLA Journal* 26.4 (1983): 273–284. Print.

Prakash, Gyan. "Who's Afraid of Postcoloniality?" *Social Text* 49 (1996): 187–203. Print.

Prentice, Chris. "Riding the Whale?: Postcolonialism and Globalism in *Whale Rider.*" *Global Fissures: Postcolonial Fusions.* Ed. Clara A. B. Joseph and Janet Wilson. Amsterdam: Rodopi, 2006. 247–67. Print.

Quill, Greg. "*Slumdog* Wins Hearts Here; While Some in India and Britain Decry Film, Local South Asians Are Saying It Deserves Academy Nod." thestarcom. 21 January 2009. Web. 9 June 2010.

Rajan, Gita. "Constructing-Contesting Masculinities: Trends in South Asian Cinema." *Signs: Journal of Women in Culture and Society* 31.4 (2006): 1099–1124. Print.

Ramchandani, Vinita. "Passionate Plots: Deepa Mehta Explains the Emotion that Connects Her Films *Fire, Earth and Water.*" *The Week Magazine.* 6 Dec. 1998. Web.

Riemenschneider, Dieter. "Of Warriors, a Whalerider, and Venetians: Contemporary Maori Film.*" *Global Fragments: Disorientation in the New World Order.* Ed. Anke Bartels and Dirk Wiemann. Amsterdam: Rodopi, 2007. 139–151. Print.

Rose, Simon. "Interview with Simon Beaufoy." *The Daily Telegraph.* 2 Feb. 2009. LexisNexis. Web. 4 Dec. 2010.

Rosenberg, Tina. "When a Pill Is Not Enough." *New York Times Magazine.* 6 Aug. 2006. Web. 15 Aug. 2006.

Rhys, Jean. *Wide Sargasso Sea.* 1966. Ed. Judith L.Raiskin. New York: Norton, 1999. Print.

Rushdie, Salman. "Interview with Deepa Mehta." *CharlieRose.com.* 12 May 2006 Web. 24 Nov. 2009.

"SA Pirates 'Hijack' *Tsotsi* Film." *BBC News*. 20 March 2006. Web. 6 June 2009.

Sacks, Ethan. "Chinese Government Cracks Down on *Avatar* and Taiwanese Man Dies of Stroke after Seeing Film." *NYDailyNews.com*. 19 Jan. 2010. Web. 25 Jan. 2010.

Said, Edward. *Culture and Imperialism*. New York: Knopf, 1993. Print.

Scott, A. O. "Final Score: Future, 1, Past 0." Rev. of Invictus, dir. Clint Eastwood." *New York Times*. 11 Dec. 2009: 1. Print.

Shargel, Raphael. "Muted Rebellions." *New Leader*. Sept.-Oct. 2004: 46. Print.

Sharpe, Jenny. "Gender, Nation, and Globalization in *Monsoon Wedding and Dilwale Dulhania Le Jayenge.*" *Meridians: Feminism, Race, Transnationalism* 6:1 (2005): 58–81. Print.

Shepard, Lucius. "A Pair of Nines." *Fantasy & Science Fiction* 118.1 (2010): 187–192. Print.

Shiel, Mark and Tony Fitzmaurice. *Cinema and the City: Film and Urban Societies*. Oxford: Blackwell, 2001. Print.

Shohat, Ella. "Ethnicities-in-Relation: Toward a Multicultural Reading of American Cinema." *Unspeakable Images: Ethnicity and the American Cinema*. Ed. Lester D. Friedman. Chicago: U of Illinois P, 1991. 215–250 Print.

Shohat, Ella and Robert Stam. "Introduction." *Multiculturalism, Postcoloniality, and Transnational Media*. Ed. Ella Shohat and Robert Stam. New Brunswick: Rutgers UP, 2003. 1–17.

Shortland, Edward. *Maori Religion and Mythology*. London: Longmans, Green, and Co., 1882. Print.

Sidwa, Babsi. *Cracking India*. Minneapolis: Milkweed, 1991. Print.

Sklar, Robert. "Social Realism with Style: An Interview with Lee Tamahori." *Cineaste* 21.3 (1995): 25–27. Print.

"The *Slumdog Controversy*." Review of *Slumdog Millionaire*. *Shvoong*. 29 Jan. 2009. Web. 2 Feb. 2010.

Slumdog Millionaire. Dir. Danny Boyle. Screenplay by Simon Beaufoy. Fox Searchlight, 2008. Film.

Snead, Elizabeth. "*Blood Diamond's* PR War." *The Envelope*. Los Angeles Times. 10 Oct. 2006. Web. 9 June 2010.

Spivak, Gayatri. "Can the Subaltern Speak?" *Colonial Discourse and Post-Colonial Theory*. Ed. Patrick Williams and Laura Chrisman. New York: Columbia UP, 1994. 66–111. Print.

Stafford, Jane and Mark Williams. *Maoriland: New Zealand Literature, 1872–1914*. Wellington: Victoria UP, 2006. Print.

Stam, Robert. "Beyond Third Cinema: The Aesthetics of Hybridity." *Rethinking Third Cinema*. Ed. Anthony R. Guneratne. New York: Routledge, 2003. 31–48. Print.

Stoneman, Patsy. *Brontë Transformations: The Cultural Dissemination of Jane Eyre and Wuthering Heights*. London: Prentice Hall, 1996. Print.

Strain, Ellen. *Public Places, Private Journeys: Ethnography, Entertainment, and the Tourist Gaze*. New Brunswick: Rutgers UP, 2003. Print.

Sutherland, John. "Some Nabob." *Times Literary Supplement* .18 March 2005:12. Print.

"Taniwha." *Te Ara: The Encyclopedia of New Zealand*. New Zealand Ministry for Culture and Heritage. 1 Mar. 2009. Web. 10 Feb. 2010.

Telotte, J.P. "Narration and Incarnation: *I Walked with a Zombie*." Film Criticism 6.3 (1982): 18–31. Print.

"The Making of *Tsotsi*." *Tsotsi*. Dir. Gavin Hood. Perf. Presley Chweneyagae, Terry Pheto, Kenneth Nkosi. 2005. DVD.

Thomas, Susan Gregory. *Buy, Buy Baby: How Consumer Culture Manipulates Parents and Harms Young Minds*. New York: Houghton Mifflin Harcourt, 2007. Print.

Thompson, Christina. "Alan Duff: The Book, the Film, the Interview." *Meanjin* 54.1 (1995): 6–13. Print.

Thompson, John. "*Invictus* Is Oscar Bound: But How Honest Is It?" *The Verge: GQ on Pop Culture*. 16 Dec. 2009. Web. 11 Jan. 2010.

Thompson, Kirsten Moana. "*Once Were Warriors*: New Zealand's First Indigenous Blockbuster." *Movie Blockbusters*. Ed. Julian Stringer. London: Routledge, 2003. 230–241. Print.

Tomaselli, Keyan. *The Cinema of Apartheid: Race and Class in South African Film*. New York: Smyrna, 1988. Print.

Tsotsi. Dir. Gavin Hood. Perf. Presley Chweneyagae, Terry Pheto, Kenneth Nkosi. 2005. DVD.

Turan, Kenneth. "*Blood Diamond*." Rev. of *Blood Diamond*, dir. Edward Zwick. Los Angeles Times. 8 Dec. 2006. Web. 9 June 2010.

Turner, Stephen. "Sovereignty, or the Art of Being Native." *Cultural Critique* 51 (2002): 74–100. Print.

Tyree, J. M. "Against the Clock: *Slumdog Millionaire* and *The Curious Case of Benjamin Button*." Film Quarterly 62.4 (2009): 34–38. Print.

Urry, John. "The Tourist Gaze Revisited." *American Behavioral Scientist* 36.2 (1992): 172-186. Print.

Vanity Fair. Dir. Mira Nair. Perf. Reese Witherspoon, Gabriel Byrne. Focus Features, 2004. Film.

Vincent, Sally. "Trying to Be Good." *guardian.co.uk*. 26 Nov. 2005. Web. 20 March 2010.

Water. Dir. Deepa Mehta. Fox Searchlight, 2005. DVD.

Wertheim, Albert. *The Dramatic Art of Athol Fugard: From South Africa to the World*. Bloomington: Indiana UP, 2000. Print.

West, Kanye, perf. *Diamonds from Sierra Leone* (Remix). Dir. Hype Williams. 2005. MTV. Web. 20 Mar. 2010.

Whale Rider. Dir. Niki Caro. Newmarket Films, 2002. DVD.

Wilson, Janet. "Suffering and Survival: Body and Voice in Recent Maori Writing." *Bodies and Voices: The Force-Field of Representation and Discourse in Colonial and Postcolonial Studies*. Ed. Mereta Falck Borch, Eva Rask Knudsen, and Martin Leer. Amsterdam: Rodopi, 2008. 267–281. Print.

Wiles, Mary M. "Narrating the Feminine Nation: The Coming-of-Age Girl in Contemporary New Zealand Cinema." *Youth Culture in Global Cinema*. Ed. Timothy Shary and Alexandra Seibel. Austin: U of Texas P, 2007. 175–188. Print.

Wiltshire, John. "Critical Opinion: Decolonising *Mansfield Park*." *Essays in Criticism* 53:4 (2003): 303–322. Print.

Wotzke, Anders. "Interview with *Disgrace* Director Steve Jacobs." *Cut. Print. Review*. 14 June 2009. Web. 11 Jan. 2010.

Wright, Laura. Writing *"Out of All the Camps": J. M. Coetzee's Narratives of Displacement*. New York and London: Routledge, 2006. Print.

Zacharek, Stephanie. "Heading South." *Salon.com*. 7 July 2006. Web. 20 Mar. 2010.

Index

ഇൗ൫ഌ